MW00412916

Redesigning School

Redesigning School

Lessons for the 21st Century

Joseph P. McDonald

Jossey-Bass Publishers • San Francisco

Substantial discounts on bulk quantities of Jossey-Bass books are available to corporations, professional associations, and other organizations. For details and discount information, contact the special sales department at Jossey-Bass Inc., Publishers (415) 433–1740; Fax (800) 605–2665.

For sales outside the United States, please contact your local Simon & Schuster International Office.

Manufactured in the United States of America on Lyons Falls Pathfinder Tradebook. This paper is acid-free and 100 percent totally chlorine-free.

Library of Congress Cataloging-in-Publication Data

McDonald, Joseph P.
Redesigning school : lessons for the 21st century / Joseph P. McDonald. — 1st ed.
p. cm. — (The Jossey-Bass education series)
Includes bibliographical references (p. 253) and index.
ISBN 0-7879-0321-3 (acid-free paper)
1. School improvement programs—United States—Case studies. 2. School management and organization— United States—Case studies. I. Title. II. Series.
LB2822.82.M38 1997
371.2'00973—dc20 96–25339
CIP

FIRST EDITION
HB Printing 10 9 8 7 6 5 4 3 2 1

The Jossey-Bass Education Series

For the schoolchildren who showed us their schools,

and for Beth, who runs a school

Contents

Preface xi

The Author xxi

Introduction: New Schools for a New Century 1

Part One: Believing

1 A New Belief System 23

2 Leading with Belief 53

Part Two: Wiring

3 Wiring Fundamentals 89

4 Rewiring a School 120

Part Three: Tuning

5 Tuning Challenges 155

6 A Tuning Protocol 202

Conclusion: Scaling Up by Scaling Down 243

Appendix: A Glossary of Terms 249

References 253

Index 261

Preface

In 1990, several colleagues and I looked for some schools that had taken on the challenge of educating all their students to use their minds well. We sought schools that had genuinely responded to the reform rhetoric of the late 1980s about combining equity with the pursuit of intellectual excellence—schools that refused to have different standards for different students. We knew that such a refusal was then and still is hard to initiate and to sustain. Many of the beliefs that underpin American schooling encourage different standards for different students. We knew, too, that the way most schools are organized prevents teachers from working in the ways necessary to teach all students to use their minds well. Finally, we knew that schools ordinarily enjoy scant opportunity to inquire into what it means to use one's mind well. In short, most schools are not designed for the task. We knew, therefore, that the schools we sought would necessarily be involved in redesign. We wanted to study their experience of redesigning, as well as their new designs.

In contrast to studies of reform that focus on state or national educational policy, or on curriculum and teaching, our study was to focus on schools as both the targets and the agents of reform. Our goal was to try to describe the look and feel of serious reform from the perspective of the schools themselves. I say "serious reform" to suggest the enormous shift of purpose implied in the idea of educating all children to use their minds well—a shift that reverses the emphasis of schools throughout most of this century on serving different children in different ways and on emphasizing goals other than intellectual power and resourcefulness.

Encouraged by our principal funder, the IBM Corporation, our project took a long view, and so does this book. That is, in searching out school partners, we sought not model schools but ones with a serious commitment to serious change across a variety of contexts. That is one reason why this book is different from many others about school reform. It does not portray schools or school programs that really work. This is not because we found no practices worth emulating in the schools we worked with and studied. Rather, even the most promising practices are still rudimentary given the scope of the undertaking, and the failures are quite predictable. Indeed, I do not believe that even the best designs of today's school reformers will last beyond the first few years of the twenty-first century. Nevertheless, within the best efforts of schools, including those we studied, there is a kind of map for the long term that can help us to target explorations, conserve energies, and mark off the route of the journey.

Readers searching for models may not be satisfied with what they find in this book. "Ah, only more talk," they may conclude. I respond that the talk is authentic—the result of its having rubbed up against real schools in real places—and that authenticity is valuable inasmuch as it can ground our planning for twenty-first-century schooling and remind us that we have to get there from here. Moreover, the talk has been turned over by more minds than mine, including some who understand in personal terms, with an intimacy outside researchers cannot acquire, what it is like to work for serious change in real places. The last point is especially important. Although I am the sole author of this book, and accept full responsibility for it, the ideas it reports are really the product of a kind of seminar. I do not mean a real seminar, conducted for a semester around an actual table. I mean a virtual seminar whose parties were some school-based educators, some researchers at Brown University, and some people from IBM. Like a real seminar, it involved conversation and writing, it prized diversity of perspective, and it focused especially on questions of meaning: What does it mean to use one's mind well? How can schools mean what they say when they commit to teach all children to use their minds well? The parties raised and tested tentative answers to these and other hard questions by the light of our own experience, expertise, and invention. Meanwhile, as in a real seminar, their purpose was to enlarge understanding rather than define it precisely. If this had been a seminar on *Romeo and Juliet* rather than on school reform, its purpose would have been to ensure that every participant walked away with a broader and richer understanding of that intricate text, one better grounded in its actual intricacies. However, its purpose would not have been to ensure that everyone walked away with the same understanding, as if only one understanding of *Romeo and Juliet* could be the correct one.

Now that our virtual seminar is over—having run for nearly six years—it has fallen to me to report on it. Thus I have had to impose a shape on its participants' thinking and experimentation. That is, I have had to figure out what was learned and to organize that material to benefit others' learning. In doing so, I have tried to serve diverse readers. Some will find the information in this book helpful in their efforts to redesign their own schools, whether as teachers, administrators, or parents. To this end, I have culled from our research notes as well as other writing done within the project what I take to be some useful lessons, concepts, and tools. Other readers, with less obviously utilitarian purposes at stake, may find the book's images and stories helpful in understanding the current state of the American school. With such understanding, these readers—citizens, parents, neighbors, and employers—can make a difference in determining the design of the twenty-first-century American school.

Research Design

In 1990, I was a senior researcher at the Coalition of Essential Schools. Under the leadership of Theodore Sizer, the Coalition has struggled since the mid-1980s to understand how the systems of the conventional school might be reordered to serve the purpose of teaching all students to use their minds well. As a network, the Coalition combines insights from hundreds of particular contexts. As a famous network, it provides cover for bold experiments. And for those schools smart enough to seek it, it provides an opportunity within the network for peer critique and collaborative reflection.

The Coalition's discourse and experimentation are guided by nine principles. These include a dedication to the intellectual purpose of school, a belief that schools should hold high expectations for all students, a determination to provide students a decent environment where they can be known and taught as individuals and where they can be active rather than passive learners, a sense that schools today are too cluttered with subjects and that the curriculum should be simpler, and a resolve to graduate students on the basis of their demonstration that they have actually learned what their schools set out to teach (Sizer, 1984, 1991). It was this last principle especially, often expressed by the shorthand phrase "graduation by exhibition," that guided our selection of schools for this project. Indeed, we called our project the Exhibitions Project. We hypothesized that schools that asked students to exhibit the knowledge the school valued would likely be institutions that had at least asked themselves what they valued and how to recognize it in students. We knew that this is not all one would hope to find in a school design aimed at excellence and equity, but we thought it a crucial first step. We also had some ideas about succeeding steps, but these ideas proved faulty, as I explain in Chapter Two.

Sensible and not a bit radical, the principles of the Coalition of Essential Schools are only rarely evident in the practice of schools today. The rarity is by design. The twentieth-century school was built on other principles (Cohen, 1985). That is why today's schools pursue a purpose that seems more social than intellectual and why their intellectual expectations sell most students short. High schools especially seem to foster an impersonal environment for all but the stars and the troublemakers, and graduation requirements often amount to little more than putting in time (Powell, Farrar, and Cohen, 1985; Boyer, 1983; Sedlak, Wheeler, Pullin, and Cusick, 1986; Goodlad, 1984). I do not blame schools for functioning in this way, since this is exactly how the twentieth century has designed them to function. Indeed, we began our project with the assumption that even schools that have committed themselves to the Coalition's principles cannot be expected to undo a century's influence quickly or quietly. Moreover, we assumed that practical designs for a different kind of school in the future are not likely to surface on a predictable schedule, as the result of an orderly growth of insight, or by a rational process of trial, adaptation, and adoption. To look for good designs, we thought, we should begin with schools that seemed committed to producing them, although we should also expect fickleness in the circumstances favoring commitment. One rationale for pursuing serious school reform within a coalition of schools is that innovations can be passed around and in this way survive fickleness of circumstance.

In early 1991, after a process that involved self-nomination by a relatively large number of schools, as well as recommendations and site visits, we invited ten schools, located in nine states, to join the Exhibitions Project: four urban schools in large cities, five suburban schools in a variety of socioeconomic contexts, and one rural school in a poor community. They were all secondary schools, reflecting the fact that the large majority of schools in the Coalition of Essential Schools are secondary schools. As the project progressed, we also made a point of visiting a number of elementary schools, and there are references to these visits throughout the book. Most of these elementary schools were not associated with the Coalition of Essential Schools. We visited them because we wished to know whether our emerging ideas about redesigning school might be relevant across the entire age spectrum of schooling.

The bulk of our attention, however, remained on the original ten schools, and most of the stories, images, and quotations in the chapters that follow come from these schools. We visited eight of the ten schools at least ten times over the course of three years, and the other two schools three times. On these visits, each generally lasting two or three days, we observed the teaching and learning in these schools, conducted both in-depth and casual interviews, elicited documents relative to each school's reform experience, provided technical assistance, especially on assessment and technology issues, and in other ways tried to understand and assist the schools. Over the course of these three years, we also convened conferences to which various subgroups of the ten schools were invited to send representatives. On these occasions, our virtual seminar became an actual one, as we sat around conference tables in Boston; Chicago; Louisville; IBM's Thomas J. Watson Research Center in Hawthorne, New York; Simsbury, Connecticut; and Brown University. At the end of the three years, IBM generously supplied another two years of follow-up funding, resulting in more visits to some of the schools, more tool development, and more writing. In the end, the project produced fifteen papers written by researchers and by people in the schools;[1] a short book coauthored by a principal, three teachers, and me (McDonald and others, 1993); a videotape and a CD. It also produced a number of tools, some of them technology based, and most of them described in the chapters that follow.

Acknowledgments

I follow the convention of masking the identities of the schools we studied, but somewhat reluctantly; I would prefer to celebrate their resourcefulness, inventiveness, hard work, and courage. The courage manifested itself in many ways, not least of all in inviting us to study them and in acknowledging to us their failures as well as their successes. For the most part, however, neither the public as a whole nor even the school reform community is yet prepared to let schools acknowledge failure without incurring penalty. That is one of the great impediments to redesigning schools. It is also why anonymity is necessary here. However, I am pleased to list the names of all the schools we visited during the course of the research, hiding the ten among others that provided crucial background information. I am grateful to the following schools, listed in alphabetical order: Brookwood Elementary School, Snellville, Georgia; Cape Elizabeth High School, Cape Elizabeth, Maine; Carrie Tompkins Elementary School, Croton-on-Hudson, New York; Central Park East I Elementary School, New York, New York; Central Park East Secondary School, New York, New York; Chatham High School, Chatham, New York; Croton Harmon High School, Croton-on-Hudson, New York; Eastern High School, Middletown, Kentucky; English High School, Boston, Massachusetts; Euclid Elementary School, San Diego, California; Fannie Lou Hamer Freedom High School, New York, New York; Federal Hocking High School, Stewart, Ohio; Fenway Middle College High

1. All of the papers of the Exhibitions project are available from the Coalition of Essential Schools, Brown University, Providence, Rhode Island. Many have also been published elsewhere, including McDonald, 1992c, 1993, and 1996; Podl and Metzger, 1994; Sizer, McDonald, and Rogers, 1992; and Allen and McDonald, 1994.

School, Boston, Massachusetts; Greenbrook Elementary School, South Brunswick, New Jersey; James Rutter Middle School, Sacramento, California; Magnet Middle School, Stamford, Connecticut; Narragansett Elementary School, Gorham, Maine; Norview High School, Norfolk, Virginia; O'Farrell Community School, San Diego, California; Oceana High School, Pacifica, California; Pierre Van Cortlandt Middle School, Croton-on-Hudson, New York; Puyallup High School, Puyallup, Washington; Rippowam High School, Stamford, Connecticut; Rochester Memorial School, Rochester, Massachusetts; Salem High School, Conyers, Georgia; Satellite Academy, New York, New York; Sedona Red Rock High School, Sedona, Arizona; Sullivan High School, Chicago, Illinois; Thayer Junior-Senior High School, Winchester, New Hampshire; University Heights High School, Bronx, New York; Walbrook High School, Baltimore, Maryland; and Zamorano Arts Academy, San Diego, California.

A very special acknowledgment is owed to David Allen among my research colleagues, who conducted many of the interviews I draw on in this book and provided more than his share of the project's insights; and to David Niguidula, who managed the Exhibitions Project and invented or co-invented most of the project tools. Other colleagues who made important contributions are Michelle Riconscente, Jody Podl, Jill Davidson, Sarah Alpert, Carrie Peterson, Jan Hopp, Christine Caldwell, Karen Thompson, and Elsa Christiansen. Jan Hawkins served us well as an outside consultant during the follow-up funding period. I use the word *we* in this book whenever I write about the conduct of the research that informs it, since my colleagues and I are jointly responsible for that conduct. However, I change the pronoun to *I* when it comes to most interpretations of the data and to the efforts I make at certain points in the book to go beyond the data. As I said, the purpose of a seminar is not to ensure that every party to it emerges with the same understanding. And although I am referring here to research—that is, to systematic inquiry—this was research aimed at provoking broader understanding rather than validating particular understandings.

As I claim at several points in the book, the work of redesigning schools for the twenty-first century is an immense undertaking. It is therefore problematic to try to forecast much about it based on the experience of a relative handful of schools in the early 1990s. Nevertheless, I attempt to do so anyway, and in the process I sometimes go beyond the data. At such moments, I seek support for what I say from others' data, others' speculations, and the logic of my own arguments. Because the book is, in this sense, a more personal construction than is conventional in research-based writing about school reform, I introduce each chapter's themes with a story from my own experience. I want readers to have sufficient orientation to my values to support a critique of what I conclude. This is also one way I do what Michelle Fine (1996) calls "working the hyphen" between self and other—between my privileged perspective as researcher and the experience of the people I studied.

Still, my personal interpretations of our data and the speculations that go beyond them are not idiosyncratic, having been enriched and critiqued already within the fine company I keep. I refer not only to my project colleagues but to other colleagues as well in both the Coalition of Essential Schools and at the Annenberg Institute for School Reform at Brown University. First among them is Ted Sizer, without whom there would have been no project and no book. His thoughtfulness and patience served unobtrusively as compass. Other colleagues who enriched our work are Deborah Meier, Dennis Littky, Rick Lear, Sid Smith, David Green, Pat Anderson, Sherry King, Paul Schwarz, Eileen Barton, Pat Wasley, Nancy Mohr, Karley Meltzer, Bil Johnson, Herb Rosenfeld, George Wood, Bob Brazil, Marian Finney, Julie Gainsburg, Sam Billups, Margaret Metzger, Jim Sexton, Frank Miles, Dot Turner, Bob Cresswell, Connie Goldman, Bethany Rogers, Lisa Lasky, Kathleen Cushman, Joel Kammer, and Bianca Gray.

I am grateful to a number of people who were willing to read early manuscripts of this book and provided valuable feedback, especially Pat Wasley, Paula Evans, Seymour Sarason, Paul Schwarz, Richard Sterling, Julie Gainsburg, Peggy MacMullen, Carrie Peterson, Grace McEntee, and three anonymous reviewers.

The generosity of the IBM Corporation in supporting our work for five years deserves special mention. Indeed, our most important guide and confidant throughout the Exhibitions Project was IBM's Sam Matsa. My colleagues and I are forever grateful for his insight, his patience, and his occasional nudging. Other IBM staff who provided valuable assistance include Stanley Litow, Robin

Wilner, John Porter, Bob Meisel, Ron Frank, and Janine Meyer. During the early years of the project, we also received generous support and valuable counsel from the UPS (United Parcel Service) Foundation. Both IBM and the UPS Foundation, in addition to funding the research, provided developmental support to some of the schools involved.

Finally, I acknowledge the contributions made to this book by my wife, Beth McDonald. Without the benefit of her guidance as an elementary school principal, I would never have dared to extend our inquiry into elementary schools. Without the benefit of her company, I would not have understood half of what I understand about schools, or anything else.

Providence, Rhode Island
September 1996

Joseph P. McDonald

The Author

Joseph P. McDonald is director of research at the Annenberg Institute for School Reform, Brown University. He has worked at Brown for a decade as a teacher and as senior researcher at the Coalition of Essential Schools. Previously, he was a high school teacher and administrator for seventeen years. He holds a doctorate in education and a master of arts in teaching from Harvard University. He is the author of *Teaching: Making Sense of an Uncertain Craft* (1992), and of many other publications about teaching and about school design, policy, and reform. He lives in Providence, Rhode Island, with his wife, who is an elementary school principal.

Redesigning School

Introduction

New Schools for a New Century

One afternoon, near the beginning of the research that led to this book, I visited the school in a suburb of a major city where my cousin's daughter was a second grader. At the time of my visit, her mother was starting up a new business. Whether it would be successful seemed to depend on certain qualities of judgment and habit in her mother. Had she taken the right risk in this new venture? Had she risked enough? Had she planned as well as she might have? Would she manage all the shocks of starting up smartly enough? Was she tough enough and nimble enough and patient enough? Did she know what she needed to know, or know how to learn it?

People call these practical qualities, but they are also intellectual—a matter of using one's mind well. And they are moral too. That is, one can have these qualities, but too meanly or too narrowly. Having spent several childhood summers in the close company of my cousin, I felt I had some sense of where she might have acquired some of these qualities. They did not come from school. She had not invested much in school. She would have gotten them instead from the intimacies and scuffles of growing up in a family of twelve, from a close relationship with a wisely practical father and a strict and loving mother, from the adventures of days spent with me and others roaming streets and woods, from the experience of negotiating a life across class and ethnic barriers, from the challenges of single parenthood. But why not from school too? Is there something about the conventional design of school that precludes such learning? These were among the questions in my mind as I visited my cousin's daughter's school.

It was a nice school—different, at least superficially, from the schools her mother and I had attended. The rooms were better equipped and organized for children's exploration, the teachers seemed better educated and more attuned to children's differences, the children were more diverse. Having spent only a single day there, I thought that this might be a school whose aims were broader than the ones my cousin and I had attended, one that might add real value and depth to the practical, intellectual, and moral education my cousin's daughter, like her mother before her, was bound to acquire outside school. But would the difference I sensed now hold up over the long haul? In the end, would schooling really matter any more in the daughter's life than it had in the mother's? Would it make the daughter smarter—beyond the rudiments—in living in a diverse and interactive world, earning in a quick and global economy, growing in wisdom and citizenship? Maybe, I thought, if she happens to take to school and learns how to work it toward these ends—as her mother did not but as her mother fervently hopes her daughter will.

Second grade is just the beginning of the path, though, and the easier end at that. So things are going well now, I surmised, as I took Melissa's tour of her classroom on a late afternoon in May while we waited for her mother to pick us up. For one thing, her teacher seemed to know her well. There was evidence of this in what Melissa told me of their interactions. For another thing, there seemed to be time and culture enough for intellectual immersion and ownership in the way this room functioned every day. There was evidence of this in the projects still under construction, the files and display spaces stuffed with former projects, the pride with which Melissa shared her work with me. Yet I know how rarely one teacher's rich knowledge of a child's growth is passed along to the next teacher, and so on down the path, and I know how choked the path gets with things that must be covered, things that preclude immersion and the assumption of intellectual ownership, the exercise of real judgment.

I asked Melissa lots of questions that afternoon, which she readily answered, and I asked myself some questions too—ones about her future in school and indirectly about the future of school itself. How might all the teachers on this or any other child's path plot her growth and nurture it? How might they plan backward from some compelling image of the person she might become? How might they enlist her mother and grandparents and even faraway people like me in helping them to construct that image? How might they respectfully but resolutely move Melissa's community's expectations of her past College Board scores and homecoming pageants? By what means might they best press Melissa—and help her acquire an interest in pressing herself—to think deeply and broadly, to be empathetic and critical, to assess risk thoughtfully?

After visiting many more schools in the next three years, both casually and intensively, I concluded that these questions are a matter of design. Now, near the turn of the century, even good, well-equipped schools like Melissa's are poorly designed to handle the issues the questions raise. Many are numbed by antiquated beliefs about what is worth knowing, how learning works, and what learning demands of children. Most are also too hardwired: they run well but cannot manage to learn continuously about what they are teaching or the people they are teaching it to. Nor can they adjust that teaching easily, although adjustments are continuously needed. Moreover, even many of the most well intentioned of them, the most politically sensitive, are too closed in on themselves, too distant from the issues that matter outside their walls.

So one of my first informants in the research I report in this book—my cousin's daughter—got me thinking about themes that later informants enriched. Like some of these later informants too, she stopped at one point on our tour to ask me suddenly, "What are you really doing here?"

"I'm beginning a book," I explained, "a book about how schools might be changed."

"My school?" she asked, hitting on a central point.

"All schools," I answered.

Later, heading up to bed from the kitchen, she turned to call down to me below: "Will you dedicate your book to me?"

I smiled, and agreed to think about it. And I thought about all the changes she might see in school design—if we are lucky—and of the courage she would need to live through some of them herself and to support others for her own children's sake. I thought particularly of the shift she would have to make from the ordinary perspective of her mother's generation and mine—that my child's school is fine, but those other schools have to change. This involves the shift that Robert Bellah and his colleagues (1985) describe: from a radical individualism in which the American identity is dedicated to its own "lifestyle enclave," toward a commitment to community among all Americans.

I decided that such prospective shifts of mind and heart warrant a dedication. But as readers will notice, Melissa shares it with other schoolchildren I met in researching this book—for example, the girl we meet in Chapter One who dared to take me and her classmates below the surface of her school's rhetoric about racial equality; the boy in Chapter Two who let his rage against the premature deaths in his city become an occasion of learning for me and others; the third grader in Chapter Three who has learned to use technology to take control of her own record of progress, and in the process may herald a fundamental shift in design; the remarkable students of the school depicted in Chapter Four, who are partners with their teachers in an important but tortuous change effort; the young woman in Chapter Five who by showing her distress with the state's new assessment helped me understand an important issue of educational policy; and the students in Chapter Six who helped pilot the tool I describe there.

Emerging Specifications

Throughout the twentieth century, reformers have squabbled recurrently about the purpose of school, and these squabbles have deeply influenced its design. Some reformers have focused on knowledge, wanting to ensure that schools pass on the best of it to children. Others have focused on the children themselves—on their presumed capacities and interests, and on the need to accommodate these. Still others have kept the economy uppermost in mind, wanting schools to produce the right kind of future workers. Finally, some have sought above all else to use school to improve or even reconstruct society.

At various times, each of these interests has seemed dominant in the rhetoric of school reform, although the others have always played a part too (Kliebard, 1986). Thus some of the most important design features of the twentieth-century school are products of compromise among the interests. There is a little bit of each interest in the consolidation of small schools into big ones, the proliferation of curriculum offerings, the growth of guidance and related services, and the reliance of schools on textbooks (Cohen, 1985). Meanwhile, certain design questions, like arenas of dispute in an old marriage, have long served to keep the separate interests sharp within an overall framework of togetherness. The question of whether students should be homogeneously or heterogeneously grouped for instruction is one of these, as are such related questions as whether curriculum should be sliced into levels of difficulty, whether it should be more or less academic or more or less practical, more or less moral or more or less intellectual, and whether testing should be against fixed criteria or a normal curve.

Today in the United States there is much talk about redesigning schools to suit the new century looming just ahead. The subtext of all the talk is that the interests that shaped the design of the twentieth-century school, and that continue to compete for influence within it, may be undergoing some fundamental change. The evidence of this change is hardly conclusive, but it is increasingly noticeable.

First, the conception of school as dispenser of knowledge has been undercut by the proliferation of knowledge. It has also been complicated by a pervasive reconsideration of what it means to know. Psychologists now hold that the mind constructs knowledge within constraints of prior belief, experience, and understanding; it cannot simply accept new knowledge as a bank accepts a deposit.

Second, the century-long view that schools must accommodate variety in children's intellectual capacities—the focus on children's "needs"—has recently lost nearly all its theoretical underpinnings. New conceptions of intelligence regard it as multidimensional and situational rather than unidimensional and prewired. The timeworn strategies of distinguishing the more or less smart children from the more or less dumb ones suddenly seem problematic in a theoretical sense, even if few know how to practice "schoolkeeping" in any other way.

Similarly, the focus on the economic purposes of schooling has lost its prior grounding in the concern for efficiency. It is not just that the economy has no interest any longer in a schooling for assembly-line readiness, but little for bureaucratic dutifulness either. In the face of an often volatile economic environment, one wants smart, frontline responsiveness rather than the faithful application of centralized decisions. To educate for this quality requires an enormous shift of emphasis in both the curricular and organizational habits of the school.

Finally, the consensus around the idea of the common school as an engine of social improvement and guarantor of democracy, now two centuries old, seems to be coming undone. Arguments across the political spectrum hold that choice, charter, and privatization schemes that distribute public resources for schooling may better serve the public than school districts that monopolize and in some cases squander these resources.

Of course, from the limited perspective of the last decade of the twentieth century, we cannot be sure how these phenomena will develop or what their individual or collective impact may be on the school. Moreover, they coexist with a great many other possible influences. Given all the possible influences, what are the chances, really, that the coming century will demand more thoughtfulness of more people than the current century has? What are the chances that an immensely diverse nation of disjointed communities might actually decide to educate all its children for thoughtfulness? And what are the chances that over the course of, say, the next two decades, we might actually discover how to do this?

It is clear, for example, that most of the talk today about school reform falls well short of these aims. My colleague at the Annenberg Institute, Deborah Meier (1993), has observed that the phrase one hears so often now, "All children can learn," is either a banality or an incomplete sentence. Learn what? Learn to grapple with matters of real intellectual weight? Learn to use their minds well? And, if so, how? Very few schools have yet dared to face these questions squarely, and the incentives to do so are still much weaker than the disincentives.

We can take heart from the example of Meier and other reformers who are facing the questions squarely, and I do. References to their work are scattered throughout this book, and my hope is that these references may provide guidance to other such work in other places. Whether the sum of all this work will amount to much in the end, however, remains an open question. It will depend on where the history of the early twenty-first century takes society and of what happens in the process to people's ideas about education.

Designing Against Common Sense

The teachers and principals who cooperated in our research and their colleagues in school reform throughout the United States today are not the first to have taken up the challenge of creating genuinely thoughtful schools. Some good school people took it up also at the turn of the last century. John Dewey hoped then that their mindful teaching might secure for our time a widespread and mindful citizenry. But the dream was hijacked early by large social forces that eventually imposed a different common sense. One of these was the shock of widespread industrialization and its impact in vastly diversifying the incomes and status of Americans and their children. Another was unprecedented immigration and a resulting transformation of American identity (Tyack, 1974). The shock of diversity was assuaged then by a conspiracy to associate difference with deficit. The deal was sealed with a new technology of assessment that aided academic sorting (Gould, 1981; Resnick and Resnick, 1991). The sorting served the needs of the emerging economic order. Thus, by degrees, the dream of schooling for thoughtfulness became schooling for social adjustment (Kliebard, 1986).

What happens to a dream deferred? Does it stay around waiting to be realized in another new century? Or does it get deferred again, the work of enacting it marginalized again? This is a crucial question for the reformers of our time, one that ought to keep them reading the history of their professional forebears' work at the start of this century and pondering the subtleties of sameness and difference between then and now. It is important to note, for example, that our era, like theirs, is experiencing the pain and opportunities of an emerging new economic order. Of course, it is partly these circumstances that fuel the impetus to develop new and more mindful schools. The argument is that broadly distributed intellectual achievement may be the only means to salvage American prosperity. But it is an argument made within a climate poisoned by already declining prospects of prosperity. Some children—and some parents on behalf of their children—scramble today rather more fiercely than a generation ago for the security of comparative advantage—to be designated as more "gifted" than another, to attend a "better" school, to have a more prestigious degree. Thereby they hope to escape the likely prospect (likely if one is white and middle class, that is) of becoming economically worse off than their parents.

This occurs, as it did at the turn of the last century, against the backdrop of immigration unprecedented in its sheer numbers and in its non-European sources. Many of the children in this immigrant wave will do better economically than their parents did, as will many of their native, nonwhite peers. The difference of expectation, threatening a long pattern of entitlement in the society, puts pressure on many schools to maintain tracking (the designation of curriculum levels to suit ability levels), even while the rhetoric of reform assails it from the other direction.

Finally, we are busy again, as we were almost a hundred years ago, at inventing a new technology of assessment and a new, more "systemic" educational policy apparatus. Then it was standardized tests and the bureaucratic school district (Tyack, 1974). Now it is performance assessment designed to elicit and evaluate complex work samples, and coherent national and state accountability policies (Fuhrman, 1993). An important difference is that we explicitly aim the new assessments and policies toward the achievement of richer learning outcomes for all children. Yet these innovations may serve more the purposes of sorting than of teaching, as they did at the turn of the last century (Darling-Hammond, 1992). Meanwhile, a century-old ideology has also reasserted itself—one that would hide human diversity beneath the simplistic construct of IQ and substitute eugenic efforts for educational ones (Herrnstein and Murray, 1994).

These circumstances and others are evidence of a grain of tacit assumptions about people and schools that runs deep in the American society. The new school designs we seek must cut against this grain, or they will fail. The designers must do what is always difficult and dangerous to do: contradict what has become common sense. Therefore they must have great perspicacity, ingenuity, and political courage. Because these qualities are always in short supply in any society or profession, no one can say with any assurance that the prospects for more mindful schools this century around are any better than they were the last time. Nor can we say now whether the American people will be willing to bear the financial costs of redesigning the school. As I write, there are powerful coalitions of interests emerging around scaling back even the costs of maintaining the school as it is. Given the pressures likely to be exerted by these coalitions, it is conceivable that we will open the new century with a greatly weakened resolve to maintain free and public education in any design.

Meanwhile we know that the prevailing habits of practice in schools today are extensions of values deeply embedded in the larger society. They will not give way to policies or inventions of practice as a dry hillside gives way to rain. To dislodge them will take an earthquake—a serious shift in basic public attitudes, a massive unlearning. In what follows, I sketch out an agenda for this unlearning. In the process, I offer some grounds for optimism that it might actually succeed if we can manage to hold on to enough hope and enough dollars.

The Unlearning Agenda

Among the most important things to be unlearned by the public—a public of parents, other citizens, professional educators, purveyors of serious and of popular culture, and policymakers—is the attitude that waylaid change at the last turn of the century: *the association of difference with deficit.* In the best of circumstances, the new immigration might actually free us from some of the ethnic and racial bias the last one installed, and the new technologies of assessment might actually help us discern the value of difference in the ways of knowing and working (Wolf, Bixby, Glenn, and Gardner, 1991; Resnick and Resnick, 1991). But things could easily go the other way again, making us "surer" of our false perceptions.

Nevertheless, in the past ten years, a remarkable body of research on cognition has radically redefined certain basic conceptions of human psychology as they relate to teaching and learning (Jones and Idol, 1990; Cohen, McLaughlin, and Talbert, 1993; Gardner, 1983, 1989, 1991; Perkins, 1992, 1995; Bruer, 1993). Whereas psychology by and large supported the association of difference with deficit at the turn of the last century, it is in a very different place now (Gould, 1981). As a result of the recent shift in the basic theory of learning and in basic theories of intelligence, learners are now presumed to construct knowledge rather than simply receive it, using prior knowledge, skills, values, and beliefs as construction material. And the intelligence they bring to this construction is presumed to be more complex than was once presumed; it is multidimensional, socially distributed, and tool dependent. Suddenly the image of intelligence as a finite capacity carried quietly inside a person's head seems antiquated. We are urged instead to think of intelligence as the flexible and expandable capacity of a work team with access to powerful information tools, or as an array of capacities that are personal and interpersonal, native and acquired. These basic conceptual changes may be said to support deep reorientations in the system of schooling as we know it. They justify the transformation of the teacher's role from that of "deliverer of instruction" to that of cognitive coach, one who stands watchfully on the sidelines of a rich learning environment he or she has prepared (Collins, Brown, and Newman, 1989; Collins, Hawkins, and Carver, 1991). Similarly, they justify the transformation of organizational contexts for learning from that of direct instruction in isolated classrooms to that of a community of learners, supported by norms of intellectual striving, habits of metacognition, and, most powerfully, respect for diversity of perspectives (Brown and Campione, 1994). This last element, pursued tenaciously against the common sense that difference means deficit, can help the public acquire a sense of variety in intellectual excellence (Gardner and Kornhaber, 1993). This is critical for any serious effort to educate all children well.

Getting there will be far from easy, however. An important obstacle is one that deserves its own place on the unlearning agenda: our *habitual association of the intellectual with the academic.* This is one source of the American anti-intellectualism that commentators from Alexis de Tocqueville to Richard Hofstadter have noted: many of us find serious intellectual study unappealing because we associate it with the effete, the impractical, and the class conscious. Children imbibe this attitude from many sources in the culture, including, ironically, intellectual ones. One boy, for example, whose life was chronicled in my hometown newspaper, meditates on his life after the close of basketball season: "Man, life has been boring without basketball. . . . I miss the practices, the games, the hype, the sweat, the basketball-smelling hands. But I'll live. I've got plenty of things to do—Dungeons and Dragons, Beth, pick-up ball" (Miller, 1993, p. A8). There is nothing conventionally intellectual on this list of things to do, as there would not have been on either Huck Finn's or Holden Caulfield's lists. Deborah Meier, in a 1993 address with the provocative title, "Why Kids Don't Want to Be Well Educated,"[1] claims that this young man is following a route common among young men—and among many young women too—in devoting the bulk of his energy to pursuits that are marginal to his school's intellectual agenda. Kids don't want to be well educated, she says, "because they can't even imagine what it is that we claim could be 'wantable' about it" (p. 8). The problem, she continues, is that we have restricted our definition of "well educated" to a narrow band of academic competence. It excludes the skills that some youths, like the one quoted above, exercise on the basketball court, with their romantic partners, playing Dungeons and Dragons, holding down a part-time job, and so forth—things like figuring out another's intentions, managing complex moves, assessing risk, picking up the pieces when things fall apart, and so on. These moves matter a lot to young people, and they continue to matter to them as they grow older. Although the moves clearly depend on thoughtfulness—or fail for want of it—we call this kind of thoughtfulness merely "practical," and say that the "intellectual" is only about doing calculus problems and, yes, reading required novels like *Huckleberry Finn* and *Catcher in the Rye.* Of course, the dichotomy is false from the perspective of life outside school, and even from the perspective of *Huckleberry Finn* and *Catcher in the Rye.*

Meier claims that "we cannot get kids to be something we don't genuinely want them to be" (1993, p. 12). Throughout the twentieth century, we have asked them to be academic because we intended to sort them on the basis of their response. In the process, we have disassociated the academic and the intellectual, and made the former a relatively narrow set of competencies. If we now want all kids actually to be intellectual, then we cannot continue to ask them to be academic. There is not enough room within this concept to accommodate them all, or enough room for the actual intellectual exuberance we could stimulate if we wanted to.

---

1. A version of Meier's essay appears as Chapter Nine of her 1995 book, *The Power of Their Ideas.*

Designing against the commonsense confusion between the intellectual and the academic is a big challenge for school designers. If our intellectual goals for students are not to be defined in conventional academic terms—knowledge of algebra, ability to write a research paper, and so on—then how are they to be defined? Depending on our answer to this question, we inherit another question: How might the academic disciplines inform teaching and learning in some other way than by structuring them utterly?

The third item on the agenda for unlearning that I propose is subtly related to the first two. It is the public's commonsense perception that *personal competition is a necessary training ground for work in a competitive economy.* It too rests on the assumption that the school's essential function is meritocratic, that is, sorting out the winners from the also-rans. Much of what is demanded by new economic circumstances, and justified by new conceptions of intelligence and learning, runs counter to the idea of school as a sorting machine, but the idea is deeply ingrained. "All students will achieve at high levels," says the school, in accordance with the state's new goals, but in the hearts of principals, teachers, and parents, conditions are added: "in proportion to their abilities," "within the traditional hierarchy of achievement," "consistent with their family background," "given their probable career paths," and so on. And as in all other winnowing organizations, the worth of individuals is often defined by very narrow criteria: one's grade-point average, one's dutifulness in completing assignments, one's capacity for speaking and thinking like the majority or elite group.

In terms of serving the needs of a competitive economy, the problem is that this winnowing may well winnow out the diverse talents and viewpoints that enterprises need to stay responsive within their markets. Moreover, it threatens to accustom future workers to performance conditions that may be counterproductive in the workplace. The vitality of certain postindustrial manufacturing sectors is now considered dependent on production workers' cooperative skills (Marshall and Tucker, 1992; Commission on the Skills of the American Workforce, 1990). The same is true of so-called knowledge industries, from software development to medicine, where the individually competing entrepreneur is increasingly obsolete. It has become commonplace among school reformers to argue that the current organization of schools matches a workplace that began to emerge at the turn of the last century but is obsolescent today. But redesigning school to fit the values of a new workplace is so difficult partly because the meritocratic scheme embeds more than economic values. It also resonates with deep-seated American moral assumptions. We Americans like to live on our own, work on our own, be judged on our own, find our own salvation.

The fourth attitude in need of unlearning also has moral roots. It is the organizational preference for *central control in cellular institutions*—that is, institutions that are not highly integrated, where work happens in compartments. Most school principals today have more power over school policy, and teachers more power over classrooms, than either can wisely or effectively wield on their own. This dysfunctional separation of powers is sanctioned by a tacit treaty in most schools whereby teachers maintain instructional autonomy in return for their silence about school management—the closed classroom door (Johnson 1990; Goodlad, 1984; Goodlad and others, 1970). It is a key feature of the school as Taylorist workplace—an organization of hierarchical, rule-bound, and compartmentalized behavior—the epitome of organizational design at the turn of the last century but anachronistic today (Callahan, 1962). What is lost in the Taylorist workplace is the capacity of the school to articulate common standards or to digest those it has been handed, to develop collective images of excellence over time, to reflect on their application to actual student performance, and to direct the school's systems accordingly (Sizer, McDonald, and Rogers, 1992). All of these require broadly distributed powers to generate information as well as challenge it, to command resources and attention, and to take action.

Nor is power enough. Opportunities to wield power in the interest of genuine learning often seem constrained by debilitating school norms, consequences again of centralized controls. These are the givens of much current school design and include the compression of work time into short and errand-filled days and years, inflexible parceling of teacher and student effort into subjects and grade levels, inflexible and often inequitable apportionment of resources by bodies per classroom, a persistent wariness toward parents and other "outsiders," and a tendency to keep information and information-processing tools privileged and scarce.

Despite all this, there is ground for optimism in unlearning this organizational addiction. First, there is as much ambivalence about central authority in the American tradition as there is a yearning for it. Furthermore, new initiatives in industry offer an alternative image of control, one that includes generous training time and reflective capacity built into work schedules, heterogeneous and integrated work groups, flexible and responsive use of resources, valuing of all clients and suppliers as integral participants in organizational life, and information-based decision making at the front line (Senge, 1990; Deming, 1986, 1994). In fact, a tenet of current industrial theory is that decentralized production processes respond more facilely to turbulent markets than centralized ones can.

On the other hand, schools might easily remain insulated from these trends until most of the next century has elapsed, so isolated are they now, and so much the prey of an unthinking reaction to their "crisis" that would actually make them worse in this regard. All that the "ineffective" school needs, some continue to proclaim, is a strong and visionary principal and a management design that puts all the power and responsibility in this principal's hands. Or all it needs is more "accountability," a word that on many tongues means more and tougher tests and teacher evaluations. Again, there are tacit moral conceptions ingrained here, not just economic ones.

Finally, a distinctly moral habit in need of unlearning is the *suspicion that children incline naturally toward trouble.* It is a habit that seems to thrive in this era when a growing number of children—a plurality in many communities—fail to resemble the adult establishment in skin color and social class. So the tendency of the adults is to lock away the students in conditions of extreme custody, where boredom threatens to smother anything active, including learning. Sometimes these conditions are physically appalling, as Jonathan Kozol (1991) has documented. But even where the custodial facilities physically resemble the average suburban shopping mall, the custody itself remains a serious impediment to achieving a mindful school (Powell, Farrar, and Cohen, 1985). I call it the intellectual lockdown.

One thing we have going for us at the moment by way of encouraging a shift away from this attitude is the fact of its manifest failure to accomplish its aims. Keeping young people cooped up and bored tends to make at least some of them act up rather than shut down. This is partly because they suspect the stated rationale of their confinement. It seems intuitively obvious to them that the custodial arrangements of ordinary school life are not really about safety, since they are enforced within a society manifestly unconcerned with the safety of children—a society that exercises little supervision except in school, that keeps many of them in poverty, that surrounds them with enticements toward danger, that seems, according to the evidence of milk cartons and tabloid television, to be full of kidnappers and molesters. So what is the real rationale? Again, children and young adults intuitively sense that it is about control rather than direction—the attempt of one generation to dictate rather than guide another generation's thinking and feeling (McNeil, 1986). This sense becomes especially salient in circumstances where the custodial arrangements lack evident caring, respect, and an appreciation of individuality. Such circumstances are common in large, public, secondary schools (Sizer, 1984; Sedlak, Wheeler, Pullin, and Cusick, 1986).

Yet we know how to create schools, at all levels and in all kinds of communities, that combine custody with caring, respect, and the appreciation of individuality. We know also that students who attend such schools tend to reach higher achievement levels, at least as these are commonly defined (test scores and course levels, for example), than do their peers who attend ordinary schools. The key seems to be to ensure that the school is a purposeful community rather than a collection of individuals pursuing their own self-interest (Bryk, Lee, and Holland, 1993; Newmann and Wehlage, 1995). Purposeful communities in which members feel some stake do not require coercive custodial arrangements. They are self-regulating.

On the other hand, they are not necessarily the kind of powerful intellectual environments that we wish to design for the twenty-first-century school. Purpose and caring are necessary but insufficient. Based on the research that I will be reporting in the following chapters, I would say that the following are also needed:

1. Access for students to the intellectual expertise of others besides their teachers and to good intellectual work done by others outside their school
2. Allocations of the school's time, space, and other resources in proportion to the demands of intellectual projects
3. Opportunities for students to learn to manage their own intellectual work, uncover their own intellectual resources, and exercise their own intellectual judgment

Systemic Design

The theory of redesigning school that my colleagues and I developed, and that I will elaborate on in the rest of this book, is a theory of systemic design. It takes account of the school reform cycle of the 1980s, when the perceived unresponsiveness of schools to state directives was followed by the design of stronger directives and then by the schools' perverse adaptations to the resulting pressure (Darling-Hammond and Wise, 1985). It holds that the unresponsiveness of schools to directives—whether they take the form of 1980s-style minimum competency exams or 1990s-style curriculum frameworks—is at least partly the result of the school's necessary attention to interior complexities (Elmore and McLaughlin, 1988). Schools are simple only when viewed from the outside. At the same time, our theory holds that interior complexities do not account for the entire design of a school. Exterior relations matter too. In short, schools are both the nodes of a complex system and also complex systems themselves. It will not do to ignore either aspect of their complexity in trying to redesign them. On the other hand, we began the Exhibitions Project with a bias for understanding both the interior and exterior complexities of school from an interior point of view. We wanted to help correct what we saw as an imbalance among the school reformers of the early 1990s toward thinking of schools as objects rather than agents of reform. Indeed that was our charge to ourselves: to capture the inside story. By inverting the ordinary perspective of systemic reform, however,

I think we gained more than access to the inside story. I think we also found a fresh way to think about school design in its entirety.

Design Arenas

Schools differ in shape, size, structure, culture, political environment, and still other dimensions. My colleague Ted Sizer likes to say that no two good schools are alike. I would say the same of bad schools: each has been poisoned in a unique way by history, leadership, and circumstance. Certainly the ten schools in which we conducted the bulk of the research I report in this book were extraordinarily different from each other along many dimensions, though they were also unusually committed to change. Because we spent enough time in each one of them to know them well, we came to realize not only their obvious differences from each other—such things as large and urban, small and rural, middle or high school, midwestern or southern, and so on—but also their subtle differences. These are the things one catches a whiff of early but only later tracks down enough to name: idiosyncrasies of personality, subtleties of attitude, differences of rhythm and emphasis.

At the same time, however, hopping from one to the other over the course of three years, we came to think also that the most important characteristics of each of the schools were features of the same three general properties. The schools all had core beliefs. Some of these beliefs were actively up for reconsideration as a consequence of the schools' reform agendas, though others seemed hardly noticed. Second, the schools were all organized—we came to say wired—so that certain kinds of functions involving the exchange and distribution of energy, information, and power were ordinary, while other kinds were nearly impossible to carry out or sustain. And, third, the schools had ready access—we came to say that they were tuned—to certain ideas and values emanating from the world outside their walls, while they remained oblivious to other ideas and values. Gradually we realized that these three properties of schools constitute arenas for design. That is, one cannot hope to redesign the whole school without dealing in depth with issues of belief; issues involving the distribution of power, energy, and information within the school; and issues involving the schools' links to outside values and ideas. There are two obvious benefits of thinking about the problem of redesign in this way. First, it avoids the trap of regarding schools, at least tacitly, as either utterly independent systems or as mere outposts of a larger system. The three properties cut across the distinction. Second, they break down the whole task of redesign into approachable parts, while nevertheless preserving a sense of the whole and of its interrelatedness.

The Process of Redesign

In some respects the terrain within which we redesign school is hospitable and in other respects quite hostile. In any case, it is what it is, and we would be foolish to think of it otherwise. We must do our designing with the real terrain in mind. It helps also to be as broad as possible in our conception of design. This is where the research reported in this book may be most helpful. Current school reform efforts often emphasize only one of the three arenas that we found in the designing work of the schools we studied—the arenas we dubbed believing, wiring, and tuning. Some reformers, for example, put all the stress on the formulation of missions, goals, outcomes, and ideology. They imply that the right beliefs alone can transform a school. Still other reformers tend to ignore beliefs in premature but often passionate efforts to restructure. They try to lay the wiring before anyone is clear about the purposes it must support. Finally, a third set of reformers puts entirely too much stock in tuning, as if the existing beliefs and structures of schools really do not matter. Just get the incentives right, these reformers say, and everything else will fall into place.

The thesis of this book, by contrast, is that all three arenas make important claims on our attention if we are serious in our redesigning efforts. Yet it is possible to deal with these claims one at a time. Another way to put this is to say that the problem of redesigning school systemically can be approached systematically. The discovery is akin to the realization that writing has a process that can be taught and learned. It is comforting to see that what otherwise seems an impenetrable tangle of demands can be approached in order. So, for example, in writing, the writer gathers whatever raw material is of interest, then shapes that material, and finally finishes the shape. Of course, these phases are not utterly distinct. Yet the writer does well to approach them as if they were—to keep gathering even in the face of shaping's incessant demands to impose itself prematurely, to dare to shape despite the gnawing sense of having left so much ungathered, to hold off finishing until the last possible moment but then to devote oneself to it as the guarantor of meaningful communication.

Similarly, the arenas of designing or redesigning school are an ordered threesome. First, one has to work on crucial issues of believing before committing to a new wiring plan. Otherwise, one will lay new wiring as if for the old house. This is not to disagree, however, with Michael Fullan's (1993) quip that the motto of school reformers ought to be, "Ready, fire, aim." In fact, believing has much more to do with readiness than with aiming. I too despair of the change strategies that would have schools spell out all their goals and objectives before they make a single move. In school reform, impetuousness is a virtue. Furthermore, what Fullan calls aiming and what I call tuning are much the same, and they are most effective when there are some new systems to aim or tune.

When one approaches the arenas of design in order—believing, wiring, tuning—the unique challenges of each become more decipherable, and the greater clarity stimulates improvisational energy. That is why I have organized this book in the same way. Of course, there is a drawback to approaching redesign in this systematic way, whether as designer or author. It is that one may come to overrationalize a process that remains in practice very messy. In fact, whether the design process involves designing a new school from scratch or redesigning an established one—and our research included both sources of data—it can never be cleanly sequential. To expect it to be so is to doom one's efforts.

Part One

Believing

The first of the three arenas of school design, which I call *believing,* is concerned with values. What does the school believe? What knowledge does it cherish? To what ends does it wish to orient its systems? In redesigning within this domain, the school asks itself what it proposes to accomplish in the minds and hearts of the students it teaches, and it defines how it will go about this. The work always involves what is called vision, particularly the capacity to envision the school's results in the habits and attitudes of its graduates and to see the actual systems of the school in relation to these results. But it may call figuratively on other senses too—for example, what might be called taste in matters of teaching and learning.

The next two chapters are about the role of believing in school design. Chapter One explains how the focus on intellectual purpose challenges a contrary and prevalent system of beliefs. It takes up complex conceptual and strategic questions. These are important to the development of a theory of redesign. Depending on their interests, however, some readers may want to begin this section by reading Chapter Two. It examines the role of leadership in fostering new beliefs and draws on voices and stories from the schools.

Chapter One

A New Belief System

When I was young, I witnessed an event that revealed to me suddenly one of my school's deepest beliefs. Our principal stood at the top of some long stone steps and called out across dozens of children heading back from lunch: "Would someone please inform the crossing guard that I wish to speak with him?" Six boys, trained to please, raced to the corner with the message. For some reason, I held back. That is how it happened that I, but not my six friends, heard her call out sternly, "I said, '*One* boy.'" Minutes later, the six were before the principal with their hands outstretched. My classmates and I, walking slowly in formation up a creaky staircase, could see into her office just below. She raised a thick ruler above her shoulder and crashed it down on the hands of each boy. The welts that later rose on my friends' hands were intended to teach them, as well as their classmates who witnessed the scene, that exuberance was forbidden in our school—even exuberance in dutifulness and helpfulness.

I think of the incident now as a sighting, a rare glimpse of values operating below the surface of espoused belief, an empirical test of what really counts in a particular school. This school professed an ideal of service to others, but it was actually committed to control as the paramount virtue. If I had gone at the close of that school day to protest to the principal on behalf of my friends, as I had resolved to do despite the lesson, I might well have been punished too, for demonstrating an exuberant sense of fairness. Or like the James Joyce character in *Portrait of the Artist as a Young Man,* who actually did protest a similar cruelty, I might have been dismissed with a patronizing smile.

Once during the process of conducting the research for this book, I stumbled on a sighting in progress. I had been invited to observe some student performances. A teacher had asked her students to prepare dramatic presentations based on excerpts from their own autobiographical essays. A young woman, one of only two or three African American students in this class, used the opportunity to protest the school's tracking—or ability-grouping system—that keeps advanced classes mostly white. It must have seemed to her fair game; the curriculum was autobiography, and the racial partitions of her school were inescapably part of her life. "There are differences between us," this girl told her classmates, in a steely but passionate voice, "but you never see what they really are." Later, focusing on the student's public acknowledgment of difference, her teacher told me that she had tried to head it off, to get her instead to see that "fundamentally everyone is the same." In saying this, the teacher had expressed the gist of the school's commitment to desegregation. Listening politely, the student saw through this commitment. She saw that a banality like "everyone is fundamentally the same" can perpetuate the division of people by the narrowest of indicators. If we agree that everyone is fundamentally the same, then the fact that we sort them along this or that particular dimension of difference must be benign. But the teacher's teaching in this instance was incongruous with the student's experience: she knew that the sorting in her school was not benign. Thinking about this incongruity sparked the sighting. That is really what a sighting is: an incongruity, closely read.

Deep Beliefs

Every school is governed by deep beliefs. They shape the school's key relationships, and they ultimately determine the culture and quality of the school. Even schools that seem wholly lacking in purposefulness are deeply directed by beliefs, and ripe for sightings. Consider, for example, the high school whose social contract is characterized by Paul Hill and his colleagues as follows:

> We are obligated to run this school and you are obligated to be here. While you are here, we hope you will take advantage of what we make available. If we can help remove obstacles to your taking

> advantage of the programs here, we will do so. We will ensure that you are safe while you are here. If you ask us for specific help, we will almost surely give it. If you do not call attention to your needs, we probably will not notice the problem. We can't do much to control your behavior, but if your attendance here makes life unbearable for others, we would prefer that you leave [Hill, Foster, and Gendler, 1990, p. 40].

Like many other public schools, this one believes itself obligated to serve the public as an impassive facility—rather like the emergency room at the city hospital or a restroom at the bus station. Among some of the schools in our study—the large, open-enrollment high schools—this remained a strong residual belief, one against which much of the rest of the character of these schools was formed. As Hill, Foster, and Gendler explain, schools animated by a belief in themselves as a public facility often insulate themselves from the users of the facility by a preoccupation with the smooth running of programs. Whether particular learners thrive as a result of these programs is a more distant concern, comparable to whether the gunshot victim who receives good care in the emergency room survives, or whether the patron of the clean and safe restroom enjoys her bus trip. Meanwhile, just below the surface of the school's belief in itself as an impassive public facility may lie a belief in the futility of active teaching and personal care, a belief that the school's clients are somehow undeserving of these. Students who experience sightings in such schools, who actually glimpse this belief at work in their own education, often drop out. As an office aide in a large urban high school once confided to Michelle Fine (1991), "I don't know why they call them drop-outs, when we make them go" (p. 63).

By uncovering the operative beliefs below the surface of espoused ones or below the surface of institutional indifference, sightings get at the truth. They are therefore an indispensable tool in achieving genuine change. To build new schools focused on teaching all children to use their minds well requires the abandonment of many conventional and deep-seated beliefs, yet one cannot abandon what one cannot first discern.

While writing this book, I had a conversation with an architect who designs schools in the physical sense. The conversation confirmed for me the importance in any kind of design work of surfacing and confronting tacit beliefs. This architect believes that children will be safer as well as better served intellectually in schools that are situated in the centers of towns rather than on their outskirts, so they are integrated into the town's daily commerce rather than set apart from it. To convince his clients, however, he must first deal with the fact that their intuitions may or may not have prepared them for his argument. I, for example, who have lived most of my life in cities, feel safest and most alert intellectually in busy and noisy locations. When I see secluded rural homes, I wonder how anyone could feel safe living in them or get any work done there, so I am predisposed to accept the architect's argument, though I may not know that I am. I may think instead that I am drawn to it simply because of its rationality or its appeal to common sense. Consequently I may be unable to fathom my neighbor's utter rejection of it. Nor may the neighbor understand that her own childhood spent in a remote and quiet place has predisposed her to think the idea utterly irrational and contrary to common sense. To design a school for both our children, this architect must first get us to notice our respective orientations in these matters and their grounding in our different experiences. Then he must somehow manage to get us talking with each other about the differences and help us appreciate the irony of our having become neighbors. From such talk and appreciation, he can then nurture the consensus of belief necessary to build a school. To say that none of this believing work is the architect's work—to confine the architect's work to the drawing table—is to ensure design failure. It is also to reject one of any designer's richest possible sources of inspiration: the different perspectives people bring to everything and the power unleashed by their reflection on these differences.

The Current Belief System

Enunciating a set of new beliefs is among the least difficult challenges of redesigning school. Dislodging old beliefs is much harder. That is because beliefs really matter. They are deeply and systemically implicated in all the dimensions of schooling. The power of their hold is defined by their generativity and by an ensuing coherence. So they tend to generate layers of assumptions, attitudes, and habits of practice, which reinforce each other in an evolving and dynamic way. The result is what we call a belief system. As in all other systems, one part affects all other parts. Genuine change requires a deep transformation in the system's coherence. It must be taken apart and put together again on an utterly different basis.

In the following pages, I explore this idea of systemic change by first considering two pervasive beliefs about children and teaching that have a systemic influence on schooling today. In my view, this influence is among the most serious impediments to redesigning schools so that they teach all children to use their minds well. Then I critically examine two change strategies aimed at uprooting these beliefs. One is a strategy pursued by many school reformers today; the other is one my colleagues and I articulated when we reflected on our earliest findings in the study of the ten schools. Next I reflect on our ultimate findings in order to suggest still a third strategy, one that I think improves on the first two. Finally, I take up the question of what might replace the belief system that all three strategies oppose. I propose one that I think can support the actions needed to turn all children into thoughtful and resourceful citizens of the twenty-first century.

Two Prevailing Beliefs

The first of the beliefs is that children can be easily sorted intellectually. Schools today tend to believe that children differ from each other principally in age and in how much brain power they were born with. Children are, in this view, just as sortable by one dimension as by the other. Among the practical consequences of this belief are grades, ability grouping, and differentiated expectations.

The second belief, also widely shared now, is that teaching is a form of telling. On a deep level, though often not avowedly, most schools tend to believe that telling and repeating what one has been told constitute the elemental relationship of schooling—defining the teacher's intellectual subordination to higher expertise even as it defines the student's intellectual subordination to the teacher.

Enhancing their generativity, these two beliefs dovetail nicely. The givenness of a neat range of abilities seems to require that knowledge be tailored to the range. Since telling is not a reciprocal activity, this tailoring can be accomplished outside the messiness of actual encounters between real teachers and real children—for example, through the production of textbooks, the design of course syllabi, the articulation of curriculum scope and sequence plans, and so on. Together the two beliefs generate and reflect commonsense notions of human intelligence and the nature of knowledge. They seem to justify and be justified by actual student behavior and the products of student work. A few children do learn readily to identify the Gadsden Purchase and the Oregon Territory in matching tests, while others lag behind at predictable intervals. Meanwhile, some children—at the bottom of the class, of course—will not even sit still to be told where the Oregon Territory was, while others seem to hunger for even harder facts. Third, these beliefs seem so well tuned to other circumstances. So the economy seems a pecking order based on individual achievement, neighborhoods seem arranged in hierarchies of class and taste, and the principal work of citizenship seems to lie in following directions and filling out forms on time. Finally, the beliefs fit "naturally" with professional teaching practice, guiding it into comfortable, century-old patterns: group the children according to their instructional level; present the algorithm for "borrowing" in subtraction and have the whole class practice it at their seats; make sure that no one collaborates in answering the questions.

Yet many educators today regard these teaching behaviors as antique. That is because they have been influenced by the new theoretical environment I described in the Introduction. This environment is the result of a confluence of disparate intellectual forces including cognitive psychology, so-called constructivist epistemologies in the disciplines, the new rhetoric of industrial productivity, the abiding American rhetoric of educational equity, and the century-leaping mentorship of John Dewey. The environment is similar to those that supported reforms earlier in the century—in the 1910s, 1930s, and 1970s—except that psychological and economic arguments have now been added to long-standing philosophical and political ones. The result is that educators today seem to have less confidence overall—theoretically speaking—in the default values of the school as these have emerged during the twentieth century. Is intelligence really given, singular, assessable, finite? Is diversity really a disadvantage in teaching and learning?

Is control the prerequisite of creativity? Is understanding actually conveyable from head to head? These questions, relatively well settled at the century's midpoint, now seem problematic, insofar as one can judge by articles in professional journals and by the frequency of certain ideas on the professional development circuit.

Still, theory is not enough, even when it begins to affect ordinary professional discourse. Worse, its presence there can sometimes mask its absence in practice. The principal of one school we studied, feeling discouraged one day, warned us not to mistake all the talk of change in his school for change itself. "It's hard," he warned, sounding like a professor of research methodology, "to hear what's said and look at what's happening without imposing drama on it that is not really there." It is just as hard, he might have added, to make one's deepest and most operative beliefs yield to a new idea. Although the leaders of all the schools we studied were explicitly and sometimes passionately committed to a new intellectual deal for the schools' students, and although they found their faculties responsive to this ambition for the most part, they also found old beliefs very hard to budge. Under pressure, the prevailing belief system underlying practice may grow stronger first, rather than dissipate quickly. One teacher explained to us how this dynamic unfolded in her school:

> One of the outcomes of all this talk about high standards is that people began to panic. Teachers were afraid that this thing was just going to keep on spreading, that standards were going to be raised in every area. And the principal's idea was that if the regular kids were going to do it, then the special education kids were going to do it too. And I think that really scared a lot of people.

What unnerved this teacher's colleagues is that they might be forced to cope with the uncertainties of teaching absent the security that leveled children and correspondingly leveled curriculum seem to provide. Even among teachers who are conscious of the falseness of such security, the attachment may die hard—if not on a conscious level, then on a subconscious one. So, for example, one teacher, deeply involved in her school's effort to dismantle tracking, nonetheless told us that she worried about "the lower-level kids who have always been used to having somebody standing right over them, telling them, giving them a worksheet, really leading them step by step." In her comment, the teacher failed to make the distinction one might expect, given her own interest in detracking, between lower-level experience and "lower-level kids." The two categories had fused for her, as for so many other teachers we talked with and also for many of the students we met. Meanwhile, her comment also reveals the impact of the other belief. She worries about what "low-level" students will do without the telling they have grown used to.

Indeed, the association of teaching with telling is just as difficult to shake as the idea of naturally leveled children. In the schools we studied, we noticed it most frequently within environments that seemed expressly designed for a different kind of pedagogy. In one school, for example, I visited a horticulture class meeting in a workshop and greenhouse stuffed with plants and tools and worktables, a space with easy access to school grounds and gardens. The principal, who was among the most active of the principals we studied in trying to foster what he called active learning, thought that I would find it here. But in each of my two visits to this class, I found the teacher spending the entire double teaching block on tenaciously didactic instruction and his students fiercely fighting his effort to control their every move. The physical environment he had created with an evidently deep and personal investment of many resources seemed just an ironic backdrop. In another school's theater class, I found many opportunities for students to improvise and otherwise engage in creative activities, but I also found the teacher regularly giving notes on dramatic literature. These were invariably banal: a dictated list of a particular play's main and secondary conflicts, the teacher's definition of its theme or moral. In still another school, I entered the art room one day expecting to find students at work there on different projects, animated by their own distinct interests, coached by a teacher whose teaching took its cue from these projects and interests. I knew that the teacher believed expressly in what her school termed student-centered, project-based teaching. But a deeper belief was showing the day I visited. The teacher had just halted all work in the room in order to demonstrate to everyone a particular drawing technique. Only one student clearly needed the demonstration at this moment, but the teacher thought that all her students might need it at some point. The problem was that the others were then immersed in their own work. Some students looked up at their teacher's call for attention, but others groaned and kept on working. Their reaction triggered another in her, one that was perhaps exacerbated by the fact that I was watching. She demanded loudly that everyone pay attention and put down their tools. One young man disgustedly threw his brush onto a nearby table, while another mockingly picked one up. The teacher refused to proceed with her teaching until the latter put the brush back down again. The room grew thick with tension. "Man, you got a control problem," the student said finally. "And you got a respect problem," the teacher countered.

As an observer, I thought both accusations true, though I also saw the benefit of the frank exchange. One cannot change what one cannot see or frankly say. Although this was the most painful of the three classes to observe, it struck me also as the most hopeful. That is because a theory of art as a constructive activity had clearly infected both students and teacher (even if the latter may have violated its spirit in this instance). It is also because a theory about the role of speaking up in acquiring an education was in the air here too—the consequence, I suspect, of its deliberate cultivation by the school as a whole. Most schools weigh tact as a greater virtue among students than assertiveness. Not so here. The result is that such an encounter as the one I witnessed is more likely here than in many other schools to turn into a learning experience for both student and teacher rather than into just another detention or suspension.

Yet although the art class seemed to me the most hopeful, the horticulture and theater classes seemed far from hopeless. Of course, it helps enormously that all three classes involve school subjects that have conventionally been taught in other than exclusively didactic ways. This is how the alternative theory got into the picture in each case. Since it is there, it can function as a catalyst for change under the right circumstances. So the horticulture teacher's now-distant attachment to a theory of learning by doing first caused him to fill his rooms with plants and tools for working with them. Although his teaching is now dominated by telling and his students' learning is dominated by unreflective resistance, still the stuff all around them mocks this status quo. Such environments are ripe for sightings. Some day a student may say to this teacher, "I don't get it. Why do you have all this stuff here if we can't use any of it?" And such a statement might awaken the dormant theory. Similarly, although the theater teacher is now trapped in an ineffectually segmented pedagogy, where the didactic and the active do not touch each other, their juxtaposition offers at least the chance that the theories undergirding each might someday come to rub. Here again, a student might spark the process: "How come they call them plays, if you can't play around with them?"

By themselves, sightings make only a psychological difference. Yet perhaps a revolution can grow from such a difference, as Paolo Freire ([1970] 1981) has argued. The principal of one school we studied made a similar argument in a memo to her faculty: "People's minds are harder to change than buildings, timetables, and monitoring devices. The task is to create a useful dissonance between the latter and the former, one that encourages new habits of mind, heart, and work." This often requires some clever moves on the part of a school's leaders, a matter I explore in Chapter Two. But such moves matter little where there is no irony available to give them greater reach.

In one of our interviews, we found a teacher pausing at an ironic intersection in his own daily practice. At that point, he was not ready for a full-fledged sighting, but his concluding metaphor hints of one:

> I find that when I have my hat as a computer teacher on, it's a lot different for me than when I have my hat as a math teacher on. When I'm a computer teacher, I'm not really dealing with a concrete answer. What I'm dealing with is a methodology of arriving at an answer. Maybe one kid is more elegant than another—in other words, uses fewer steps. Another kid takes twice as many steps, maybe takes twice as long, but still comes up with a perfect answer. Both are good, both are fine, as long as the kid understands that one answer could be better than the other because it's shorter.
>
> But, I think math is a hard area—how do I want to say this?—to be more creative—like what I'm doing across the hall—I've just

gone over the same problem three times. Each time a kid asks me the same question, which is really something they should have had three years ago. Either it's right or it's wrong. There's not really a thought process which they go through.

There are some times when I almost say to myself, "My God, I'm being so black or white or right or wrong," and it upsets me that I have to sit down and actually figure out averages when I'm grading a math class. And I have to say this kid never made up this test, whereas in a computer class if a kid misses a class it's not a big deal. Last year, I had a database class with about eight or nine kids in it, and one of the kids had just gotten his license and had four of the other kids in his car and it snowed. They got into an accident, and all went to the hospital with broken bones. It knocked out half of that class for two weeks. But then we came in one Saturday and spent from nine to three and made up the two weeks. So, in computer class, I don't have to be so . . . I don't have to have those blinders on. I like that a lot better.

The dissonance this teacher noticed, the irony he felt, and the possibility of a future sighting—that is, of the emergence of real awareness on his part of the need for change—are all products of considerable work under way in his school to redesign its system of beliefs. But the leaders of this work—the principal, a half-dozen teachers, one of two assistant principals—had to fight off continually a feeling that their work was forlorn. In fact, such signs of its success as what the math and computer teacher told us might well have struck them more as evidence of its failure. Notice again his line, "There are some times when I almost say to myself. . . ." "Why still *almost*?" his reform-minded colleagues might have answered. How will you ever get past *almost*?

What, indeed, might get this teacher past *almost*? What else do his colleagues need besides patience? Even if all four of these teachers had sightings, so what? What is the link between a sighting and a revolution? What can bring theory to the ground?

The Lure of Leverage

There is a tantalizing consequence for school reformers of the neat fit between the idea of children as sortable intellectually and the association of teaching with telling. If one could only find the right lever, they think—or, like Archimedes, the right place to stand—then one might be able to dislodge the whole prevailing belief system in a single lift. One could also then replace it with another coherent system. It happens that there is also a neat fit between the idea that all children are smart enough to construct valid understandings of the world and the belief that genuine understanding requires active exploration. If all children can figure things out for themselves with good guidance and rich materials to work with, then a teacher can teach without telling.

But how can the prevailing coherence be replaced with this candidate one? Is there some lever to be found that might do the job, say, in a couple of heaves? And in the enormous sprawl and fragmentation of the schooling system in the United States, is there a good place to stand in order to use such a lever?

What does it mean, anyway, to supplant a reigning coherence? It is obvious, for example, that one cannot argue it away, since arguing is a form of telling, and telling is one of the culprits. Nor can one teach it away, since teaching is under its spell—not only in schools but throughout higher education and the particular branch of it that we call professional education. This presents no small problem inasmuch as the preprofessional and continuing professional education of educators has long been reform's favorite lever. Yet by privileging the perspective of the outsider—the professor, the consultant, the curriculum supervisor—most professional development activities for teachers inadvertently reinforce the givenness of an intellectual hierarchy, in which the teachers who are presumed to need development are clearly at the bottom. Even when the overt purpose of such activities is to teach teachers that their students cannot be sorted into hierarchically arranged bins, the hidden curriculum steals the show. It is indeed often a show: one for an audience of 150 teachers assembled in an auditorium for the superintendent's bimonthly in-service day, or one for 250 educators in a hotel conference room, in which some currently prominent author tells everyone the limits of telling as a teaching strategy.

But if argument alone is a poor strategy, and ordinary professional education too, then what is to be done?

One Strategy of Leveraged Reform

Some reformers today are addressing this question with a bundle of ideas they pack into a single word. The word is *standards,* and their various efforts comprise what Anne Lewis (1995) calls the standards movement. Those involved in this movement often seek to exert leverage in three places. The first place is where teachers get their ideas of what to teach. Here, *content standards* seek to lift teachers' sights. Content standards are propositions concerning what all children should know and be able to do, both within particular domains of knowledge and across them. Following the cue of the standards movement, the federal government has funded a number of national efforts to devise such propositions, and many states have done so also. The 1994 federal legislation that enacted the Goals 2000 program, and also the latest version of the Title I compensatory education program, are premised on the availability of content standards as touchstones for policy, practice, and the design of state-level assessments.

The second proposed point of leverage is where teachers and others judge student performance. Here *performance standards* seek to lift everyone's sense of what is good enough. Performance standards are definitions of satisfactory performance, keyed to the content standards, and applied in assessments rich enough to capture what is actually valued. Such assessments may use the emerging technologies of performance assessment: exhibitions, portfolios, constructed-response testing, and so on (Mitchell, 1992; Wiggins, 1993).

Finally, the third proposed point of leverage is where students gain the supports they need to meet the challenge of the content and performance standards. Here, *opportunity to learn* standards seek to lift the prospects of all students. If the new paradigm for practice is not to be simply a fancier sorting factory, say many standards movement activists, then all children must have access to good teaching and other resources necessary to achieve at the unprecedented levels desired and in unprecedented numbers. But how might such opportunity-to-learn standards be employed? And exactly what form should they take? Most reformers agree that simply counting resources—the proportion of teachers teaching within their certification area, the number of books in the library, the number of electives offered at the high school, and so on—is not enough. David Green and Tom Wilson argue that policymakers should put aside their habit of specifying abstract indicators that travel by paper up the policy chain and ensure opportunity to learn by inspecting for it (Wilson, 1995). Others seem to associate opportunity to learn almost exclusively with professional development incentives and programs for teachers (Porter, 1994). The Goals 2000 legislation requires that participating states pay attention to opportunity to learn, but is largely mute on the form that this attention should take.

Perhaps the best articulation of the hopes of the standards movement and of the assumptions of belief that underpin it can be found in the New Standards Project, cofounded and led by Lauren Resnick at the Learning Research and Development Center and by Marc Tucker of the National Center for Education and the Economy. With philanthropic funds as well as public funds committed by member states and cities, the New Standards Project has developed a set of content and performance standards well illustrated with samples of actual student work (New Standards Project, 1995). It has also conducted many professional development activities aimed at enhancing opportunities to learn. Finally, it is developing an assessment system in core areas—literacy, math, science, and so on—designed to be used as the basis for awarding a national certificate of initial mastery (CIM) at about age sixteen. One point of the CIM strategy is to permit national and international benchmarking of student achievement—with a level of initial mastery well delineated and acknowledged. In organizational terms, the strategy is highly rationalist. It is intended to induce a sequence of changes in structure and attitude such that the belief system I have been sketching above will be undone. A primer on the CIM, produced by the Workforce Skills Program (1994) of the National Center for Education and the Economy, imagines some of these changes from a teacher's perspective, capturing in the process the rationalist quality:

> Imagine that you were a high school teacher of mathematics in a school district and state that had adopted the Certificate of Initial Mastery system. There is a very clear measure of your success—the

> proportion of your school's students who get the Certificate of Initial Mastery before they leave school. . . . For many years, the elementary schools passed their failure up to the middle schools, the middle schools passed their failures up to the high schools, and the high schools gave diplomas to youngsters who could often barely read and write. But now, everything in your world has changed. Now there is a clear standard in place and everyone is expected to meet it. You and your students and their parents all have handbooks that explain what the standards are, and provide clear, vivid examples of the kind of student work that will meet those standards [pp. 11–12].

Here is the lure of leverage well expressed: that a clear standard expressed in a single assessment poised at just the right point in the complex system of schooling might at once dispel the effects of years of tracking and of differentiated expectations for students, might provide all students a compelling reason to work hard, and provide their teachers the energy they need to ensure that the hard work pays off.

A Second Leveraged Strategy: Planning Backwards

My colleagues and I began the research I report in this book with a search for leverage quite similar to that of the standards movement, though significantly different in scale. We formed our hypothesis with the perspective in mind of a small number of actual schools, rather than the perspective of national education policy. Scale makes a difference. Ours helped us quickly discern a key problem facing the standards movement, the one David Cohen (1995) describes in writing about Goals 2000:

> This statute is perched atop an education system in which there is little experience either with formulating or using content and performance standards. Everyone involved has almost everything to learn. . . . Standards set high enough to exemplify truly outstanding work could be irrelevant because they would be so far from current practice as to alienate or mystify most potential learners. But standards set close enough to current practice to be more easily understood and attained could fail to stimulate much improvement. Most American educators are quite unfamiliar with

> high standards, as are most Americans. Our ignorance on this matter is one crippling inheritance of a school system that has long refused to offer intellectually demanding work to most students—in good part because few Americans have wanted it. That inheritance is a good reason to adopt higher standards, but it is also a great barrier to achieving or even seriously comprehending them [pp. 753–754].

The schools we worked with knew quite well what they were up against in trying to dislodge the prevailing belief system. I think now, however, that they were smarter than we researchers in avoiding the search for leverage. Indeed, leverage struck many of them intuitively as the wrong change strategy. From the beginning, they expected us, as a condition of our relationship with them, to try to understand this intuition and to help them make its terms explicit. It took us a long time, however, to fulfill this expectation, though the relationship conditioned us for eventual insight.

As I acknowledged above, we began our work with the same hypothesis as the standards movement and proceeded accordingly. We also focused on the importance of surfacing things submerged in the ordinary running of the system—for example, the decision rules that teachers use when they decide what to teach or what is good enough in student performance. And we looked to the emerging technologies of performance assessment.

In our case, this technology was what the Coalition of Essential Schools calls exhibitions. The term derives from the eighteenth- and nineteenth-century academies—the precursors of the high school—where the school year often ended with public exhibitions of what students had learned (Sizer, 1964). Building on this etymology, school reformers today generally use the term to refer to an assessment in which students exhibit for some public audience the results of a project they have undertaken or the understanding they have gleaned from a set of texts or experiences. More generally, the Coalition of Essential Schools uses the term also to signify a major design objective: to graduate students on the basis of demonstrated performance rather than on the basis of course credits earned (Sizer, 1991; McDonald and others, 1993). One way to do this is to require students to exhibit what they have learned at various points during their progress toward graduation or promotion, and perhaps to make a culminating exhibition as well—one that in some way integrates what they have learned or demonstrates that in the most important respects, they now match the school's expectations. The Coalition calls this "graduation by exhibition," and many of its schools have evolved systems for managing it.

A prime objective of many in the standards movement is also a performance-based system for promotion and graduation. That is one point of introducing the CIM, for example. As researchers, my colleagues and I shared the hypothesis of the standards movement that this objective, seriously pursued, would disturb deep beliefs. We thought that exhibitions might therefore be a good lever at the school level to undo the prevailing belief system. We called this "planning backwards" from an image of what students should know and be able to do by the time they graduate.

On the basis of our earliest investigations, we claimed that the process of planning backwards follows certain steps (McDonald, 1992c; Podl and others, 1992). The claim derived from our analysis of the systems for graduation by exhibition that we found in our sample of schools. Of the ten schools we studied, seven of them had such systems in place.[1] We called the common elements of these systems *dimensions,* but for a long time, we really meant *elements.* That is, we had a static and rational conception of how they functioned. Later, as our analysis proceeded, we changed this conception. In the following description of the six dimensions, I refer to the dynamic qualities that helped us gradually make this change.

1. *Vision.* To build their graduation by exhibition systems, the seven schools first selected—from whatever consensus they could muster—a vision of student performance that conformed with their beliefs about what really matters in a high school education. In most cases, these beliefs were still inchoate, although the schools

1. The seven schools in which we closely studied exhibition systems were all secondary schools. However, in an effort to understand whether the phenomenon might also have relevance to elementary school design, we explored one elementary school example. In that school, rather than focusing on graduation, the exhibition system focused on ensuring a continuity in teaching and learning during the transition between the sixth grade and the middle school.

were working toward their recognition and articulation. One value of designing an exhibition system was that it enabled the schools to do some work with the beliefs that they had already defined rather than wait—perhaps indefinitely—for the emergence of a more comprehensive set. Meanwhile the schools acknowledged that they were leaving a lot out. This acknowledgment gave them both a valuable psychic license to perform imperfectly and also an incentive to build in reflective mechanisms.

One school declared that it believed all of its graduates should at least be able to write good arguments on contemporary issues of importance and to defend these arguments orally. Another school, long practiced in the conduct of seminars, said that it believed all its graduates should at least be able to read and discuss difficult texts in ways that enlarge their own and others' understanding and that they then should be able to express this larger understanding in writing. A third school said that it believed that all its graduates should be able to pose a researchable question, pursue it over time, and offer a public answer in three formats: orally, visually, and in writing. A fourth school, one in which all seniors pursued a year-long community internship, said that it believed all its graduates should be able to describe the setting of their internship to an audience unfamiliar with it. In doing so, they should be able to draw on interviews and documents as well as their own experience, and to answer questions like the following: What is the basic business here? How does what I do in my internship relate to the basic business? How much power do I have relative to others in the workplace? How is the business faring?

In offering these examples, I am being cleaner and more rational in my formulations than was true in fact. For example, I say that one school declared its vision to be such and such. What actually happened is that the principal made the declaration, and rather precipitously. Then for the next several years, the declaration became a focus of the school's chaotic conversation. A similar cacophony of response surrounded all the visions I cite. Initially we thought of this as noise. Later we realized that the visions we found depend on noise. Under the right circumstances, given the right leadership moves, noise can prove a catalyst in a systems transformation.

2. *Prompt.* As is evident from the examples I have given, one cannot go far along the path of defining vision without specifying exactly what students will be asked to do in their exhibition. This is a sign of dynamism and of the fact that the relationships between these elements I am listing is more important than the elements themselves. Margaret Wheatley (1992) captures a certain quality of all systems by quoting an ancient Sufi teaching: "You think because you understand *one* you must understand *two,* because one and one makes two. But you must also understand *and*" (p. 9, citing Meadows, 1982, p. 23). The *and* here is extraordinarily important. Indeed, one of the qualities that impressed us most with the exhibition systems we examined were the connections the schools were willing to draw between vision and prompt. Several of them did this quite dramatically. If it is important to us, one of the schools said, that all our graduates exhibit the learning characteristics we associate with seminars, then let us see if all the seniors we are about to graduate actually do. At great psychic cost to both teachers and students in the short term, but great psychic benefit to them in the long term, this school assembled its seniors for their seminar-based graduation exhibition less than three months after the principal first proposed the idea—this despite howls of protest from some faculty ("But our students have widely varying academic abilities") and from the seniors themselves ("It's not fair! Nobody else in the city has to do it to graduate"). The principal, pushing hard on the *and* that lies between intention and effect, responded, "Shouldn't an educated person be able to read, write, think, and articulate ideas? And aren't the seniors we are about to graduate educated people?"

His productively impetuous attitude was also characteristic of most of the other schools we studied with systems for graduation by exhibition. They dared to ask, "If this is our vision now, and these are our students now, what exactly is the connection?" *Exactly* is the operative word too. That is, in thinking about an actual prompt, the school must get specific, and the power of the exhibition as a tool for redesign is in these specifics. So in the late spring of 1991, the school that adopted a seminar-based graduation exhibition sent all its seniors a folder containing the following three readings: an excerpt from Thucydides' history of the

Peloponnesian wars, called "The Melian Dialogue"; a short story by Leo Tolstoy, called "How Much Land Does a Man Need?"; and the Universal Declaration of Human Rights from the United Nations Charter. Also in the folder were a time and place to report for the two-hour seminar (three weeks hence), a schedule for the submission of an essay based on a question surfaced in the seminar, an explanation of evaluation procedures, and a list of teachers who had volunteered to provide preseminar tutoring for those requesting it.

These last details connect the prompt to each of the next two dimensions. No more than in any other typical high school, the faculty of this one was not used to collaborating in the design of assessment criteria, nor did they previously tutor students except in matters pertaining to their own courses. But this prompt was provocative enough to prompt such changes. One could call it in this sense a lever, but the metaphor lacks chutzpah, and chutzpah made the difference. How dare any public high school, particularly a district high school in the inner city, demand as a condition of graduation that all its students read and understand Thucydides and Tolstoy! How dare it think that even its "educably mentally handicapped" seniors could manage such a task, or its seniors who had relatively recently learned English! In fact, I witnessed one of these graduation seminars and could not pick out the senior whom the state's special education apparatus had labeled "educably mentally handicapped." All the students had read Thucydides, Tolstoy, and the Declaration of Human Rights; I saw the yellow highlighting all over their copies as they shuffled through them to find passages to cite. There was a variety in the sophistication level of the comments they offered during the two-hour discussion of these texts, but everyone contributed frequently and capably, whether speaking in native or foreign accents. They also referred to each other's contributions and responded to each other's ideas. My feeling, emerging after two hours among these young people who were strangers to me, reflected the power of the prompt as a galvanizing agent: I felt proud of them as intellectually alive fellow citizens.

3. *Evaluation.* As the standards movement asserts, one of the problems with the late-twentieth-century school is the unreliability of the judgments it makes about student performance. The assessment technology with which the movement proposes to cor-

rect this problem—the use of scoring rubrics, benchmarking exercises, benchmarked samples, moderated judgments, and so on—can help solve this problem. We saw this in a number of the schools we studied. However, the assessment technology there was not installed by state or national policy; it was, instead, imported by the schools' own leaders in order to deal with evaluation problems as they emerged. So the school that dared within three months to ask all its seniors to participate in graduation seminars had to confront the fairness question head-on. How will the school know that the evaluation of their performance is consistent across numerous seminars and judges? What traits of performance will the judges look for? How much will these traits weigh relative to each other? And so on. They wrestled with these questions over the course of several iterations of their graduation seminar, adding a rubric in the second year, a form of moderation in the third year, and so on. They stayed in charge of the process throughout but sometimes called on outside expertise.

A key problem of redesigning the school to teach all students to use their minds well is how to have such genuine accountability—that is, how to ensure that the school actually cares about the intellectual development of all its students and actually seeks to ensure that no student is left out. This is quite different from an accountability that consists only of compliance with policy mandates in curriculum, assessment, and reporting. In the schools we studied, the most important external incentives for accountability were provided by networks rather than district or state policies. For example, the school with the graduation seminar would never have attempted its development if it had not been deeply involved with two school reform networks: the Paideia network—a network that encourages seminar-based teaching—that has grown out of the work of Mortimer Adler (1982, 1983, 1984), and the Coalition of Essential Schools. Meanwhile, this school and other schools with exhibition systems tied to graduation had to struggle to protect their genuine accountability against policy demands for an accountability of the more compliant variety. In Chapter Five, I tell the story of such a struggle.

4. *Coaching Context.* The exhibition systems we studied were concerned with what the standards movement calls *opportunity to learn.* They were designed to pose and answer such questions as the

following: Where does our school teach students to read material like the Melian Dialogue? Do we teach all students equally energetically and equally well? Where do our students learn the behaviors of a seminar? Do they all get the chance to do so, even the ones the state calls "educably mentally handicapped"? Do we also teach them to take understandings gleaned in a seminar and expand them further in an essay? How do we coach them in these skills? Is everyone coached?

A school that dares to ask itself questions like these expects to get some answers that require corrective action. The exhibition system fulfills its main purpose when this asking and this acting become habitual and when ordinary teaching and learning come to depend on them. It is impossible for me to think that this could ever happen solely as the result of a district, state, or federal policy intervention in the name of opportunity to learn standards. However, in the beginning stages of our research, feeling my own susceptibility to the lure of leverage, I thought that it might happen as the result of merely installing a system of graduation by exhibition. In fact, the progress of reform in each of the schools we studied proved far too tortuous to support such a hypothesis.

5. *Student Work.* Perhaps the most important way in which an exhibition system may affect a school's overall redesign is in making student work central to accountability. Here what especially matters is that the work exhibited is not just any kind of work. In the systems we studied, the work always involved what Allan Collins, Jan Hawkins, and Sharon Carver (1991) call *authentic tasks*: those that reflect the changing nature of work and life and so appeal to students intuitively as useful. Such tasks include the following components:

> 1. Understanding complex systems (for example, computer systems, electronic systems)
> 2. Finding information about different topics in a large database
> 3. Writing a report or making an argument about some topic
> 4. Analyzing trends in data
> 5. Investigating a particular topic to answer some open-ended question
> 6. Interpreting a difficult text
> 7. Learning about some new domain [p. 240]

These are precisely the kinds of tasks that the seven schools emphasized in their exhibition systems. Indeed, they are characteristic of exhibitions generally (Allen and McDonald, 1994). According to Collins, Hawkins, and Carver, authentic tasks, taken seriously, demand equivalently authentic tools—for example, computers and electronic networks, not card catalogs and arithmetic algorithms. They also demand immersion in authentic work contexts—a "cognitive apprenticeship" (Collins, Brown, and Newman, 1989; Collins, Hawkins, and Carver, 1991)—where knowledge of facts, concepts, heuristics, learning strategies, and so on mixes with a variety of problem contexts and a "rich web of memorable associations" (Collins, Hawkins, and Carver, 1991, p. 218). In effect, authentic tasks, taken seriously, demand of school that it resemble a certain kind of contemporary workplace, the one the Commission on the Skills of the American Workforce (1990) calls a high-performance workplace, where people work cooperatively as well as alone, where diversity of perspectives and expertise is an asset, where access to appropriate tools is a given. By insisting on a conception of the intellectual as situated, they create room for more people to be smart. They alert the incipient pedant that it is more important to apply knowledge than recite it, and they address the interests of students otherwise lost in a schooling where *Macbeth* and the multiplication of fractions seem totally unrelated to any context they know or any life they might imagine for themselves (Collins, Hawkins, and Carver, 1991, p. 216).

I would argue too that authentic tasks, taken seriously, demand more than high-performance, in-school workplaces. They also demand authentic opportunities to engage with people and places beyond school. In effect, they demand a pedagogy radically at odds with that of teaching as telling. They demand of teachers that they function as guides to realms of information and experience they do not control and have perhaps not fully explored themselves.

Yet as we discovered in our research, statements about what authentic tasks demand of schools are rational abstractions of how they really function. What they really do is introduce the possibility that a complex and much more vital system may emerge. They facilitate what Dee Hock (1993) would call organizationally beneficial chaos. To the extent that the school is limber enough to adapt to the possibilities within this chaos and is reflective enough to notice them, then the possibilities may be realized.

6. *Reflection.* All the exhibition systems we studied had mechanisms for ensuring that they worked as expected and stayed useful. They all generated data—for example, videotapes of student performances, paper portfolios, scoring tallies—and they included mechanisms for reading and analyzing these data. This typically took the form of a committee of teachers, but at least one of the schools added other stakeholders too. Initially our analysis restricted the dimension we called reflection to these mechanisms. Later, however, we acknowledged that all the other dimensions depend on reflection too, and the acknowledgment ratcheted our analysis up to a higher level.

Throughout my discussion, I have insisted on attention to the connectedness of these dimensions. The reader may have thought I mean that the dimensions are linked serially. But does length follow width, or width link with depth? In fact, reflection is a dimension of an exhibition system, as length, width, and depth are dimensions of concrete objects. It is not a part of the whole but an aspect of it. The same is true of all the other dimensions. A prompt is not the element that comes after vision, as our original conception of planning backwards might suggest. The two exist simultaneously, but in different dimensions. Schooling and teaching are not linear enterprises. Teachers do not tend to prepare their teaching by first constructing abstract goals or consulting the state's content standards. Vision and prompt occur to them as interconnected facets of planning. The trick is to ensure that, as facets, they share a wholeness that is characterized by what Donald Schön (1983) calls reflection-in-action: the turning back of a thought on itself, yielding a reframing.

Planning Backwards Reconsidered

The schools we studied were mostly in the early stages of their experimentation with exhibitions. We found evidence, nonetheless, that the experimentation was straining the coherence of their old belief system— straining, though not yet breaking it in most cases. The difference is crucial and led later to our rethinking the steps of planning backwards. Still, the strain was notable. One student told us, for example, how startled she was by the evidence in her exhibition of her own intellectual capacity: "Speaking in front of your peers, explaining something more—it surprises you." A teacher we interviewed expressed a similar surprise in commenting on the exhibitions he witnessed in a colleague's class: "She had even her low levels doing really neat things!" Witnesses at one exhibition marveled at how the students, encouraged to pursue an intellectual interest, seemed to have gone far beyond what most had produced in ordinary classwork. Of course, such surprised reactions as these—lacking evident theoretical grounding, absent a commitment to test again the momentarily disturbed assumption—may lead to little redesign. As I say, strain without break.

It was in the process of trying to understand this strain without break that we began slowly to abandon our initial conception of a process of planning backwards, a rational one involving definite steps, one premised on leverage. What we developed instead over the course of the next several years was an image of school design that informs the ideas and structure of this book. Exhibition systems continued to play a part in our thinking, and whenever we consult now with schools, we advise them to build some. But we stopped thinking about them as levers—powerful enough by themselves to begin and sustain fundamental redesign. The experience of the seven schools taught us otherwise. There, the exhibition systems proved useful, but not in this linear way.

My hypothesis now, informed by the experience of the seven schools, is that the usefulness of systems for graduation by exhibition depends on the fact that they capture in the microcosm the entire breadth of design. Working to build such a system, the redesigning school gains access to all the arenas of design—belief, wiring, tuning—as if in a scale model of the larger design challenge. If the school uses the scale model to understand the larger system and acts on this understanding, then the process of redesign may be greatly strengthened. Recently I shared this new understanding with one of the principals of the schools we studied, a school that has indeed used its exhibition system to powerful effect. "I never believed in levers, anyway," he told me. "I believe in chaos."

Briggs and Peat (1987) say that wholeness is "what rushes in under the guise of chaos whenever scientists try to separate and measure dynamical systems as if they were composed of parts" (pp. 74–75, quoted in Wheatley, 1992). An exhibition system is a good tool for redesigning school because it captures the chaotic whole in miniature. It embeds and highlights the relationships among the key challenges of design, and it forces us to deal with them as a system. Then it connects us to the larger dynamics of the whole school, though not in a mechanistic way. Margaret Wheatley (1992, p. 42) explains the difference:

> Acting locally is a sound strategy for changing large systems. Instead of trying to map an elaborate system, the advice is to work with the system that you know, one you can get your arms around. If we look at this strategy with Newtonian eyes, we would say that we are creating incremental change. Little by little, system by system, we develop enough momentum to affect the larger society.
>
> A quantum view would explain the success of these efforts differently. Acting locally allows us to work with the movement and flow of simultaneous events within that small system. We are more likely to become synchronized with that system, and thus to have an impact. These changes in small places, however, create large-systems change, not because they build one upon the other but because they share in the unbroken wholeness that has united them all along. Our activities in one part of the whole create nonlocal causes that emerge far from us.

But how does this work? What ties the local to the nonlocal? How, for example, is an exhibition system different strategically from a pilot reform—such as setting up an innovative program within a larger school as a demonstration? My own observation and the research of my former colleagues Pat McQuillan and Donna Muncey (1991) suggest that such pilot reforms tend to isolate and stymie reform rather than promote it. The truth is, exhibition systems can isolate reform too. Both strategic devices can avoid this trap, however, when designed to furnish continuous data for the whole organization to reflect on. Here is Wheatley (1992) again, on the organizational power of such reflection:

> As a consultant, the most important intervention I ever make is when I feed back organizational data to the whole organization. The data are often quite simple, containing a large percentage of information that is already known to many in the organization.

> *But when the organization is willing to give public voice to the information—to listen to different interpretations and to process them together*—the information becomes amplified. In this process of shared reflection, a small finding can grow as it feeds back on itself, building in significance with each new perception or interpretation. . . . From this level of understanding, creative responses emerge and significant change becomes possible [p. 115, italics mine].

These creative responses identify and act on previously tacit relationships of the system. They are based on sightings.

Today the seven schools we studied with exhibition systems in place have them in place still, but in only three cases have these systems had the broad impact we first hypothesized with our notion of planning backwards. These three schools happen to be among the smallest of the seven, small enough, perhaps, to become genuinely reflective. Within all the arenas of school design, we found smallness a benefit. In the larger four schools (though I make this judgment now from a distance) the exhibition systems seem somehow to have been swallowed up by the larger systems they once threatened. Deborah Meier (1995) has an explanation. She says that "school change of the depth and breadth required, change that breaks with the tradition of our own schooling, cannot be undertaken by a faculty that is not convinced and involved" (p. 107). But, she claims, the convincing and the involving require that the faculty be small enough to sit down together and talk with each other regularly in a room no bigger than an ordinary classroom.

Conclusion

Several deep-seated beliefs sustain the school designs we now have, and we must understand and rethink these beliefs in order to have better designs. I have suggested a way to approach this work, while pointing out some drawbacks of other ways. In the process, I have made plain some of my biases, though I have not laid out an exhaustive set of beliefs for schools of the future. Indeed I would encourage a diversity of beliefs for the schools of the twenty-first century, as well as a diversity of operating systems.

To avoid carrying into the new century the "one-best-system" mentality of school design that has dominated this century (Tyack, 1974), we must encourage diversity across all the arenas of design.

Nevertheless, society has the right to some common expectations of all the schools it supports with public funds, and I conclude this chapter by offering my sense of what these should be. I argue for five beliefs in common. These are deeply interrelated, and, in my view, constitute a belief system fit for the twenty-first century.

The first belief is fundamental in a strategic sense and relates to the stories that open this chapter. Schools should believe in the necessity of grounding all other beliefs in empirical tests of their presence and their consequence. In other words, schools should arrange for their stakeholders to see the evidence of the schools' work, to survey such gaps as may exist between what the schools profess and what they habitually do. This means that schools must regularly cultivate sightings on the part of all members of their community and provide opportunities for these sightings to be discussed and acted on. One good way to do this is to dare to do what several schools involved in our research have done: test for evidence of their beliefs in the actual work of students. This requires courage, since someone will always ask: "You think this is good?" To summon up such courage, schools must first believe that it is necessary.

The second belief that schools should hold in common is fundamental in an intellectual sense. They should believe in understanding as the ultimate purpose of teaching and learning. That is, they should believe that school is more than a set of invariant questions and answers. They should believe that its purpose is to equip young people to use their minds to frame some of the questions they learn by, to construct some of the answers they graduate with, and to gain habits of reasoning, skepticism, empathy, and imagination. To support such aims, schools must believe in the power of intellectual practice and must provide for it. I will argue in Chapters Two and Three that this demands a pedagogical environment starkly different from that of the ordinary late-twentieth-century school. However, I will not argue that it demands commitment to any of the particular pedagogical orthodoxies of our time, whether of basals or whole language, direct instruction or constructivist teaching. My observations in the schools we studied, and my otherwise long acquaintance with schools, has lent me tolerance for what David Green calls "the infuriating success of the wrong method." What ought to count is results, not pedagogical correctness, though the results should involve growth in understanding.

The third belief that schools should hold in common is fundamental in a psychological sense. Schools should believe in development. This means that they should believe in the capacity of all their students to grow in knowledge, understanding, and social responsibility. Most schools do not believe this now. They are constrained from doing so by contrary psychological ideas that insist loudly or quietly that student capacity is always limited and that schools can determine the limits in advance. Some are further constrained by stereotypes of race, class, and ethnicity. The consequence is a Calvinist fallacy, as James Comer once told me: their rhetoric notwithstanding, most schools today believe that all children can learn only to their preordained capacity—that they come to school already leveled. Although all the schools we studied struggled against this fallacy, it surfaced continually nonetheless in the practice of most of them. Thus I often refer to it in this book. Deep beliefs are hard to rout.

The fourth belief that schools should hold in common is fundamental in a political sense. As a condition of public support, all schools should commit themselves to prepare students to be productive citizens of a democracy. All other beliefs that schools may hold, however political and however variable, should be undergirded by the belief that school can and should make a contribution to the development and continuance of democracy. I do not think, however, that the expression of this belief demands any particular policy or governance structures. On the other hand, I think that policy and governance structures, as well as curriculum, teaching practices, tone, and the often tacit sense of a school community as to whom it includes and whom it excludes, all play important roles. "The distinctive virtue of a democratic society," argues Amy Gutmann (1987), is "that it authorizes citizens to influence how their society reproduces itself" (p. 15). Thus schools are agents of democracy, whether they like it or not. Sadly, some of them, through carelessness and a failure to reflect on this part of their work, become double agents, secretly working to subvert their students' grasp of democracy. Mindful of this problem, the principal of one school we studied proposed a novel measure of accountability. We ought to judge a school, she told us one day, by how many of its graduates choose to vote when they are in their twenties.

Finally, the fifth belief that I think all schools should hold in common is fundamental in an organizational sense. Most schools now believe in command and control as the necessary organizational basis of work in school. I think they ought to believe instead in chaos. I use the word as it is used in science, to refer to a kind of order that transcends particular efforts to define, predict, and control. Schools should believe in letting teachers, students, and groups of teachers and students pursue all the school's other beliefs in the freest, most adaptive, and ultimately most diverse ways. And I think they ought to believe that such work, conducted in the spirit of what Donald Schön (1983) calls reflection-in-action, can be more orderly and far more productive than work that is commanded and controlled. This fifth belief may be the hardest to grasp and hold—not only within schools themselves, but across the system that enmeshes them and that to a great extent insists otherwise. The influence of industrial age organizational theory is still powerful, if waning. As researchers trying to make sense of our data, we too had trouble at first professing a belief in chaos as an organizing principle of school reform. We started off expecting to find a far more rational basis, and we even thought at one point that we had found it in the lever we called planning backwards. But sightings changed our minds.

Chapter Two

Leading with Belief

As a junior in college, I found myself thrust suddenly into a position of official leadership. It was a time of great turmoil on American campuses. Many students were angry with what we perceived to be the condescension of our teachers. The truth was that normal relations between anyone in authority and us—particularly us males—had been poisoned by the Vietnam War. The draft cards we were required to carry were a constant reminder: now we are treated as children; next year will be different.

Like the others, I acted out some of my resentment. One of the things I did was to oppose a candidate for student body president whom I considered a lackey of the administration. I ran on a student power ticket as a write-in and in the process stimulated enough belief in the potential of student power to get myself elected. The belief sprang from a mass of disbelief in the prevailing power structure. The problem was that I did not know what to do with the new belief that I had helped create. I did not know how to sustain it or put it to work. In short, I was ill prepared to take the job. That is probably one of the reasons that my predecessor in the office, a very large one on the top floor of the student union, was slow to hand over the keys. Some friends and I had to break in—actually climb in through an open window. I remember sitting for the first time in my large swivel chair, mocking the accoutrements of office: a filing cabinet, a telephone, a dictating machine, a conference table, and so on. Actually I was afraid of these things, having little knowledge of how to use them. Moreover, I suspected that learning to use them would make me at best only the kind of student body president I had accused the other guy of trying to become—one who kept things running smoothly.

I had had some intuition that I could work on the inside of a complex institution and still redirect it fundamentally; otherwise, I would not have run. Yet sitting in that swivel chair, I considered the task nearly impossible.

More than twenty years later, I sometimes remembered that old panic as I talked with the leaders of the schools we studied. Although they knew how to use the tools of their office, they still faced the nearly impossible task of using them simultaneously to manage the status quo and to subvert it. School reformers are fond of saying that this is like changing the tires on the car while it hurtles down the highway. Despite the image, however, there is a difference between nearly impossible and utterly so, and part of the excitement for me in studying these leaders was to come close enough to see that difference in their work. Between this *nearly* and this *utterly* lies a small space that these leaders enlarged with beliefs—beliefs about what children might accomplish, about how schools might function, about what accountability might really mean. They provoked and activated these beliefs, coaxing them into the open in their schools and coaxing people to discuss them and adopt them. They did this by means of the following moves:

- Taking action
- Using intuition and faith
- Inventing and employing ritual
- Exercising charisma
- Drawing on networks
- Being defiant

I describe each of these moves below, taking them up in turn, drawing largely on our field notes, though also occasionally on other sources of insight too. Although I treat each move separately to help readers appreciate the unique powers of each one, the leaders we studied used the moves in combination. For example, several leaders took action, even precipitous action, to establish exhibition systems in their school (the ones I discussed in Chapter One). They used a charismatic defiance of local norms in order to unsettle the immediate opposition. They drew on reform networks for reassurance that such action made sense, for ideas about how to follow it up, for resources and other support. And they invented new rituals to help the systems become rooted.

Most of these leaders were principals, but these moves are also appropriate for other school leaders too, especially teachers and parents. Occasionally, recalling my days as an advocate of student power, I even mention students. Knowing the obstacles to school redesign, I distrust any strategy that assigns most of the work to principals. I agree with Seymour Sarason, who recently told me that he thinks one of the most important lessons of the past twenty years of school reform is that the prevailing governance system in education, including the heavy reliance on the leadership of principals, cannot create or sustain productive contexts for learning. That is indeed a lesson I take from our study. On the other hand, I also distrust strategies that assign most of the work of redesign to those higher up in the educational hierarchy, presuming that only superintendents or state departments of education can make a difference. I do not think that good design can trickle down, another lesson I take from our study and explore more in later chapters.

Taking Action

Nothing gets to be a deep belief that has not first entered the mind through the senses, nor can one assess belief except with the senses. That is why I wrote in Chapter One about sightings. In referring to belief, other school reformers too often favor the sense of sight. So we all speak of vision: cultivating it, spreading it, orienting change efforts to it. Yet many people have become adept at insulating their visions from their working beliefs. Teachers may engage in "visioning" exercises during an in-service workshop, but they return to work the next morning with their belief-laden habits intact.

I think this is partly because the teachers are not only dreaming up new visions and designs but also worrying about the change in the art specialist's schedule announced moments earlier, or the publication in the newspaper yesterday of the latest test results by grade level, or the shooting last week in plain day near the playground, or the nagging question of what to do with Joaquim. The same thing happens to parents. They may feel persuaded by the inspirational parent-teacher organization speaker that the purpose of school is to teach all children to use their minds well, yet they ponder at the same time the intellectual differences they have observed between their daughter and their son, and they worry about either of them sharing the same class with the bully who lives down the street or the child who cannot yet speak English.

To be worth a damn, visions must mix almost immediately with the problems on people's minds. That is because the best route from here to there—from schools as they are to schools that teach for genuine understanding—cannot be laid out visually in advance, as in a map from an auto club. It must emerge slowly through a process of gradually disentangling there from here—a program of action. The reformer captivated by vision may sometimes read another's reversion to concrete detail as recalcitrance. "I'm trying to get you to dream," the reformer may complain, "but all you want to do is talk about the art schedule, or whether we'll have a football team, or how your kid did on the latest test." But our research taught us that there is danger on either side of this continuum between dream and detail and that moving quickly and regularly between one and the other is the best course. So the workshop may open with the rich question: What do we want all our children to know and be able to do? But then those attending ought to move on later in the same meeting to an examination of actual student work collected that morning and to another question: What signs of our dream are in this work? Finally, the workshop should close with a discussion of still a third question: What actions can we as teachers or parents take tomorrow to ensure that the work of our children moves steadily closer to the dream?

Roland Barth (1990) captures another aspect of the typical insulation between vision and action in the following response of a principal to a question about his vision:

> I am working on a vision—but to be worth a damn it has to be a vision that comes from and reflects the thinking of the whole school community. It's a very complicated process to try to find a consensus where at the moment little exists. If and when we find that consensus, I'll be the first to engrave it over the door of the school [p. 154].

"If and when we find that consensus" is an invitation to interminable "visioning" on in-service afternoons, at community meetings in the evening, at school board retreats, and so on. Again, however, people who are experienced in making dreams real know that the dreams never simply slough off dreaminess and become reality. They require action. That is why impetuousness in school design is a virtue—why Michael Fullan's advice to reformers to "ready, fire, aim" makes so much sense (Fullan, 1993). The principal just quoted will never "find" the consensus he seeks; he must forge it bit by bit through action initiatives.

Meanwhile, the evidence of emergent new belief may be less seen than sensed as a momentum of concerted action. Asked about his school's vision, one teacher told us simply, "Our school has a thing that we hang our hats on. You can feel it. It pervades the whole place." Another teacher involved in our research, whom we invited to express a vision, warned us that she could not relate well to mission statements and other formulations of vision. "I realize an ideal in the moment and in the concrete," she said. In other words, she gropes her way to the ideal, mixing dreaming with acting. Still another teacher reminded us that the quintessential visual device, the goal, does not always provide the best orientation. "Leadership," she said, "is not just 'We're going in this direction; get in line or get out.'" It is also "making the circle full"—ensuring through caring action that any move forward benefits students here and now. The sense of the movement forward is at least as powerful as the glimpse of the goal.

Furthermore, the feel of the movement forward is a good check on the tendency of reformers to be too goal centered and overrationalize the redesign process. Michael Fullan's work (1993) suggests that the most rational reform strategy, beginning with visioning exercises and goal clarification, proceeding through progressively detailed planning, may not be tenable practically. Indeed, the schools in our study that pursued this rational course got bogged down along the way. By contrast, one of the principals in our study who planned a new school from scratch told me that she and her colleagues deliberately did not begin with a list of goals, nor did they worry first about what they wanted their students to learn. Both these emerged later as a result of groping. "We worried first about how they'd learn," she said. "The first thing we did was to imagine what a student's day would be like." They then designed a day that felt right in its intellectual opportunities and in its provision of caring. They decided much later, after they had experienced enough actual days, what they wanted all the days to add up to.

On the other hand, it is possible to be too focused on the present and to fail to ask what the days all add up to. A natural tendency of schools, given the intensity of school life, is to focus on that life one day at a time. Moreover, those who struggle against this tendency can in the process become too action oriented, too quick to reform. A common trap for school reform is the one where action initiatives abound but never link up with each other, where impetuousness is only impetuousness. So the school flits from one initiative to the next or encourages individual teachers to do so within an environment full of freedom but bereft of will. One teacher we interviewed explained how it feels to be an initiator in such an environment:

> I can always pretty much do what I want to do. I don't know if they trust me or if they just don't care—but if I have an idea, they let me take it and go. But it never fits into an overall plan. So, they say, "Yeah, that's a good idea, go ahead and do it," but you're out *there*; you're not in *here* as part of a whole thing we're doing.

Taking action is only a leadership move, in the sense I mean to illustrate here, if it helps generate or activate what this teacher yearns for: an overall plan, a whole thing, a new belief system.

Using Intuition and Faith

One of the designers of a new school we studied told us that a design process dominated by vision and action can be as futile in the end as one dominated by vision alone:

> In going from the vision to the school plan, it seems to me that there is a tendency to repress the spirit and soul of the dream and replace it with the architectural economy of a blueprint. The real question is, How do we remember why we are here? Planning backwards, student outcomes, and so on are strategies that we can take

> too seriously (very much like the language we use—*authentic* this or that, *exhibitions, interactive learning,* on and on. Does anybody know what those things look like as human behavior? Is there an expert in the house?

But what does the designer have besides vision and action? Several of our stories suggest that intuition is important too. Indeed, one of the leaders we studied claimed that intuition was his most important tool. As the new principal of a school that had fallen into anarchy, he began the redesigning process not with a vision about outcomes but with a gut reaction about process. He wanted better relationships within the school community than the ones he found there: among students, between students and the adults in the community, and between students and their teachers. To build these better relationships, he began with what might be called inaction. He thought that it made no sense to do more of what the school was already not doing well, so he cut the time students spent in school to the minimum allowed by the state. In the process, he cut himself some slack. Given this slack, he was soon able to introduce new designs for which there had previously been too little time—designs that redefined relationships. One was a new system of community-based internships. Another was a daily advisory period for all students: every professional in the building was assigned pastoral responsibility for a small group of students. Advisers were to become acquainted with each advisee's work in its whole breadth, to help him or her identify and solve academic problems, and to serve as primary points of contact with his or her parents. They were also to help their advisees collectively build a small community from their daily encounters. The hope was that these small communities might be the building blocks of a better school community.

Intuition is perhaps a more powerful shaper of belief for being a nonrational one. Faith has the same advantage. Some readers may be uncomfortable with my association of faith with school design, but I like the religious nuance it introduces. A colleague at the Annenberg Institute, Deborah Meier, then codirector of Central Park East Secondary School, spoke in the spring of 1993 to a great crowd at the annual meeting of the American Educational Research Association. Many who filled the hall surely wished to understand Meier's vision. What they got involved other senses instead, as well as a number of religious allusions. New designs for schooling, Meier implied, depend ultimately on our capacity to lead first ourselves and then our students down sensory pathways, below the surface of rational incentives and arguments, to a place of uncustomary belief (Meier, 1993). Whatever we come to cherish at the core of our schools, she insisted, must be cherished as well by the students. I would say by their parents too. Otherwise the entire enterprise of new design will fail. Here is part of what she had to say:

> They'd like to believe. That's what we have going for us. But . . . they can't buy in until they can taste what it is that we're claiming might lie on the other side. They need more than the usual drive—something powerful enough to tempt them to cross over that invisible but very real boundary that separates our worlds. It's a leap of faith into an unknown, unless the taste is already in their mouths. It helps if we show them they can cross back and forth. But mostly it takes an immersion experience—like the first time you truly experienced staying afloat, or riding the two-wheeler without anyone holding. It's like learning a foreign language. After the first success, the third and fourth come easier. You have a feel for it. But "it" has to be something you *can* feel [pp. 6–7].

Meier's religious allusions—"a leap of faith," "an immersion experience," "to cross over," and so on—are applicable not only to the challenge of motivating all students to be intellectual but also to the challenge of designing schools that would think it important to motivate all students to be intellectual. Some of the participants in our research quietly and often uncomfortably observed to us that only a kind of "evangelical" faith can dislodge the belief systems that underpin the status quo in schooling. Their discomfort in saying so reflects more than secular discretion; it is also the residue of a century of thinking about schooling as an entirely rational enterprise, where efficient structures and smart management alone may dictate success. But this hyperrationality is itself the dictate of a belief system. Overcoming that belief system, like overcoming sinfulness, obesity, or alcoholism, can seem impossible on one side of a conversion experience. But on the other side, it can seem suddenly possible, however difficult and painful. To acknowledge this is not to trivialize the work of school reform or to mystify it. It is simply to say that although good arguments and plans and strategies matter, other less rational things count heavily too: compelling visions and sounds and other sensory forecasts of what might be, testimony that moves those who hear it, and communities of faith. Professional leaders can use these things to great effect, and we saw as much in some of the schools we studied. However, I would say that these are indispensable tools for parents and students who would also be leaders of school redesign. Indeed, since they lack either a professional or a political role in most cases, their standing as leaders of school redesign depends largely on their capacity to be faithful witnesses of the impact of change.

Of course, faith can suppress thinking as well as stimulate it, and our research uncovered some suspicion in all the schools of the study—among teachers, parents, and students—that a device to prompt conversion of belief might also introduce a new and ultimately counterproductive orthodoxy. It is a matter of finding the right balance between faith and skepticism. One school we studied first emphasized faith through a strong affiliation with the Coalition of Essential Schools. Over the course of several years, the school's principal made commitment to the Coalition's ideas the touchstone for all the school's initiatives and personnel decisions. Predictably, two things happened as a result. First, the school made significant progress in redesigning itself to suit the Coalition's emphasis on intellectual purpose, universal goals, interdisciplinary teaching, and so on. Second, a small faction of the faculty—mirroring (or perhaps stimulating the development of) similar factions within the community and student body—defined itself in opposition to the Coalition. The opposition was to some extent substantive, but to a large extent, merely agnostic. The breach was addressed eventually by means of an agreement to downplay the language of the Coalition while accelerating the exploration of its ideas. The implicit basis of the agreement was the following assumption: whereas faith is needed to spur initial changes, experience alone can guide them thereafter.

Ordinarily, of course, a clash of faith and skepticism within a school community would be settled by entropy. The school's mission would dissolve to the point where it resembled the kind

Michael Huberman describes—so vague and polymorphous that "an entire staff can subscribe while carrying on radically divergent classroom practices," and parents with different views can find them all satisfied (Huberman, 1993, p. 12). The possibility that things might go differently than this in a school where faith and skepticism come to a head, depends, I think, on the work the school does in the wiring arena of school design, particularly in the area of governance. Some degree of private power is crucial for a healthy school (Fullan, 1993), but a substantial degree of the private power that exists now in schools must be rewired into collective power if we are to have in the end schools that teach all children to use their minds well.

Inventing and Employing Ritual

School is full of rituals. They govern encounters and relationships: when you talk in class and where you sit, how you go to lunch and what you do there, what you do during recess or at the pep rally, how you get computer time, how you react when the principal calls you to the office. Rituals mark most of the nodes of a school's wiring, and they are deeply invested with belief. In this sense, they routinely enact and reenact the school's deepest assumptions about the purpose of schooling, the role of authority in teaching and learning, the characteristics of intellectual achievement, the nature of children, and so on. Through constant wear, the beliefs embedded in particular rituals may grow tacit, but clever leaders sometimes tease them to the surface again, so as to confront and transform them.

I saw this happen in an extraordinary way one day while conducting the research for this book. The school I was visiting is in a large city. Its reputation as a good school within this city hinges especially on its practice of the Paideia pedagogies advocated by Adler (1982, 1983, 1984) and others (Gray, 1988, 1989; Haroutunian-Gordon, 1991). These are a deliberate mix of didactic formats aimed at "knowledge acquisition"—the use of lecture, textbooks, video, and so on—with two other rarer formats. The first is coaching with supervised practice—for example, in problem solving, writing, experimentation, and artistic performance. And the other is the Socratic seminar. In this format, which claims descendance from Plato, diverse minds struggle with a text or set of texts (usually a print text, but sometimes one in another medium) in order to enlarge each participant's understanding, without insisting on a prior and particular understanding. Seminars are an explicitly constructivist undertaking, in which students are invited to delve deeply into the text, confront its ambiguities, unsettle their initial understandings as they deal with the welter of understandings at the seminar table, and regard confusion as a learning tool. These objectives are embodied in a ritual that contrasts markedly with ordinary classroom behavior. Students gather their desks in a circle; two teachers lead; students pose questions of each other; students cite portions of text; teachers offer no answers to the questions they ask; the process takes two class periods instead of one.

At the time of the visit that I recount below (by means of an extended passage based on my field notes), this school was in its eighth year of Paideia involvement, and the seminar ritual was well rooted. Still, as the passage reveals, older wiring was very much present too:

> The first thing I see on this particular visit to this school depends on old wiring: an assembly called in recognition of Black History Month. The theme is Black Pride. It follows a standard format: kids shepherded to the auditorium by their teachers, called down a half-corridor at a time to avoid jam-ups at the door. Some students are pleased to get out of the science test they would otherwise be taking; most seem indifferent; all have been more or less explicitly warned by their teachers to behave themselves during the assembly—to sit silently and attentively for the duration.
>
> The program opens with the "Black National Anthem." The kid singing it to the accompaniment of an acoustic piano pauses in the middle to cough. The audience laughs. This is, after all, the morning after Grammy Awards night, a celebration of high-tech and high-craft music that many of these kids stayed up to watch. Next, a recitation of a poem by James Weldon Johnson—with loud feedback on the mike. The room's tattered Art Deco plaster reliefs and its hard wooden seats bounce the screech about. Kids wince.
>
> Teachers have scattered themselves strategically among the seats and along the aisles, but their intervention is seldom required: most of the audience is attentive. Half the school is here. The older half had its assembly earlier, and was disappointed when

the bell rang before the "steppers" had time to perform. This time they come on right after the Gospel dancers—twenty-two step dancers, one-third boys. They perform an intricate, vigorously rhythmical dance of steps. The audience applauds energetically, though there is a slightly hostile murmur when one solo stepper performs less artfully than the audience expects.

Following the assembly, students pass to their next class, where they finish the proof in geometry that was started on Thursday, take a quiz on manifest destiny, work on an essay in the computer lab, and so on. Some go to lunch. They either walk downstairs to the overcrowded cafeteria, or else several blocks south to a Burger King. One who goes there happens to meet someone from another gang, who stabs and seriously wounds him.

Later, as word of the stabbing reaches the school, I sit in the back of a seminar called in reaction to the assembly—a deliberate juxtaposition of new wiring with old. The teacher who called it and will lead it is also the faculty adviser to the assembly committee—in effect, the custodian of the old wiring. In this role, he conferred with the principal on a delicate matter, and they jointly decided to censor one of the scheduled performances—a student's recital of a poem by the Last Poets called "Die, Nigger." It does not reflect black pride, they decide—these two middle-aged African American men.

But, then, mindful of the school's new wiring, the teacher, with the principal's explicit encouragement, offers the student another performance context. Would he perform the poem as prelude to an entire seminar devoted to it? The boy agrees. The teacher means to use a new school ritual to problematize an old one. (I think about what my electrician once told me; it's too expensive to tear out old wiring, he said, *until you have a problem with it.*)

The student recites the long poem from memory, standing figuratively on the seminar table—the space created at the center of desks gathered in a circle. The performance is passionate, electric—several orders of magnitude more intense than what was not cut from the assembly program. He punctuates each line with the refrain, "Die, nigger, die." The students listening, mostly seniors, all African American, seem moved, saddened, angered by the idea at the heart of the poem—that African Americans are at once victims, witnesses of their own victimization, and participants in it; that to be black in America is to be painfully, continuously, casually, and cynically associated with violent death.

Following the performance, all of these ideas emerge in the seminar. They are alternately argued, disputed, and elaborated on. The talk is angry, sad, energetic, and deeply intellectual. Nearly every student participates, though several girls remain silent, sadly and attentively listening. Many comments seek to validate references in the poem—sometimes with references beyond the text. "Damn," one kid says, "a kid got stabbed today, just down the street, for doin' nothin'."

The teacher can barely get a word in, but he shows nonetheless his skillfulness in moderating a seminar—even such a passionate one, even one where his own actions are used at times to illuminate the meaning in the text. Several students read his censoring act as a pathetic and pointless defiance of the world outside the school:

"Your generation got to deny it," one kid says.

"Deny what?" the teacher asks.

"Deny the dyin', man."

The poem is so "negative," the teacher claims—partly in his own defense, partly as a spur to further insight. Indeed, it embeds no pride, no recipe for hope except insofar as it may move people to action. And that, of course, is why the poem was censored when it brushed up against the old wiring. Action is the last thing that schools want their assemblies to spur. Action overloads old wiring.

But this school's new wiring can handle heavy loads. It is designed to accommodate a very different set of beliefs than the old wiring accommodates—whereby citizenship is instilled not by means of passive encounters with displays of pride, but by means of hard thinking about tough and important problems.

To understand my characterization of this use of the seminar ritual as a leadership move, one has to set the scene I describe against the silence of the urban high school that Michelle Fine (1991) describes:

> Patrice is a young Black female, in eleventh grade. She says nothing all day in school. She sits perfectly mute. No need to coerce her into silence. She often wears her coat in class. Sometimes she lays her head on her desk. She never disrupts. Never disobeys. Never speaks. And is never identified as a problem [pp. 50–51].

Recall that my scene too included silent African American females. The difference is that they are participants as Patrice never is. And they are participants in a ritual explicitly designed to elicit and value voices. In this sense, they are young women emerging from silence (Belenky, 1986). On other visits to their school, I sat in on numerous seminars and kept track of the level of participation. How many students participated during the first ten minutes? How many by the end of the first fifty minutes? How many by the end of ninety minutes? Frequently I noted that nearly half the participants had not spoken by the end of the first of the double periods allotted to the seminar, but that everyone had by the end of the second. This is a school that has arranged its schedule in recognition of the fact that some students take time to gain a voice, to find the circumstances in which they think their voice might add value to other people's thinking and their own. It is also a school that wishes to arrange its other systems to the same end.

Yet of course this school still holds assemblies where the focus on control overwhelms interest in intellectual growth and quality. So the school too is still emerging from a kind of silence. And in this regard, the impact of this ritual was calculated to spill over. One might say that the school's overall redesign hinges on its capacity for scaling up the seminar as a ritual for voices, a ritual against silence. How much time does a Patrice need to take off her coat, raise her voice, dare to add her experience and insight to the intellectual work of her teachers and peers? And what transformations of structure, culture, and caring might enable her to use this time? Even to ask such questions is to be way ahead of most other urban high schools, because the asking signifies an enormous shifting of belief. Of course the questions raise other important ones too: How much time does this school need to redesign itself as a place for voices rather than silence? How much time is left?

Exercising Charisma

One teacher we interviewed in another school told us that the leadership necessary to create new schools involves disjunction. It arises when leaders dare to displease some set of the school's stakeholders in the interest of transforming the school's beliefs. "Although we seem to be here to please people," this teacher explained, "the actual problem is to educate people. If people get displeased with that process, so be it. You have to have disjunction. If you don't have disjunction, you don't have standards."

In the schools we studied, this disjunction was sometimes purchased with an unsettling, even arrogant attitude on the part of the principal. One principal habitually skewered colleagues and visitors with tough questions, as if illustrating the intellectual rigor she meant her school to acquire. Another inserted himself dramatically into any place or conversation he pleased if he thought he might thereby advance his mission to transform the school. Still another reveled in his reputation for jumping off figurative bridges, asking his colleagues to follow, as if he were forever illustrating the moral courage it takes to say no to ordinary expectations for minority youngsters. Three principals protected the change agents they empowered in their schools with great tents of cloth spun from their own egos. One's enormous capacity for interacting smoothly and successfully with the school's local stakeholders became the emblem of the school's transformation from cut-rate to first-rate. The second principal's prodigious intellectual interests, amplified by a similarly prodigious presence, now sweeping into a room, now ordering some momentous turn, seemed simply to swallow up the school's residual inclinations to be just another high school. And the third principal's inveterate whimsy, concealing shrewd determination, defined at once the lively culture and also the drive of what would otherwise have been a banal school.

We found in several cases that disjunction may be a consequence not simply of a principal's personal inclinations but also of his or her deliberate assumption of a persona at odds with local expectation. Two principals in the schools we studied used funny hats or ties and quirky manners to unsettle even the simple routines of social discourse in their respective schools. It was as if they meant to provoke—or at least signal—deeper changes by means of surface cracks. They knew quite well that some parents, teachers, school board members, and others would find it unsettling to deal with a principal who wore saddle shoes and a tie decorated with pictures of Tabasco sauce bottles, or, indeed, a principal with a long beard and no tie. This was exactly what these principals wanted: to unsettle these stakeholders on this superficial level and prepare them thus for much deeper change—in one case, to accept the design of an utterly untracked school, a deliberate misfit with a community deeply conditioned by region and class to think of tracking as a given; and in the other case, to accept the design of a school built on trust and intellectual challenge, a deliberate misfit with a community used to thinking of its adolescents as dumb hoodlums. In both cases, the misfit led in fact to furious political battles, which the principals eventually won. The victories appear to have led in turn to a transformation of local expectations, though one cannot say for sure until these principals have been succeeded by others.

Indeed, the norms of succession in the leadership of public schools in the United States, with their striking disregard for ensuring continuity across regimes, make the phenomenon possible that a leader might make dramatic use of his or her own person in fashioning a serious agenda for change. On the other hand, they also make possible a contrary phenomenon noted in this study: the quick dismantling of new and radical belief systems because the next principal wants to implant his or her own vision. Of the ten schools we studied, half changed principals over the course of the study. Two more changed principals during the writing of this book, and I would not be at all surprised if the remaining three changed principals before the book sees print. In one of the first changes, the principal moved to a district-level job where she continued to exert a great influence on the school's belief system. In three others, the forward momentum of reform continues, though it is still early in the tenure of the successors. In at least one of these three, it is likely to accelerate. But in still another of the schools that changed principals, nearly all the new beliefs seem to have vanished. Particularly harsh circumstances are to blame, including the loss not only of the principal, quite suddenly, but also of virtually the entire reform leadership. It is likely here too that the new beliefs had not been deeply established within the faculty. Told about what had happened there, another principal averred that this simply could not have happened in her school, where there was indeed a smooth succession. "Why not?" I asked. "Because the faculty would not have let it happen," she responded.

Yet a less dramatic return to the status quo remains possible eventually in her school, as well as in all the other schools of this study, for reasons that have to do with the power of charisma. It is, on the one hand, a comfort for reform advocates that any school, no matter how forlorn or set in its ways, may be "turned around" and "moved" by the right leader's stepping in. Indeed, nearly the entire school reform movement of the 1990s seems premised on this idea of right leadership. One teacher described its dynamics for us as follows:

> There has to be somebody in the school and maybe the community who is spearheading the whole thing, someone who's got the vision, who's saying, "This is the way it's gotta be, and here's why." I think also it really needs to be someone in a position of power—the power to make the changes. We do consulting at other schools; we see a lot of teachers there who are really excited about change, but they can't make a change because their administrators won't set up the system so they can. It's very hard for us to know how to help those people, and we always come back thinking, "Boy, aren't we lucky that our administrator is letting us do this stuff."

The problem, of course, is that following a transition of leadership, this same dynamic might well undo good change and install quite a different vision. Much depends in this regard on the pervasiveness of the new beliefs that the original leader cultivated, and on whether he or she ensured that the new beliefs were matched by new wiring. How does such a leader ensure, first of all, that his or her own beliefs spread across the school? The teacher quoted above explains how it happened in her school:

> What [our principal] does is absolutely necessary to make this kind of thing work: he's the guy with the vision, but he leaves the interpretation open to us, so that we can kind of personalize it. And the other thing that he does that will drive us crazy but it has to be, is that he keeps throwing that vision in front of us and saying, "What have you done?" So we're always being forced to look at ourselves and improve our teaching. So he gives the vision, we figure it out, and I think at some point we begin to figure it out together, instead of all interpreting our own separate ways.

This involves not simply using one's charisma to have one's own way but using it to induce collegiality along the way. Indeed, we observed a pattern of leadership in several of the schools we studied that one might call democratic autocracy. It usually begins with a charismatic leader's ordering some momentous change. In one school, it was the institution of a system of graduation by exhibition. In another, the change involved a major reorganization of the school's curriculum, including an integration of three previously separate subjects. In both cases, principals ordered the changes, then empowered faculty committees to make all the important design and implementation decisions. In the case of the curriculum change, the principal simply hired a week's worth of substitute teachers for all the members of the committee and told them that at the end of the week, he wanted the new curriculum.

Of course, this kind of leadership in itself represents only the ordinary reliance on benevolent dictatorship, albeit one that trusts the details to subordinates. However, by means of their dictatorial acts, these principals intended to do more than have their own way on important design questions. They also wished to confront and disturb a common pattern of teacher leadership, in their schools as elsewhere, that makes it a divisive rather than a cohesive force in the life of the school. They wanted to disturb the comforts of cellular organization, to pry open classroom doors. These principals did this simply by forming powerful faculty committees and expecting them to make important decisions.

To follow through, these principals should also have seen to it that the new pattern of teacher leadership they helped induce became strong enough over time to constrain their own and their successors' powers. The two mentioned above did not, but another democratic autocrat we studied did follow through in this way. This principal managed to abolish independent faculty power and reconstitute it as collective. At the same time, she also cultivated parental and student leadership in the work of redesign. This meant subverting ordinary assumptions on the part of both parents and students as to how they should behave—not simply as consumers but as active custodians of the community. This last element is crucial, since new designs can stick only if their clients are deeply invested in them, and act as faithful witnesses to the benefits.

To understand how difficult it is to do what I have just described, consider the fact that a principal's effort to transform a school's belief system takes that principal well past the power bounds of the ordinary principalship, which confine the role to "assuring that schedules are met, that paper flows in the right direction at the right time, that expenditures reconcile with budgets, and that new demands from policymakers or higher-level administrators mesh with existing activities" (Elmore and McLaughlin, 1988, p. 7). Any moves beyond this scope of ordinary activity step on a conventional prerogative of teachers, and in the process, threaten too a prerogative of parents and students. In most schools, the power to challenge the prevailing belief system is reserved for individual teachers who exercise it behind the closed doors of their own classrooms, sometimes with their own considerable charisma. These are the teachers who are often the most prized by students and parents, though they may well be unpopular with their colleagues and with principals. Indeed, a mythology of the heroic teacher is an important influence within the teaching profession, within the cultures of most schools, and in the relationships these schools have with their communities. Although its expression in Hollywood is often exaggerated, it has nonetheless a real impact on the practice of every teacher, young and old, who wishes to confront the status quo in the interests of students. It presents a hard dilemma. Shall the teacher try—against great odds, if the principal is not like-minded—to change the beliefs and operating systems of her entire school? Or shall she turn away from the school, close her door, and do the phenomenal things she dreams about with her own students within her own sphere of great influence?

A number of teachers in the schools we studied had clearly chosen the latter course. Then into their lives one day came a new principal with a vision. The encounter was not pleasant. Cultivating local circumstances and drawing inspiration from a network, this principal used his or her charisma to shut down some teachers' exercise of their own charisma. The teachers who experienced this trauma in the schools we studied were those whose careers had developed in an environment where being a lone ranger—managing to exercise one's own individual strengths on behalf of one's own students—was the most reasonable route to excellence. Often they had achieved this excellence, and were thus prized by students and parents. Then suddenly they found themselves in environments where collegiality was in vogue, where the very ground of their excellence—the teacher's cellular work world—was under assault. They found themselves being rewired out of business. Some of them reacted by rallying their special constituents—their students and the students' parents—against the reform agenda. One teacher who did this told us of the bitterness that animated his revolt:

> The school should believe very much in the teacher and in the program that the teacher has created. If you find something that's working, you fan the hell out of it. You get the old bellows there and you pump away, and make it happen more. You're very reluctant to degrade what *is* happening in the interest of some new thing that's *going* to be built. When something is going and working well, get things out of its way and say, "Fly, little bird, fly."
>
> But what happens instead, in the interest of innovation and change, is that good things get invalidated. "There's something new!" That gets to be the message.
>
> I come from the tradition of the individual. I can understand why schools need to collectivize and to unify what it is they're offering, but at the same time, I think that it can get flat, it can get predictable. Oh, here we go with the papier-mâché pyramids again. Pretty soon, you have the whole school doing these programmed things. The nature of it is supposed to be inventive, but it never gets reinvented. Here we go dropping the egg off the side of the building again.

The individualism that stoked this teacher's complaints was protective. He had been a teacher in this school for a long time and had seen administrative visions come and go. He might well have invested in some and gotten burned by their demise. At the same time, his reaction is the negative image of another phenomenon we found in the research: the resignation that teachers feel who have championed change, only to see their efforts fail when countermanded by a new principal. "What will you do now?" I asked one such teacher whose school seemed in a tailspin, "and how do you feel?" "The kids will save me," he answered. "All you can do is close your door and work with the kids." Ultimately both reactions serve as guideposts for redesigning school. The best designs avoid both the extreme of uniformity that the first teacher rails against and also the extreme of isolated excellence that the second teacher escapes to. They will also give charismatic leaders like both of these teachers something else to do than rail or flee: the chance to become constructive leaders of the whole school community.

Drawing on Networks

Most of the schools we studied were associated with the Coalition of Essential Schools. Many readers may interpret this to mean that these schools were engaged in implementing a particular reform initiative. This is not true. The reform initiatives more or less struggling to be born in the schools in this study were fundamentally homegrown. Although the Coalition supplied the schools with a basic orientation for their initiatives, its equally important role was to serve them as a network. Significantly, most of the schools belonged to other school networks too, usually regional ones. These schools were joiners. I say so in order to emphasize both the voluntary nature of these associations and the fact that the schools initiated them.

The distinction is important. These schools were not stimulated to change by the Coalition or by the other networks to which they belonged. None of them viewed themselves as "implementing" an imported reform. The evidence of our research indicates that getting school change started is much more complex than this, that it arises from a dissonance arranged by insiders and is constructed from local and personal materials, as well as from something in the air—a zeitgeist. Still, dissonance may accomplish little for want of outside support. That is because the kind of dissonance I mean, being ideological in its orientation, offends by its very nature whatever powers hold the ordinary systems in place. The leadership that introduces it may well need political cover.

Luckily the same zeitgeist that catalyzes local moves also supplies networks. Schools can choose to get involved with these networks, watch them from a distance, or ignore them utterly. Although there was a range across the schools we studied in terms of the openness and intensity of their association with the Coalition of Essential Schools, all the schools clearly chose to get involved, in most cases by a democratic vote of the faculty. But whether instituted by vote or not, Coalition membership was perceived by these schools' faculties as one important vehicle of the principal's leadership. Sometimes the principal made this manifest, as did the principal who announced at a faculty meeting: "Coalition membership represents the direction this school is taking. We are hitched to that wagon. Anybody who doesn't like it can apply for a transfer to another school."

Interestingly, this principal's belligerence in the matter did not provoke the kind of political reaction we observed in several other schools. The difference seemed to be the principal's continual association of Coalition membership, in his speeches and writing, with the school's ambition to become prominent regionally and nationally. In two other schools, by contrast, Coalition membership, through a kind of political default occasioned by the principal's decision to speak very little about it, became associated with issues unrelated to school reform. In factions of both schools' faculties, the word *coalition* became an epithet—something "they" want to do to "us." In one case, it became associated with perceptions that the principal was determined to defeat the union, and in the other case, with a perception that the principal did not understand the real culture of her school. In most of the other schools of the study, the association with the Coalition engendered some opposition from individual members of the faculty, but the opposition never coalesced into a distinct faction. In at least two cases, it gradually dissipated as the result of the principals' deliberate efforts to entice these individuals to transfer to other schools or retire early.

Although networks like the Coalition of Essential Schools accept schools rather than individuals as members, our research suggested that the real links tended to be at the level of the principal and the individual faculty member. In the schools we studied, networking was used largely as a source of new professional beliefs rather than of new beliefs for the entire school community. As a result, most of the students we spoke with in our research knew little of the Coalition, and although we made no systematic effort to speak with parents, we suspect that most of them would also evince limited awareness of it. The exception might have been three schools where the question of the school's membership in the Coalition had at one point or another become a matter of public debate, at least at the level of school board politics. But even here, the schools' leaders tried to take the emphasis off the question of whether the school should belong to the Coalition, and onto the question of whether the school should be the kind of place suggested by the principles of the Coalition. It is a subtle difference, but an important one in a system of compulsory schooling where choice of schools is often severely limited. If, in the twenty-first century, more school choice becomes available, then networking may play a more powerful role than at present in shaping the identity of schools, helping parents and students choose among them, and holding the schools accountable to their espoused beliefs. (This subject is explored in Chapter Six.)

Meanwhile, why does a redesigning school need a network like the Coalition of Essential Schools? The first reason is that conversions to new beliefs often require evangelical agency. Schools cannot redesign themselves wholly by themselves; they require the support of something bigger—a tent to enter, the inspiration of other schools' stories, the consultation of those who know what it means to undergo a conversion of beliefs, a set of clear and simple statements of what constitutes the new beliefs, and so on. The Coalition offers all these things to its member schools, as do a number of other school reform networks.

Second, networks provide good cover during the inevitable crises associated with serious change. In this regard, it is not incidental that a number of the national networks are headquartered at prestigious universities: the Coalition at Brown, James Comer's School Development network at Yale, Henry Levin's Accelerated Schools network at Stanford. Many regional networks similarly depend on the prestige of the region's university—for example, the League of Professional Schools and the University of Georgia, and the Southern Maine Partnership and the University of Southern Maine.

This is not to say that the school leaders who hitch their schools to these networks lack the wherewithal to develop and articulate new beliefs by themselves. This was not at all the case in the schools we studied. Rather, these leaders seemed to appreciate some values of this particular kind of networking that go beyond the simple provision of ideas. One is the access that networks may supply to the record of other schools' development efforts. So, for example, a prominent feature of our research project was the trading of development strategies that it facilitated among the schools we studied. A second value is the quality assurance for development work that a network may supply, particularly one with a prestigious university connection. One principal told us that she had laid down three nonnegotiable conditions for her school's redesign efforts: "First, I told the faculty, it's time for this school to change substantially, and we will. Second, we can't go it alone, so we have to find a network to support us. Third, it has to be a network based on serious research." This principal's third condition was grounded in a professional commitment to the value of educational research. It was also related to the politics of "cover." Finally, it was tied in with her own career ambitions. Indeed, she told us that she felt that her career's fate, for better or worse, was tied to the fate of the Coalition's impact on her school. With respect to all these rationales—to base development on research, to get good cover, and to advance a career—a good network connection can be indisputably valuable.

Nor were this school and this principal unique within our study. On a visit to another school, I wrote the following in my field notes: "The teachers fill in the details of the reforms here, but sometimes the details they fill in make the principal cringe. Still, he leaves them to the teachers, even when they cry out, 'Wait, we're missing some of the details!' His reaction is to shout back, 'Don't worry. The details will come along. They'll fill in.'" Later in our research, I realized that this principal's confidence was founded on his trust in the network, particularly in its capacity to help the otherwise isolated teachers in his school acquire a broader perspective and more sophisticated tools. He made some crucial investments over the years—in consultations, the use of travel funds, the orientation of staff development activities, and so on—all devised to build connections between individual members of the faculty and the Coalition of Essential Schools. I contrast this strategy with that of another principal involved in our research who, moving much faster, "played his cards too close to the vest," in the words of a thoughtful observer. This principal networked himself and the top echelon of his school's leadership, then hoped that the connection would trickle down. It never did.

Finally, a value of networks as a leadership move has to do with their use as leverage with respect to district and state policies.

Michael Fullan (1993) claims that neither top-down nor bottom-up change will be sufficient to create the kind of schools we need for the next century. The inescapable limitation of even the most thoughtful and imaginative state and district reform policies is that they depend ultimately on the willing investment of those closest to the action: teachers and their students. Such investment cannot be compelled or indoctrinated. It must arise from interest, as John Dewey insisted all significant learning does. On the other hand, the best work of the most interested local entrepreneurs of change will eventually be squashed if it fails to meet up with supportive policy contexts—if, as in several of the schools we studied, it must continually masquerade before higher-ups as something other than what it is. A great value of networks is that they amplify the voice of the pioneer school, and in the process purchase for that school the right to appear in plain clothes. We saw this effect clearly in three of the schools we studied. These schools deliberately sought to shape their respective state policies in ways that seemed to them compatible with their redesigning work. Had they acted alone on this impulse, their efforts would likely have been fruitless. But these schools used their membership in the Coalition and in regionally based networks to boost their leverage. As a result, two of the schools (in the same state) were influential in the shaping of a substantially revised state policy framework. The third, struggling against tougher odds, created a niche for itself as a demonstration school, one empowered on a regular basis to experiment with departures from policy, so as to inform policy's eventual direction.

Being Defiant

The schools in our study seemed driven to distinguish themselves locally in ways that fostered more powerful belief systems. The phenomenon concealed a dilemma: to be distinctive within their community, schools must in some sense defy the community's expectations—for example, to be better than it is assumed they might be, or even to be caring and successful in the face of people's ordinary experience of public institutions in the community. But to defy expectations is also to take a risk. Someone is bound to say, "What does that school think it's doing?" When the someone wields authority, a struggle can result.

In one school we studied, the drive to be distinctive stemmed partly from a district policy that encouraged competition among schools to enroll students. This motivation was of special interest to us in our research, since its power is much touted among school choice advocates. Here it seemed initially to have little more than a superficial impact, to induce a kind of boosterism: flashy brochures, insignia stick pins, and so on. So, for example, the principal, recognizing that any enhancement in the lure of the school would especially benefit the local real estate interests, even went so far as to solicit and obtain their support in redecorating the public rooms of the school. "I sell your houses," he told the realtors. "Buyers stop here first." The realtors responded. Today the school's main office and guidance areas look more like reception rooms in a hotel: a mahogany secretary where a gray filing cabinet might ordinarily sit, a plush loveseat in place of molded plastic chairs, bookshelves with leather-bound classics, and so on. The effect is startling, as if the school were holding a mirror to its community's pretensions.

In fact, the effect acts somewhat as a decoy. Part of a sprawling midwestern district, the school inhabits the area's fastest growing suburb, a racially integrated neighborhood where houses sell to middle-class and upper-middle-class families. Yet the school is also party to a metropolitan desegregation plan that brings some students to the school whose social class background is very different. To promote the intellectual achievement of all its students, including those who arrive on buses from less affluent parts of the district, the school must defy an often explicit assumption among the affluent and aspiring parents that their children need a different kind of education from other people's children. This assumption is a powerful force in communities all over the United States, including some of the most apparently homogeneous ones. It rests on the fear that some children bring different values to school, that they disparage intellectual achievement, and that such disparagement then comes to define the learning climate for all the school's students. How much can a school dare to defy the expectations of its most powerful and vocal constituents? In an artful move, this school strives to look impressive to its immediate neighbors, so that it can have more room to be defiant in important matters.

The suburban schools we studied faced strong challenges to their efforts to be intellectually demanding for all students. The schools tried with more or less determination and more or less success to eliminate tracking. "But," protested many parents, "won't *my* kid be hurt by having to learn among *those* kids?" One school answered the question by disputing its own excellent reputation. We are not as good as you think, it said publicly—to the great discomfort of many parents used to justifying the size of their mortgage payments with the school's reputation. "We are," said the superintendent, "just the normal labeling and sorting factory model pushed to the wall." Another aggressively defined its differences from the other high schools in town. If you want the old stuff, it said—the shopping mall mix of tracks and levels and their differing intellectual expectations—go to one of the other schools. Come here for the new stuff, the stuff of the twenty-first century. In both cases, the challenge from many parents was fierce. The second school stood its ground and won. The first school blinked and lost.

The one rural school in our sample faced a different challenge. It painfully defined itself in opposition to itself as it once was, and also as its local stakeholders had at least subconsciously come to expect it to be: once isolated, now highly networked; once sleepy, now energetic; once sullen and rowdy, now a productive community. Predictably the local opposition to these deeply cultural changes was sometimes nearly overwhelming. Severely shaken but never overcome, a nascent new belief system held on long enough to push down some roots. Meanwhile, the school also strived to become as comfortable a place for the community in its new design, as it had been in its old.

The urban schools in our study set out determinedly to be unlike other schools in their respective cities for reasons that were unmistakably influenced by the continuing American struggle for racial equality. Here community expectations were no problem. They drew support from the community. The problem was district expectations. "You have marked us as a school for the 'other,'" these schools seemed to say to powers higher up, "but we are other than you expect." In only one of these schools was this stance a self-consciously political one, and in another it was clearly attended by some ambivalence. Yet all rejected their respective city's default option: to be just another high school, a "minority majority" school with low expectations and a low profile.

In the circumstances of the big cities especially, such rejections are not made once and for all, like passing through a single juncture in a decision tree. To be worth anything at all in terms of redesign, they must become intense and sustained states of refusal. Such an existentialist attitude—provoked by local circumstances, fed by personal strength, and supported by networks within and beyond the city—can create sufficient chemistry for an institutional transformation. That happened to varying degrees in three of the four big-city schools we studied.

On the other hand, a defiance of local expectations can result instead in smoke and fire without lasting change, and that is what happened in the fourth. The leader of this school recalled the story for us during an interview. I quote from that interview at length here because it portrays vividly the grip of beliefs that characterizes the status quo in many schools, urban and otherwise, and also the courage and political power necessary to undo this grip. As is clear from his account, the principal knew what he was up against, but he also knew that there could be no winning without taking on the forces that ultimately defeated him: no winning without challenging the core of beliefs that governed the relationships in his district and ended up dictating the relationships in his school. So he turned up the school's defiance. Had the tactic succeeded, he might have later adjusted it back down for balance. But one can infer from his story that a balance struck too early can mean an even greater loss.

Question: How did the war start?

Answer: I was there for eight years, and all the time, no matter what changes we made—we put in schools within schools, and what I thought was an emerging, exemplary assessment system, and we had a lot of neat things—but they were always against the mandates of the school department.

Even when we went from a seven-period to a six-period day, and some of us wanted to move to a three-period day, I ended getting called on the carpet by the associate superintendent: the Office of Information Services couldn't handle our report cards, they couldn't collect data because we were different from all the other high schools. So we had to deal with this crap all the time.

Last year, we sent a whole new set of standards for the school tied into performance assessments and new course requirements to the superintendent and associate superintendent. This was the second year in a row that we sent it, because we didn't get it to them the first year until May, and they rejected it on those grounds. The next year we started sending it in September, and they kept refusing to respond, refusing to respond. Then, finally, they said there was too much going on now, and besides if we did this, then our expectations at our school would be significantly different from the expectations that other schools have of their kids and that wouldn't be right. And it should go to the school board, and if it happens for your kids, it should happen for all kids, which—bottom line in this city—means it's going to happen for nobody.

It had really turned sour earlier when the previous superintendent asked two principals—I was one of them—to write a reorganization plan for the city's high schools and we did. Unbeknown to us he had also asked our boss—the associate superintendent for high schools—to write one at the same time. And so they were both presented and were almost contradictory from beginning to end. Bad blood developed as a result of that because we felt very passionate about what we had written.

Question: Could you characterize the differences between the two plans?

Answer: The big difference was that—and this is me talking, it's not my boss, so if you talked to him, he'd probably call me a liar—but we felt that the expectations we had of kids were just so much higher. His plan was one that was built on what I consider a social work model, where you have to care for the kids and give them all the soft, kind, pulling in, counseling, and support stuff in order for them eventually to rise to the occasion academically. Now we didn't say that you shouldn't give them all those things, but we believed that you have to set incredibly high—but reasonable—standards in academics and behavior first—and the kids will respond because they know better. Poor schools are the ones that don't do that, and consequently they fall apart, and that's why you have to get into the social work model.

Meanwhile, I knew that my school had more social service agencies working in it than any other school in the city, but that was not our modus operandi, our raison d'être—to bring social services to kids. That was the support to help us continue to maintain standards.

My boss's plan was the other way around. So our biggest arguments were about our behavioral expectations of kids and our academic expectations of kids. He said that they were not reasonable, that we were too strict, asking too much of the kids.

Question: When you say they thought you were asking too much of the kids, what were they afraid of? That kids wouldn't graduate, that kids wouldn't pick your school, would drop out?

Answer: Right, they were afraid of those kinds of statistics, and they were saying that we were just trying to get rid of kids, the marginal kids. Our point, honestly, was that we were trying to save those kids. I must have said this a thousand times: the best person to be honest with a kid is someone who loves them and cares about them now. The best person to tell them the truth is us now, not some employment officer they go and see after they leave here, because those people will tell them the truth.

But they just didn't buy it. The school board came to my school last December—they go to different schools for different meetings—and as part of that, the principal and anybody else gets to welcome them to the school. Word got out that my welcome was going to be a statement about how I thought things basically sucked. They wanted me to talk about all the good things going on at the school. I prefaced it by saying that we have a lot of good things going on in the school, but I have even more important stuff to talk about, and that is all the things that happen in this city that put all of those good things in jeopardy.

To make a long story short, well before I even started, the superintendent had his administrative assistant come up to me and tell me that I was not to give the presentation. Basically, I told him I was going to speak anyway. Then I did. Before I was finished, the president of the school board told me to cease, and I said, "Sorry, I have two more sentences." So I finished my two sentences and said, "Now I'm finished."

The superintendent found me insubordinate, and the media jumped all over it. The mayor—and this is ultimately what crushed me in terms of having any hope of working this thing through—the mayor came to the school with the media trailing, and he told me that he was glad to hear someone speak up for standards and he was behind me and so on. Well, the superintendent and the mayor were already in a tussle and so things went downhill from there.

Basically, from that point on, they stonewalled all my budget revisions and all my recommendations for the next school year. That's the way they ice you out.

Conclusion

In this chapter, I have examined some moves that leaders might make in order to stimulate and deepen new beliefs about school and its purposes, and about children's intellectual potential. I drew the list from our observations in the schools we studied. It is hardly an exhaustive list of all the leadership moves that committed redesigners might imagine or make, nor do my illustrations, heavy with principals, honor the possibilities even in this limited list. Still, this tool kit makes at least a good starter set.

I have deliberately ended the list with an illustration that some readers may take to be a negative one. We are used to thinking about leadership moves as being winning strategies, but the defiant principal quoted at length clearly lost. Or did he? The fact is that the district leadership that iced him out and provoked his resignation a few months after the events he recounted to us was itself iced out a year later. The principal's defiance—bold, public, and played out to some extent in the local media—helped stimulate the disenchantment of the city's leadership with the superintendent. Today the principal is back in town, working as a special assistant to a new superintendent, one as determined as he to institute a new belief system, this time citywide. Whether these two leaders will be any more successful in their current effort than the principal was when he battled alone remains an open question. The point I wish to make is merely that the leadership created by his charismatic defiance of the status quo was not lost, even if the move seemed at the time a losing one. If, by contrast, he had decided on the basis of the odds not to be defiant, then I think he would indeed have lost—lost an opportunity to displace, if even a little bit, an oppressive belief system.

But what is the point, some readers may ask, of displacing an oppressive belief system a little bit? In answering, I draw my inspiration from chaos theory as applied to organizations—that a small change in a massive system, when reflected on, can transform the system in an unpredictable way. In this case, a defiant act in one part of a system failed to have an immediate impact there, but it showed up later in another part of the system—the consequence of some reflection undertaken by the city's power brokers. Meanwhile, because this school and this principal were networked, the act also had an impact on an even larger system by means of his writing and other work on behalf of the network. This is an impact that is no less real for being difficult to trace.

What makes any leader's move powerful in this nonlinear, nonleverage sense is its foundation in belief. The image of leadership I have presented in this chapter is not that of a technical phenomenon. I am convinced that technical moves and innovations will not create the kind of schools we need for the twenty-first century. We need a kind of spiritual leadership instead, a leadership steeped in beliefs about what schools and children can be and passionately focused on enacting these beliefs, willing in the process to risk loss. Indeed, it is such leadership, exercised not only by principals and teachers but also by parents and other adults in the community, that can accomplish the kind of revolution in child rearing advocated by my Brown colleague Bill Damon (1995). "When we teach children to concern themselves first and foremost with their own senses of self," he warns, "we not only encourage self-centeredness but also fail to present a more inspiring and developmentally constructive alternative: that they should concern themselves about things *beyond* the self and *above* the self" (p. 81, emphasis in the original). Children must acquire much of their capacity to believe in more than themselves from their parents and from other adults they interact with outside school. But separation of church and state need not mean that they can acquire none of this capacity in public school too. One important source—the one I have tried to highlight throughout this chapter—is the example of school leaders willing to express and act on their beliefs in the intellectual power and promise of all children, even when such beliefs are risky to hold. One leader we studied put it succinctly: "To do any good, I have to be the kind of principal who is willing to be fired for what I believe."

Part Two

Wiring

The second arena of school design, which I call *wiring,* is all about relationships. It deals with how beliefs may be activated in the distribution of energy, information, and power. It thus focuses design work on the interlocking relationships of curriculum, accountability, and governance.

In this arena, what Seymour Sarason (1982) calls the constitution of schooling, as it has endured throughout this century, comes up for revision. This section of the book begins with Chapter Three, which presents what I take to be the fundamentals of wiring. It is the more theoretical of the chapters and makes a series of arguments against the "common sense" that underlies schools as they now exist. Chapter Four follows with an account of a school in the midst of rewiring; the reader gets to smell the plaster dust. Again, depending on their interests, readers may begin with either chapter. Some may wish to treat the story in Chapter Four as a classic case study, pausing at the most complicated moment of the plot to engage in a conversation with others about what the school might do to resolve its dilemmas.

Chapter Three

Wiring Fundamentals

In 1988, when the fall of the Berlin Wall seemed still inconceivable, I visited East Germany as part of a larger scholarly exchange. I crossed the strange frontier in the middle of the Friedrichstrasse subway station. It proved to be a kind of time lock. That is, I went underground, waited anxiously through a long fuss with my visa, then emerged in the early 1950s—or so it seemed by the war-worn look of the train station my escort hurried me through and of the war-era train we managed to catch. My visa problem had left no time for the lunch she had planned, or for the telephone call I had planned, to tell my wife I had arrived on the other side. Within minutes, we were heading north, clacking past the woods and fields of Mecklenburg, on our way to Rostock.

When we arrived, my escort passed me off to another. He helped me clamber aboard a trolley, packed with shipyard and other workers headed home to their "new village area," one of a string of high-rise housing developments that surround the town's medieval center. I would live here for the next couple of weeks, in a small apartment with no telephone. As I entered the apartment for the first time, I remembered that I still needed to call home.

After unpacking and arranging to meet my escort again the next morning, I took the elevator downstairs and headed to the public telephone in the lobby. I dialed an operator and, in halting German, asked her to place a collect call to the United States. She replied in perfect English that it would not be possible to make such a call from this telephone. I thanked her and hung up. Then I dialed again, thinking I would get a different operator. "I told you," the same one scolded in a tone more fearsome to my ear for her German accent, "it is not possible to make such a call from this telephone."

When I returned to my building from a short walk to the grocery store, the lobby attendant approached me. "You may not use this telephone to make foreign calls. You must go to the post office, where there are special telephones."

Reeling that she knew about what had happened well out of her earshot, I asked quietly, "Where's the post office?"

"About twenty kilometers from here," she replied. "You had better wait until morning."

But morning and afternoon and another evening passed before I had time to get to the post office. Once there, I passed my call request in writing to a clerk, who told me to wait to be summoned to one of a number of booths that lined a nearby wall. An hour later, he summoned me instead to his desk, where he informed me that the trunk line to Berlin was down and that I should try again tomorrow. Since the exact scenario repeated itself on my second visit, I suspect now that the delay was a convenience for the Stasi, the secret police, whose information processing was apparently slow enough to require more than an hour to determine who I was and whom I was calling.

I learned over the next several days that I was in a country without many telephones, public or private, and where modems and fax machines were rarer still. "It is a matter of resources," my apologetic hosts explained. "Ours is a relatively poor country, and we have had to invest in other things than communication infrastructure." This seemed true enough, but it seemed true too that something else was going on. Although some of the otherwise hospitable people I encountered during the following days had private home or office telephones, none could risk letting me use them to make my call home. I learned this by causing one host great consternation when I asked casually during a dinner party if I might use her telephone to call the United States. I had not thought about the Stasi's listening—or worse, not listening but simply recording that such a call had been made from this professor's personal telephone. It was not until days later, having taken the trolley to the post office near midnight and having waited an hour again, that I finally phoned home.

Wiring mimics belief—whether in the information investments of nations or in the design of schools. That is the point of my story, though its analogy may make some readers wince. Why is the proportion of telephones to people still so low in most schools? Why are modems, fax machines, direct lines to the outside, and other commonplace communication devices of the information age still so scarce there? Why is it often easier for schools to get funding to buy another lab of computer workstations than to network their existing computer workstations? Why are teachers still among the dwindling number of workers in America for whom workplace access to ordinary information tools remains a rare and regulated privilege? Why, even when they get access to a telephone, can't they dial to get an outside line? Why is student access to photocopiers, modems, telephones, and even computers often strictly regulated and rigidly constrained? Why, in even some of the most technologically sophisticated schools, does the internal or local area network not connect to any external or wide area network (Newman, 1994)?

It is a matter of resources, as the East Germans put it. Schools are relatively poor institutions that have had to invest in other things than information infrastructure. And unrestricted use of a precious few machines makes them wear out faster. But something else is going on too. I do not mean a top-down conspiracy to thwart dissent or impose ideology, but something far subtler. Although it sounds odd when put so plainly, schools today believe by and large that the tools of the information age are not useful for learning. The East Germans thought they were not useful for living—that is, for living an ideologically correct and socially useful life. The assumption in both cases rests on the value assigned to control. The distributed availability and use of information tools like telephones, faxes, computers, and photocopiers seriously disturb authoritarian organizations. They enable people who function within such organizations to elude controls and to open unsupervised channels of communication among themselves, and also between themselves and the outside world. This is why the current wiring of schools precludes the full use of such tools, quite apart from the cost of purchasing enough of them and providing enough support for their use. This cost is not insignificant and would likely require a major shift in existing resources, but it is not the primary obstacle. The primary obstacle is the prevailing belief both within schools and beyond them that teaching and learning, accountability, and leadership all require hierarchical control. And, as I say above, wiring mimics belief.

I use the term *wiring* here and throughout the rest of the book to refer to much more than technology infrastructure. I mean the entire infrastructure of school supporting the distribution of power, energy, and information. The real wiring problem of the school today is not the scarcity of telephones or computers or network connections; it is the habitual maldistribution of power, energy, and information. Until we begin to deal with this deep problem, any new technologies the schools manage to acquire will not be integrated into teaching and learning. They will be baubles rather than tools.

Like the actual wiring of the Pompidou Center in Paris—a museum turned inside out—the figurative wiring of a school is visible. One sees it in the stark division of activity between classroom and hallway, in the massiveness of some activities like the provision of lunch or of the daily announcements, in the scarcity and marginality of other activities like tutoring or study groups or private conversation that lasts longer than thirty seconds, and in the dependence on a central office. It is also apparent in the tones of human interaction between students and teachers, among teachers, between teachers and parents, between any insider and any outsider, between any insider and the principal. And one can hear it as well as see it almost any day:

I said listen up, children. Did you hear me, Fatima? Do not turn on your computers until I tell you to. Marcus, take your hands off the keyboard.

Excuse me, girls, but this is study hall. If you two have to talk, I will sign you a pass and you can go to the cafeteria.

It's not my fault. I swear I didn't hear the announcement. My homeroom is such a zoo.

Classrooms on the north side of the third floor may now release students to come to the gym for the pep rally.

Sally: Karen, what happened last night with Josh?

Karen: Ssh. I'll meet you third period.

Sally: Where?

Karen: The handicapped stall of the first-floor girls' room.

In this chapter, I will not criticize schools for discharging their custodial obligation to children. That is necessary for safety and for learning. Nor will I make a neoromantic argument that what is most needed is for schools to "free" students to learn. I will argue, however, that the energy channels, information flows, and power arrangements characteristic of most schools today and suggested by the images I have offered are not conducive to deep and sustained learning, do not permit children to benefit from the availability of powerful new information tools, and ought not to be carried forward into the twenty-first century.

The core functions of teaching and learning, especially the ones we associate with curriculum, accountability, and governance, are constrained by what is now antiquated wiring. Showing its origins, the school at the turn of the twenty-first century is wired to ensure the linear communication of a pre–information age bureaucracy and to discourage the lateral communication or the external communication that is becoming commonplace in other institutions. The presumption is that teachers are workers on a line. They receive some cohort of students on one end of a segment of that line, treat them with lessons wired linearly to a framework of curriculum supervision, then turn them out at the other end. Except at the margins of their workday, they lack the space and time to collaborate with each other or to meet with students individually. They often lack the powers they need to teach responsively: the power to call in another perspective, to alter a faulty placement, to reorganize a set of resources, and so on. Similarly students often lack genuine opportunities to work independently or to collaborate with each other in any other way than under the watchful eye of a teacher monitoring their cooperative learning groups. The presumption is that they too are workers on a line, who need no greater work space than the surface of the little desktop attached to their chairs.

Of course, as anyone knows who has worked in schools or studied them closely, teachers do not actually function linearly, nor do students. They subvert the presumptions of the wiring. Most teachers close their doors to the influence of linear higher-ups with a little cunning and great resolve, then do as they like behind the doors (Johnson, 1990; Lortie, 1975). Doing as they like, they may greatly benefit students. Indeed, some teachers privately create the most remarkable environments that are exactly opposite in their emphasis from the sketch I offer above. Most do not, however, for an obvious reason: it is very hard to create such a remarkable environment all by oneself.

Meanwhile, many students mimic their teachers in subverting the presumptions in the wiring, particularly at the secondary level. Some manage in the process to create powerful roles for themselves. Think of the media aides, for example, who seem to run the communications apparatus of many schools and go about their troubleshooting absent strict scheduling constraints. But most students conduct their subversion less openly and without any benefit to their learning: they sit all day long as required in their little desks but let their minds wander. The wiring mocks who they really are and what they are capable of doing, so they close themselves down during instructional time, and save their energy for before and between classes, after school and evenings. R. G. Des Dixon (1994) captures the irony:

> The very young consume all types of information via television and computers, while our model of childhood still views them as ignorant and innocent. Teens spend most of their time working for pay, listening to music, and watching television, but the model still pretends that school is their primary activity. They are indispensable to such major industries as fast food, supermarkets, gas stations, retail stores, and hospitals, but the model sees them as outside the labor force. They are looking after themselves and running households for absentee adults, but the model sees them as helpless [p. 362].

Whether from the perspective of teachers or of students, the consequence of all the linear wiring in many schools is not the humming hierarchy its installers intended and that, even now, many reformers would restore, though on a grander, more systemic scale. Rather, the consequence is an unreflective institution composed of isolated units, one that blocks and distorts information, saps energy, and ultimately disempowers teachers and students. It is a massive failure of communication.

To see this more clearly from a student's point of view, consider the hypothetical case of a high school student named Felicia. She attends a quite ordinary, medium-sized high school nearly anywhere in the United States. One evening, just before the annual school-home communication event called Back to School Night, Felicia's parents ask her a question. It is one that parents frequently ask their school-age children at dinnertime and at other times too —all of the times inconvenient from the point of view of the children. "So, Felicia, how are you doing in school?"

Although they offer a vague question, Felicia's parents hope to elicit a reassuringly detailed answer. Instead, they get: "Oh, I don't know, Okay, I guess."

Is Felicia lying? Is it possible that she really does not know how she is "doing" in school?

Worried by the response, her parents go to the school later that evening, armed with the same question: "How is Felicia doing?" The first thing they discover is that the question simply does not fit the school's wiring. As a global and integrated, yet intimate question, it cannot survive the parsing it gets right away: "Do you want an academic or an affective response, a norm-based or a criterion-based response?"

No one, of course, explicitly responds this way, but they may as well. Felicia's parents take the question first to her homeroom teacher because he is the first one they encounter in the ritual that has them follow Felicia's daily schedule. He answers in terms of her attendance record and also what he calls "her generally cooperative attitude." By this, he apparently means that she shuts up when the announcements come on and stands appropriately for the flag salute. Next, they ask her math teacher, who speaks only of math grades; her English teacher, who speaks only of English grades; and so on down the roster of Felicia's day. They save some time at the end of the busy night to sneak downstairs to try out the question on Felicia's guidance counselor. She offers them a printout of Felicia's ninth-grade standardized test scores and promises more information next year, "after Felicia has taken the Preliminary Scholastic Assessment Test." Finally, on the way out of the building, they try the question on the school's principal, who is standing in the corridor shaking hands with departing parents. He cannot recall even having met Felicia but assures the parents with a chuckle that that is probably good news about how she is doing.

The problem here is not just that there is no single adult in Felicia's school who knows her in any integrated way, or who therefore can care for her in any integrated way, or advise her in the matter of caring for herself in an integrated way. That is bad enough. But neither is there any facility in the school, with the possible exception of the special education apparatus, whereby those adults who know Felicia partially can come together to pool their knowledge or take concerted action on her behalf. The result is not just that Felicia's school lacks a comprehensive sense of Felicia, but that, for want of the capacity to know its actual effects, the school also lacks a sense of itself and its mission. In short, Felicia was not lying when she claimed not to know how she was doing in school. She lacked comprehensive information and, just as important, good criteria. "Doing in school?" Relative to what? No one at school had provided her more than the most partial images of what schooling might help her do.

This is partly a problem of belief. Felicia's school needs to reorient itself radically in its sense of obligation to Felicia and the other students. The principal's little joke was very telling. But new beliefs will not be enough. This is also a case of inadequate wiring. Even if the principal were secretly disconcerted by having to confess his ignorance of Felicia, he would face immense obstacles in trying to remedy the core problem. That is because the system whereby information, energy, and power are distributed in Felicia's school is not conducive to serving Felicia well, or to serving him well as he tries to serve her and her parents. It cannot pool information about her, build sufficient energy on her behalf, or act in a timely way to press her or rescue her if needed.

Of course, Felicia is a high school student, and the wiring problem that I describe is particularly prevalent at that level. But it exists at other levels of the system, too, and across the levels of the system. Recall from the Introduction that I felt good about my cousin's daughter's opportunities to be known by a caring adult and to have serious intellectual adventures while she was still in the second grade. But at the time of my visit to her classroom, she was nearing the end of the second grade, and I was not confident that the transitions ahead in her schooling—to the third grade, then to middle school and high school—could accommodate rich transfers of information or amplify rather than extinguish her energy for learning.

Nor could I feel confident that any of her teachers, current or future, shared a powerful image of the person they hoped she might become. High school faculties are often too specialized to notice the absence of such an image. They presume that it is enough for students to be "college bound" or "vocational." Often parents go along with the decision. Although, like my cousin, they may know intimately the complex intellectual and moral challenges of living and working in the United States near the end of the twentieth century, they put this knowledge aside in the face of the school's distortions. For their part, elementary school faculties are often too divided between those in the upper grades who mimic the specialization they see further on and those in the lower grades who may attend to children's development as if the ends of that development need not be kept in mind. They may resist efforts to imagine the end for fear that it will be imposed prematurely. Indeed, in some cases it is—by means of grade-level gates, retention policies, or other inappropriate installments of expectation. Still, in the process of resisting such impositions, these teachers may also fail to provide a compass for development, one their students might learn to read for themselves, one that might help them later when direction is left to their own devices or to the insensitive guidance of the track they happened to land in.

Miswired for Communication

Writing about higher education, but with implications for schools too, Peter Denning (1992) argues for new designs that reflect certain characteristics of emerging workplaces. First, he says, educational organizations should become organizations that listen and then identify the concerns of their clients and form individualized partnerships to address these concerns. Listening, he says, means being as open to the unique qualities of a particular case as to the question of what it is a case of. Listening also means responding to what is heard by preparing plans and proposing models that capture details, nuance, and preference. To listen thus, says Denning, organizations must cultivate opportunities for their members to inquire deeply and openly, to discern and describe difference, to appreciate diversity and anomaly, to link analysis and intuition, and to act on what they learn. As Peter Senge (1990) would put it, they must become learning organizations. Second, Denning suggests, educational organizations must become practiced at completing what they start. They must be rigorous about keeping their commitments, delivering on time, and achieving client satisfaction. In a word, they must be accountable.

These functions of listening and completing are the heart of communication. Typically their absence is the source of our disappointment when we speak of a failure to communicate: either the message never got through, or it was never acted on. One might say that the wiring of a school, as I use the term, denotes the school's communication system—its system for listening and completing and, in Senge's terms, for learning. It is a measure of the problem we face in redesigning school for the new century, however, that many readers may regard a school's communication system as a relatively marginal thing. They think of the school's public address system, with speakers hanging in every classroom—occasionally interrupting the real business of school, but otherwise peripheral to it. Or they think of the daily bulletin that is printed on paper or produced each morning as a tag-on to the Channel One broadcast. It starts the day in a ceremonial sense but is almost always about matters that have little to do with the substance of the day's work. Or they think of the parent communication apparatus—for example, the number that parents call for information but that only rarely connects them with the teacher they want to speak with, and then only after the school secretary has run down to the teacher's classroom to retrieve her; or the machine that calls parents to tell them that their child is absent but cannot record the parents' response. Or they think of the faculty communications apparatus—the attendance bulletin that offers data without circumstance, for example, concealing whether Tanya was absent yesterday because she missed the bus again, or had to take her mother to the hospital again; or the monthly faculty meeting where hardly anyone but the principal ever talks, and where the talk is almost never about teaching and learning.

Yet every school has at least two other communication systems too. First, there is the informal one that tries to make up for the deficits of its formal counterpart. This is the system whereby some faculty members manage to share lesson ideas with each other over lunch or on the playground. It is the one the principal uses when she manages to insert an idea about teaching or learning into a quick hallway conversation that is otherwise about completing the classroom census of students eligible for free or reduced lunch. It is the system that eventually manages to let teachers know why Tanya is absent again, although its informal status precludes it from checking the accuracy of this information and often from acting on it in a timely way to benefit Tanya. It is the system that eventually communicates with parents, although often only after there is a problem. And it is the system that spreads word rapidly when there has been a shooting over the weekend involving one of the school's students, when the cafeteria is serving mystery meat again, when the gym teacher's husband has cancer, and when the sixth-grade teachers have had a great row with the playground aides. In short, it is a system of gossip and other furtive exchange, emergency alert, and stolen moments.

Then there is the school's third communication system. This is the core one, the one that deals deliberately with teaching and student learning, even while it impedes organizational learning. This is the one that is premised largely on what are called classrooms, typically cellular allotments of space and time within which individual teachers instruct relatively large groups of students. Some of them are highly specialized in function: the art room, the chemistry lab; others are merely personalized: Ms. Sanchez's or Mr. Maroni's room; still others are bland intersections of space and time: the nondescript environment where a health class meets every other day during first period, followed by a special education math group, and so on. Students spend nearly all their school time in these classrooms, shuttling regularly among them more or less frequently, depending on their grade level. For this reason, classrooms are the focus of most of the system's attention. When the assistant superintendent introduces the new reading program, she expects that it will be implemented in classrooms. When the team of professionals confers to develop an individualized educational plan for Robin who is so easily distracted and so far behind, their planning is framed in terms of how much Robin should be taught in or out of these classrooms and of how to handle her there. "How can I use this in my classroom?" asks the teacher at the in-service workshop. "Ultimately, all that matters," intones the school reformer, "is what happens in classrooms."

In elementary schools, these classrooms are frequently the sites of vital communities, full of varied places to work and talk, meet and be nearly alone, although they are often crowded sites. In secondary schools, particularly high schools, they can be stark environments, even intellectual lockdowns, where twenty to forty young humans sit still for nearly an hour while one grown-up human talks to them. But whether in elementary schools or secondary schools that have lately tried to make their classrooms livelier, the classroom itself as chief element of an overall wiring design has two major faults. First, it pockets too much of the energy of school, distracting everyone from the learning potential of what is not classroom based, arrogating to itself experiences that would have greater learning potential if they happened somewhere else. Second, it steals away much of the power that schools might otherwise use to build common cultures. That is because it keeps teachers from interacting with each other and too severely partitions students' awareness of the intellectual work of their larger environment.

New Wiring

It is interesting to recall that the midcentury efforts of school reformer Lillian Weber to transform elementary education began with the simple but bold provocation of moving student work and activity into the hallways of New York City schools (Perrone, 1991). When, as part of the research reported here, I first visited a school that owed something to Weber by virtue of a line of progressive inheritance, the school startled me with its disregard of ordinary classroom design. Its older students especially seemed to come and go on some basis other than a mass schedule and seemed to use the facilities of school in a more individualized way. Even when they were scheduled to be together in a particular space with a given teacher, they seemed directed in their activities there by a set of expectations extrinsic to the particular grouping. In fact, they were simultaneously taking a course—in chemistry or the novel—and also using the experiences of the course to help them prepare part of their graduation portfolio. This represents a radical departure from the ordinary curricular wiring of high school, whereby teaching and learning energy is presumed to be utterly carved up into these packets of space and time called courses.

Throughout our study, my colleagues and I got glimpses of a future school in which the classroom was not elemental—which is to say, glimpses of a very different kind of curriculum. A number of the schools we studied had replaced the ordinary fifty-minute class scheduling typical in secondary schools with longer blocks of time. One consequence was that the habit of thinking about learning and teaching as synonymous with carefully planned and well-bounded class time was weakened. When we observed in these schools, we sometimes had trouble finding "the class"—the attentive group gathered for its lesson of the day. Instead we might find students engaged in a wide variety of activities, some of which took them outside the "classroom"—to the library, for example, or even into the community beyond the building. Adding to the effect was the fact that these blocks of time were often directed by a team of teachers rather than by an individual teacher and were often focused on more than one subject. In one school we studied, three teachers were responsible for teaching math, science, technology, and social studies to sixty-five ninth-grade students over the course of four hours every day. At the beginning of each week, during their planning meeting (while their students were off to band, community service, physical education, or some other area), the team decided how to allot its time and space for the week. Typically during this planning time they also talked about the needs of individual students, discussed what they were teaching and how they might teach it, and created the policies that governed the considerable chunk of school life that they controlled—the homework and disciplinary policies, for example. The learning environment of this entirely team-taught high school in some respects resembled an elementary school in its allotment of space and time and in the quality of relationships between teachers and students. In another respect, it resembled a college inasmuch as students did not wander furtively in the hallways or wave hall passes defiantly or smugly. They just walked from one place to another, looking productive in an ordinary way, suggesting in the process that they regarded their school as something other than a set of classrooms strung along a no-man's-land.

Throughout our study, we also glimpsed governance systems radically different from the norm of the late twentieth-century school. The team meetings offer such a glimpse. Several schools also had schoolwide councils or steering committees, some including students. These tended to be consultative rather than formal governance bodies, but they had great influence and in at least one case ensured a smooth transition between principals. One school evolved all its policies through an elaborate constellation of team meetings, cross-grade (or vertical) meetings, cross-curricular (or horizontal) meetings, and periodic faculty retreats. The schools that had built the exhibition systems I describe in Chapter One had also created governance committees for these systems. These committees defined the exhibition tasks, oversaw the evaluations, used examples of student performance to reflect on the schools' other systems, and so on. In the process, the committees acquired significant, if informal, powers with regard to curriculum and policy.

A third area where we glimpsed emerging and significantly different wiring involved accountability systems. The exhibition systems are good examples of this. Several of the schools we studied had gone well beyond these, however, to create elaborate accountability systems, all of them anchored by a framework of expectations for student performance. Integrating such frameworks with the ordinary business of teaching and learning in school is not easy, as the case in Chapter Four recounts. They are nonetheless essential to any school's effort to be accountable for all its students' learning. That is because in constructing and tending these frameworks, the school raises up its many eyes from the close work of shepherding this or that particular group of students through the third grade or introductory Spanish, and focuses them on a bigger scene. In this way the school gains reflective power, and the students gain an integrative perspective. Yet a framework of performance expectations is hardly enough to build an accountability system, as I suggest below.

Six Unconventional Lessons

I would say that we learned six lessons about wiring across the schools we studied. The first two focus on curriculum or the energy exchanges of school, the next two on governance or power relations, and the last two on accountability or the capacity of schools to generate, share, and use information to benefit students. In what follows, I present each of these lessons as a confrontation with conventional wisdom.

1. *The conventional wisdom is that curriculum is what teachers teach to students.* A better way to define curriculum is to say that it represents one point of a triangular relationship, with the other two points being the teacher and the students. In other words, curriculum is not something the teacher possesses (or can hope to possess) and hands over to students by various means. From the teacher's as well as the students' perspective, the curriculum is something that must be continuously constructed. The question that first confronts the teacher is not whether to teach the binomial theorem to these students, but whether he or she shall invest in the binomial theorem such that the teacher's knowing may enable their knowing (McDonald, 1992c).

I am not suggesting that the teacher must continuously construct curriculum from scratch, though I am mindful of the teaching energy some teachers get from doing so. I merely mean that some significant degree of construction is needed. The teacher gets her mind, so to speak, around some bit of knowledge in the world. It may come her way as the result of what is called a curriculum framework, perhaps produced by a statewide committee, or as the result of an afternoon's walk in the woods. In either case, she must turn her mindfulness into an enticement and a direction for her students' mindfulness. John Dewey (Archambault, 1974) called this "psychologizing a subject":

> [The teacher's] problem is that of inducing a vital and personal experiencing. Hence, what concerns him, as teacher, is the ways in

> which that subject may become a part of experience; what there is in the child's present that is usable with reference to it. . . . He is concerned, not with the subject matter as such, but with the subject matter as a related factor in a total and growing experience [p. 352].

Although the teacher and her students have a relationship with each other independent of the curriculum, each also has a separate relationship with the curriculum, and they have as well a relationship with each other through the curriculum—through the binomial theorem, the poem, the making of applesauce, or whatever else. It is this latter relationship that lends meaning and power to the other two. It completes the triangle.

This revision of conventional wisdom has many implications. One concerns a favorite pastime of the twentieth-century educational system. If curriculum is at its heart of set of relationships, it is inane to think of "teacher-proofing" it—of so polishing it in frameworks, guidebooks, or textbooks that the teacher can pass it on without having to invest in it. But a second implication concerns many prescriptions for a twenty-first-century system. It is equally inane to imagine a curriculum that requires no teachers—a curriculum that can be delivered, for example, by the information superhighway to every child's home.

Perhaps the most important implication of this way of thinking about curriculum, however, is that it requires of school that it become a place for teacher learning too. This requires extensive rewiring: introducing opportunities for teachers to meet in learning groups, study privately, gain access to teaching resources, get their minds around what they teach.

Some may say that teachers do this now in the brief but daily preparation periods they nearly all get during the school day and in the hours many devote weekly to preparation at home. But I am not speaking here of preparation in the ordinary sense—the effort to create lessons, grade papers, fill out report cards, and so on. I am speaking of the kind of learning that now happens for many teachers only in such special summer programs as those run by the National Science Foundation or the National Endowment for the Humanities, or in content-focused university courses, or by means of private reading and travel and projects.

Not every teacher cultivates such opportunities or takes advantage of those that may arise without deliberate cultivation. There are many reasons for this, including the fact that learning is always difficult as well as enjoyable, but the main reason is that such learning is not considered part of the job of teaching. The job is wired such that one may, if one chooses, construct all teaching out of previous learning. There is literally no time built in for learning on the job. Indeed, learning on the job is disparaged to some extent. School life is full of cautionary tales of teachers who foolishly tried to stay one chapter ahead of their students. Good teachers are supposed to come to teaching already knowing what they must teach. The effect of such lore and such working conditions is that many teachers try to stretch thin knowledge too far, for fear of looking foolish or for want of opportunities to learn more.

When in their work life might teachers find time for learning? Anyone who has ever practiced or studied school reform knows that there never seems to be enough time. However, most complaints about time accept two features of conventional wiring as given: the short day and the short year. Of the schools we studied, three dared to attempt some rewiring in this area. Two of the schools managed, by means of voluntary commitments within a powerful school ethos, to create an eight-hour teacher workday. The point of their effort, however, was not to create more time on task for students—more productivity in a narrow and counterproductive sense—but rather to create more learning time for teachers. It was still not enough learning time, but it was symbolically very valuable because it came during rather than after the workday.

In the process of gaining more learning time for teachers, one of these eight-hour-workday schools inserted a block of recreational time for students in the middle of the day. Ordinarily, recreational time comes at the end of the day, when many students play sports or the most privileged have private ballet, music, or karate lessons. By incorporating such time into the middle of the day, this school not only gained prime time for teacher learning but also acknowledged the educational value of the recreational activities and broke up an otherwise long stretch of academic learning.

The third school in this set tried, though without immediate success, to tackle the other half of the time problem by initiating a proposal to change to a year-round schedule. It proposed substituting smaller, scattered chunks of vacation for the longer summer break. Such scheduling, now becoming common in California and other fast-growing areas of the country, does not fully address the problem of an artificially short year. It does, however, have great symbolic value, particularly if it leads to efforts within the community to provide enrichment and recreational experiences for children during break weeks. These address the deep core of the opposition to year-round schooling: the sense among some parents that the experiences many children have in summer are deeply educational, and more so for being informal and not associated with school.

2. *The conventional wisdom is that good schools require good teachers.* Call this the Jaime Escalante fallacy, after the remarkable teacher who taught heroically but alone and whose work was chronicled in the Hollywood film *Stand and Deliver* (Matthews, 1988). The idea depends on the fact that nearly everyone has had a "good teacher" at some point during the school years—that is, one who stood out from other teachers as a result of passion, skillfulness, caring, and effectiveness. If only every teacher were like Ms. Epstein, we tell ourselves. How might we arrange teacher education, certification policies, career ladders, tenure laws, collective bargaining agreements, and so forth to produce more Mrs. Escalantes or Ms. Epsteins? In plotting such policy moves, however, we fail to ask two crucial questions. First, is the apparently severe scarcity of such teachers—one or two out of perhaps forty or ninety teachers in a student's career in school—really remediable through policy interventions? And, second, did everybody who had her for a teacher really like Ms. Epstein as much as I did?

Our study convinced us that good schools depend on good teaching but that good teaching is best thought of as a distributed property—a quality of schools rather than of teachers. Our evidence is that good teaching is more stable, reliable, and pervasive when groups of people rather than individuals are expected to supply it. When the wiring of a school permits them to work in groups, gives them time to plan together and confer with each other about the students they share in common, teachers can build on each other's strengths and compensate for each other's weaknesses. In the process, they can collectively reach the children that one or another of them could not reach individually for reasons of personality, style, gender, or a dozen other factors that are not faults.

Good teaching as a distributed quality facilitates accountability. But I refer to it here especially as a curricular innovation in order to emphasize the way in which it may also facilitate a shift in what is learned in school. Our attachment to the idea of teaching as a matter of highly individualized practice is deeply implicated in our attachment to the idea of separate grades and subjects. For all practical purposes, the fourth grade becomes the child's complex relationships with Mr. Barr, and geometry becomes Mrs. DesRoche's teaching. Most of the schools in our study that dared to disturb these associations broke another old habit in the process: they combined grades and dissolved some of the conventional divisions between subjects. They could do this because team teaching gave them more flexibility in the distribution of teachers' expertise. In combining grades, they freed themselves from the constraints of faulty developmental benchmarks, giving children more room to grow. In combining subjects, they gained more time during each day for learning in depth. And in doing both, they gained for teachers and students that much more sense of school as something other than a set of cellular experiences.

3. *The conventional wisdom is that the faculty—for better or worse—is the source of a school's stability, while its administration is the source of change.* Even this book may reinforce this assumption. Recall that the "moves" I described in Chapter Two were nearly all made by principals. Often the examples of drag that I cite involve recalcitrance among teachers. Finally, the one case of complete design collapse that I mentioned came as a result of a change in leadership.

As I suggested in Chapter Two, however, these tendencies are symptomatic of a problem in the wiring. Although the principal's strong leadership was crucial in initiating the new design work in nearly all the schools we studied, the concentration of power invariably proved problematic later. In the end, our sense was that in most of the schools we studied, entirely too much power resided in the principal's office. Too many decisions ended up there, and too many expectations hovered there. In most cases, the principals we knew handled these decisions and expectations well, but a culture of deference developed despite their best intentions and sapped energy from the rest of the school. Moreover, the problem

I discussed above with regard to teachers held here too: "good principals"—that is, heroic figures—are hard to come by. When power has to be handed over, the chances are good that it will be handed over to a lesser figure.

Sorely exacerbating this problem in most of the schools we studied was a related one. Where a leadership transition occurred, there was no governance envelope to supply stability across the transition—to ensure, for example, that the new leader believed in the changes under way in the school. This is the function that is served, for example, by an independent school's board of trustees or overseers. Most of the schools we studied, all of them public schools, had nothing like this. Instead, some had volatile school board politics or indifferent bureaucracies or both. In one school, the selection of a new principal was handled with utter disregard for the state of the school's redesign and the hopes of the school community.

Nevertheless, two of the schools we studied were exceptional in this regard. In one case, an elected school community council of teachers, parents, and other citizens was empowered by law to choose the new leader. It chose conservatively and wisely, protecting the redesigning process. In the other case, the school was deliberately wired for predictable transitions. That is, it had a complex and distributed leadership of codirectors, division chairs, team leaders, and so on. The distributed leadership was predictably conservative, fiercely guarding the school's beliefs and rituals. By similar means, it ensured a smooth transition in leadership: when one codirector left, the distributed leadership made compatibility with the remaining codirector a key criterion in the selection of the successor.

Meanwhile, this school moderated the conservative influences of its leadership system in two ways. First, it engaged in a number of tuning practices, opening itself up in an extraordinary way to external scrutiny and critical feedback. Second, it established a policy of encouraging a rather high degree of faculty turnover: hiring young teachers whose sense of adventure was bound to take them elsewhere within a few years, hiring interns whose term of employment was limited to two years, encouraging some of its most capable and experienced teachers to move on to positions of leadership in other schools with which this school was networked. The tactic worked to a limited extent, creating more vacancies than would otherwise be expected in a good school, and also some insulation from the ordinary trauma of budget cutbacks. Its real significance was symbolic, however. This school, much admired and often visited, flouted the conventional wisdom related to public school governance. It inverted the ordinary pattern of looked-for stability and hoped-for creative stir.

4. *The conventional wisdom is that the productivity of a school depends on good control mechanisms.* We were persuaded by our research that the productivity of a school depends more on its capacity for generating and sustaining what I call slack. No matter how successful a school is in developing purposefulness, it cannot put this purposefulness to work for students without having a significant supply on hand of undirected resources. Slack is flexibility of key resources, especially time, space, and human expertise.

People who do not work in schools often have difficulty comprehending why schools seem so inertial in allocating resources, or why principals have to be guerrilla fighters to find the resources necessary to implement good ideas on short notice. One explanation for the phenomenon is that they have so little practice matching resources to purpose. Traditionally, time, space, and human expertise are preallocated by curriculum. The third grade is here, and the fourth grade there; the seven periods are carved up into five major subjects, one elective that alternates with gym, and lunch; and the Title One teacher does this, while the Reading Recovery teacher does that.

This habit of preallocation is reflected in budgets. One elementary school we visited has an overall annual budget of $2.3 million. Of this total, 59.8 percent is tied up in salaries. Although the school may be said to have some discretion on an annual basis to adjust this figure up or down—say, by deciding that prospective enrollment in the kindergarten warrants only three teachers and three aides rather than four teachers, or that the school can get by with three custodians rather than four—the figure cannot be easily adjusted except annually. The next largest share of the budget goes to routine costs, which for all practical purposes are fixed: transportation, building maintenance (everything from fuel to toilet paper), and general supplies (photocopier paper, sticky notes, and other essential stock). This part of the budget also includes the school's share of the cost of maintaining a superintendency with two other small towns. The third largest item in the budget, accounting for 16.7 percent of the total, is special education (for example, salaries, out-of-school tuitions for severely disabled children, and contracts for occupational and physical therapies). What is left over after all this is 2.9 percent of the budget, or just $66,007. This is the only truly discretionary money, but it is hardly mad money. It must pay for all books and classroom supplies for 470 students, professional development activities for 34 professional staff, technology purchases, and anything else that the school may decide it needs during any given budget cycle. Meanwhile, $5,000 of it comes from federal grants that are passed on from the state in a way that makes them neither predictable nor timely in terms of the school's budget cycle. The result is that these federal dollars are the least likely dollars of all to be used in any strategic way.

My point in providing this example is that many schools, lacking practice in matching resources to special purposes, may not know what to do with slack when they find some. At one point during our research, we were asked to administer a small planning grant to three of the schools in our study sample. It was to have lasted for two years. Fully five years later, two of the three schools had not yet spent their share. This happened because in the matter of allocating resources, these schools were ill prepared to act any other way than compliantly. They simply rolled along each year, spending down the lines of the budget handed them from central office.

A symbolic way to think about the need for slack in school is to consider it from the perspective of introducing new technologies. Because our research involved the exploration of a number of innovative information technology applications, I often found myself demonstrating these to people interested in the research. More than once, however, the things I was demonstrating did not come on at the flick of a switch or mouse. Or, after coming on, they did not work as expected. Of course, when these technological glitches interrupted my presentations to a large group, there would invariably be one or two people present who could rush to the rescue and fix the problem —stop the horizontal scroll, get the juice to the dead outlet, make the LCD panel project, or whatever else needed to be done. I knew nonetheless what all the teachers who watched the rescue were thinking: "What if *I* were depending on this contraption, and what if I were alone?" This is the conditioned response of one used to the fact that the period is only forty-two minutes long, that the only adult in the school who knows how to fix wayward machines also has five classes of his own, that one can sign up for the computer lab only one day a week, that when the photocopier jams, it stays jammed for half a day because the key operator also has to answer the telephones in the main office, and so on. Having been a teacher myself for a long time—one who remembers what it was like to have the 16-mm film suddenly split in the middle of a showing, or to have a lesson plan ruined by a blown projection bulb—I adopted a stock response to these snafus in my presentations. To the annoyance of my technologist colleagues, I would invariably say, "Well, you really didn't expect the technology to work, did you? You ought to know by now that technology never works." Then I would go on to explain that it never works within the constraints of time and other resources assigned to it. It always needs slack—time to reset it, people to troubleshoot it, flexibility in the circumstances surrounding its use, patience in the system. Of course, my listeners knew as well as I that these are rarities in school.

Occasionally in our research, we found slack in a school. One incident I recall vividly involved technology again and a third-grade classroom. The classroom was in a remarkable school in a small town of mixed-income families. The teacher in charge had jerry-rigged an electronic portfolio, aided by the district's computer specialist. This was one of the ways in which the school was remarkable: it encouraged experimentation, called itself a center of inquiry, and stretched its modest resources accordingly. The hardware sat in one corner of a bustling room: a Macintosh computer, a scanner, a zap camera, a microphone for audio input. I was talking to the teacher about other things on my visit to this classroom one day, when, out of the corner of my eye, I saw a little girl approach the hardware. I watched her use the keyboard to call up the portfolio software and the mouse to select several options. Then she put a large piece of paper on the scanner and entered more keystrokes. Finally, she picked up the microphone and said within my earshot, "I think this is the best poem I wrote so far this year, because I really like the picture it makes in my mind." Then she did something more with the mouse, and returned to the table where she had been writing earlier.

I interrupted the flow of our conversation to ask the girl's teacher about what I had just seen. She explained that she would later read the girl's poem in the electronic portfolio where she had just placed it and would add her own voice annotation. She also told me that the girl might later invite some of her peers to call up the poem too and to record their reactions. Finally, she told me that several of the students in her class had made a video—working by themselves to direct it, shoot it, and act in it—one intended to explain the electronic portfolio to the children who will use it next year.

I watched this video that same evening and was astounded by the children's comfort with what seemed to me to be two complex tools: the electronic portfolio and the video camera. But thinking about it, I realized that what astounded me involved more than technology and that it need not be so rare in school as to be astounding. I was simply seeing what happens when children become accustomed to piloting their own way through a rich learning environment—one full of both relatively new technology and ordinary production materials, plus time and space for production, opportunities for conversation and critique among multiple partners, opportunities for taking initiative and for delving deeper into matters of special interest, books and other information resources of all kinds, including those that must be accessed by telephone or modem. I was marveling, in short, over a teaching and learning environment that for once had some slack.

Then, in my mind, I pictured the electronic portfolio in use in the average secondary school, with its eight-period day, its hall-pass requirements, its concentration of computer technologies in computer labs. The scene I witnessed in the third grade would be impossible in this other place. When would students have the time to scan in their work? How could they be trusted to do so given the expensive machines, the time it would take "off-task," the security and confidentiality issues, the problem of access to the lab, and so on? The teachers or the guidance department would have to do it, but where would they find the time? These are questions that a number of the high schools we studied deliberately confronted, with my colleagues and I eagerly assisting. I therefore know firsthand that they are not impossible questions. Here I highlight a generic answer that fits all of them: slack. The principal of one of these secondary schools, who began his career as a kindergarten teacher, told me once that he often makes design choices in favor of whatever option will make his school more like kindergarten.

5. *The conventional wisdom is that a school's accountability depends on the strength of its agreement on standards.* On the basis of our study, however, I would say that the real work of accountability is in facing up to disagreement. That is because accountability depends ultimately on reflective conversation about student performance, and, however it eventually plays out in judgments, reflective conversation entails disagreement along the way. Sadly, such disagreement is often preempted.

This happens, for example, as a result of the pervasive influence of standardized achievement tests. They have become a mainstay of accountability in the late-twentieth-century school system. They are constructed to be highly reliable, such that one child's scores can be compared with another child's scores, and one school's average scores can be printed in the newspaper next to another school's average scores. The premise here is that such comparisons will facilitate improvement. This will happen, however, only if the test data become a basis for reflective conversation within the school.

One reason this seldom occurs is that the high reliability of these tests has been purchased at some distortion of their validity, and the high-stakes circumstances surrounding the testing—for example, the scores in the newspaper—emphasize the distortion. The typical standardized reading test, for example, represents reading in a way that is quite different from the way we find it nearly everywhere else. Test takers read brief passages extracted from context, then select from among preconstructed answers to questions about the passages. These activities are tokens of reading, not reading itself. What often happens, however, to the test takers who score poorly—and to whole schools of them—is that they are drilled on the tokens so that they will do better on the next testing. For them, reading becomes practice test taking (Brown, 1991).

One way to characterize this problem is to say that it is one of premature and unreflective agreement. Important questions about what reading is, how you know when somebody is getting better at it, and how you help children get better at it have been settled before the schools have had any opportunity to struggle with them. Their possible disagreements have been preempted by a set of hollow agreements:

Question: What is reading?
Answer: It is what the test asks students to do.
Question: How do you know that students are getting better at it?
Answer: When their scores on this test go up.
Question: How do you get the scores to go up?
Answer: You drill the children on test questions.

A second area where premature agreement stifles opportunities for deeper teaching and learning in school involves grading. Here there is little scientific basis for assuming reliability, but schools and stakeholders often pretend that it is there anyway. In the process, they protect themselves from the uncertainties and messiness of disagreement. So teachers often assess student work by assigning the letter grades A through F. They may base these grades on a quantitative standard—so many points off for such and such an error, so many points added in for such and such a feature. Near the end of report periods, they average all the numbers behind all the letter grades, weighting them as they judge appropriate—so much weight for a quiz, so much more for a unit test, and so on. By means of all this data crunching, they manage to satisfy themselves, the school's authorities, their students, and the students' parents that the grades are fair, valid, and objective. In fact, there is rarely anything more than private and subjective judgment underlying all the analysis: whether to deduct five points or no points for a failure to indent paragraphs or label angles, whether to put more weight on the book reports or on class participation, whether book reports are even a very good way to assess reading, whether to count effort. The reliability of such a grading procedure across students, teachers, grades, and courses—that is, the likelihood that one A or C is equal to another—is utter illusion because different graders are typically not linked by even the barest conversation about standards. Moreover, because grades in a gradebook are often all that remain of the work they are supposed to represent, graders lack a basis to check on the reliability of their own grading from one episode to another. The idea that grading is reliable across schools and communities— that an A is an A is an A—is utterly preposterous. Yet, as I say, we may pretend otherwise. Many parents in a school district in my state became quite upset recently at the prospect of losing report card letter grades in their elementary schools. One parent told a reporter that she opposed the change because the letter grading format is universally understood and tells parents "exactly, precisely, where our children stand. It's so objective" (Olsen, 1995, p. 26).

The attachment to such imperfect agreement derives from fear that open disagreement will loosen the schools' standards from their presumed moorings, that standards will become negotiable rather than objective. Our study, however, convinced us that where standards are not negotiable—that is, where they are not the product of continuous conversation between teachers and students, among teachers, and between the school and its community—there are no real standards at all (Berger, 1996). There is only superficial agreement masking deep and private disagreement.

The wiring challenge here is how to create opportunities for productive disagreement. This challenge is derivative of an ethic, as Amy Gutmann (1990) claims, that makes a virtue of disagreement—one that is absolutely central to democracy. It demands an idea of standards as tentative, lively, and open to all manner of possibility, and it demands a facility within which they can both operate and be disputed. Such a facility will have the characteristics of what Maxine Greene (1988) calls an authentic public space:

> The aim is to find (or create) an authentic public space . . . one in which diverse human beings can appear before one another as, to quote Hannah Arendt, the best they know how to be. Such a space requires the provision of opportunities for the articulation of multiple perspectives in multiple idioms, out of which something common can be brought into being. It requires, as well, a consciousness of the normative as well as the possible: of what *ought* to be, from a moral and ethical point of view, and what is in the making, what *might* be in an always open world [p. xi].

The idea of exhibition as the central feature of school accountability—a crucial tenet of the Coalition of Essential Schools—and experimentation with exhibition systems are expressions of the search for an authentic public space.

6. *The conventional wisdom is that assessment is the heart of accountability.* Based on our study, I believe instead that the heart of accountability is an inquiring attitude toward student performance. Assessment is one way to generate the performance, but not the only way. Moreover, even the cleverest or most comprehensive assessment is worth little if the school lacks opportunities for reflective conversation about the results.

The key question, therefore, is not how the school conducts assessment but rather how it designs for reflective conversation about student performance. In the next several paragraphs, I advocate a four-part response to this question.

First, the school must generate student performance that relates directly to the school's goals. Many schools today are not in the habit of doing so. They may want students to write well, for example, but they may give them only worksheets on which to perform writing. Or they may want students to speak well, but they may give them only opportunities to complete the blanks in teachers' sentences. Moreover, some significant amount of the performance the school generates must be public—the stuff of exhibitions, exhibits, recitals, and so on. And the school must be willing to take risks in the process of generating these public performances, not try to limit them to only the best.

Second, the school must provide some means for recording the student performances it generates, so that they might later serve as texts for reflective conversation. Here, students' investment in the process is crucial. The third grader mentioned above took the trouble to enter her new poem into an electronic portfolio because she perceived a growth opportunity for herself. She would not have been so eager to participate in a process designed to audit her learning for the sake of the teacher's skill building or for the sake of the district's accountability reporting to the state. Another way to put this is to say that accountability, like it or not, is in the hands of the children. One may as well, as my Brown colleague Bil Johnson (1995) puts it, "give the kids the keys"—that is, design the system so that students run it. One school we studied graduates its students on the basis of their demonstration through recorded performances that they meet the school's performance requirements for graduation. The students present this evidence, one folder at a time over the course of two or three years, to a graduation committee consisting of the student's adviser, one other teacher, a third adult of the student's choosing (sometimes a family member), and another student. As in graduate school, the student runs this system. She is in charge of deciding which performances to record and how to record them, of presenting and defending the records of these performances as evidence of achievement, of putting her committee together and of convening it as necessary. Her incentive in taking on this responsibility is that this is the only way she can graduate; simply putting in time and collecting passing grades is not enough in her school.

Third, the school needs some overall information system that can archive and retrieve all these records of performance. This is not an easy system to design, as the case in Chapter Four reveals. John Fredericksen and Allan Collins (1989) suggest that schools think of the task as the building of a multimedia library of benchmarked performances—that is, performances across a range of quality that have been reflected on by the light of some set of standards. The retrieval system must be easy to manage, and the performances need to be readily accessible to students as well as teachers, available for coaching and private consultation, as well as reflective conversation. Recall the third grader's teacher's prediction that she would likely ask some of her classmates to call up her poem later that day and discuss it with her. When one thinks of such a system on a larger scale—a function of the whole school rather than of one teacher's experiment—many design problems arise. Privacy issues are involved, for example, as well as difficult technology hurdles. But both are minor problems compared with the challenge of redefining the daily work of school such that examining and talking about others' performances is as common as it is, say, in sports.

Fourth, the school must invent rituals, or what in Chapter Six I call *protocols,* for reflective conversation about student performance among all the parties to accountability, especially the students themselves, their teachers, and their parents. Many of the schools we studied, as a result of their interest in exhibitions, had such protocols for generating and discussing feedback on particular student performances. Several used them for the private examination of portfolios of collected performances—by student and teacher, by student and parent, and by all three parties. And the school I described with the graduation portfolio system had a protocol for teachers' reflective conversation about these portfolios. It was quite simple. Every Tuesday afternoon, a different group of teachers met to discuss two complete portfolios—ones that had justified the students' graduation the year before. The teachers first read through all the work, and all the comments made about the work by the students' respective graduation committees; then they talked about what they saw. Sometimes this talk was difficult because it surfaced disagreements with colleagues' judgments. But the moderator of the discussions was clear about the purpose: it was not to worry about judgments now past and final; it was to gain a better, more collective sense of how the school does its most important work.

Conclusion

In this chapter, I have claimed that new beliefs are not enough to create the kind of schools that teach all children to use their minds well, and that even the best new beliefs will be distorted if they have to accommodate late-twentieth-century school wiring. By wiring I mean the channels that schools now use to process information (for example, about how children are doing), exchange energy (for example, between a teacher excited about Shakespeare and a student who has never read him), and exercise power (for example, with regard to the allocation and use of resources). I have recommended new wiring designs in three areas: curriculum, where I suggest we abandon our fixation on the classroom and create opportunities for teacher learning on the job; governance, where I suggest that we learn to share power in school, especially with regard to making decisions about particular children's needs and how to expend resources to meet them; and accountability, where I have advocated a focus on student performance and have suggested ways to make that performance more accessible for learning. In the process of making these recommendations, I have demonstrated again the habit I revealed in the Introduction of taking issue with common sense—this time, commonsense definitions of curriculum, governance, and accountability.

Looking across all the claims, recommendations, and propositions I have put forward in this chapter, I would say that they all reduce to three basic and interrelated specifications for rewiring the school. The first specification is for slack. People who work in schools, both adults and children, need more time, space, power, and freedom of movement to do that work, if the work is to be done well. School need not be a lockdown for any of them so long as the right beliefs pervade the place. The second specification is for reflective conversation about learning and teaching. The absence of such conversation in most schools now is the consequence of an outmoded association of teaching and learning with telling and remembering. In fact, teaching and learning at their heart depend on reflection and conversation. Schools that allow for neither cannot truly conduct the business they are assigned to conduct. Finally, the third specification is for communal responsibility in setting the direction of teaching and assessing its impact on learning. Both words are crucial: we need schools where no one works alone and that do not hide behind statements of their best intentions.

Were we to work very hard to install new wiring in accord with these three interrelated specifications, then we would have the wiring we need to get us through at least the first years of the twenty-first century. Of course, good wiring is much easier to specify than to install, as the next chapter reveals.

Chapter Four

Rewiring a School

While writing this book, I had the chance to tour the construction site of a new school, where I could see its wiring in the barest state. Indeed, I got to see this school before all its roofs were in place, before its doors and window frames were attached. I even got to see through its interior walls, which were still just steel studs, dangling cables, and empty receptacle boxes. The sky was blue, the sun warm, and the nearby mountains beautiful through the school's unframed windows. Visiting a school in summer, one that is not only without its children but also without walls, doors, or an entire roof, helps one focus on what school is for. That is because one can appreciate so directly on such a construction site the considerable belief, as well as energy, imagination, illusion, and plain expense, that construction requires. Yet because it is summer, one also feels the old American suspicion, stoked by Huck Finn, Nancy Drew, and Bart Simpson, that school may not be worth all the bother it occasions and that it may inevitably be irrelevant to the most important kinds of learning.

I asked for this tour because I feared that my writing about school design was becoming too ethereal. I wanted to walk in actual construction mud, touch the concrete subfloor, see the steel partitions bolted to it. I especially wanted to see these things in the company of my friend who had just been appointed principal of this new school and who would have to turn the physical facts of this emerging school into a human organization. I needed to be reminded at that moment about who I was writing this book for.

I hope it is now clear that *wiring* is the metaphoric term I assign to the facts of school: some of them hard facts—where the walls, doors, and windows are, and whether there are receptacles for network hookups and telephone jacks—and some of them soft facts—how the schedule is configured, and who has the power, and how energies are channeled. These are all means by which a school organizes the attention of its students and teachers, turning them for better or worse away from other concerns they might have in the world, trying to convince them that it does so for the sake of a larger good—battling, so to speak, against Bart Simpson. A school's wiring is nearly everything about a school that mediates successfully or otherwise between a world that is full of attractions, dangers, and unorganized opportunities for children, on the one hand, and, on the other hand, the set of beliefs the school holds about the kinds of people these children should become and why.

Sometimes a school with strong and explicit beliefs actually gets to install the right wiring to match them. This was true of the new school I toured and one of the schools we studied. But all of the other schools in our study had to adjust as best they could the wiring they inherited from another era of belief. They had to engage in lots of rewiring—not only the literal poking of holes in walls and ceilings to string cable for a computer network but also efforts to move from an eight-block daily schedule to a four-block one, to introduce public assessment where there had previously been only private and even furtive assessment, to shift from habits of isolation to habits of collaboration in teaching and planning and administering, to substitute for an intellectual lockdown a learning environment full of inquiry and access to diverse expertise, and so on.

The first time you know your wiring is antiquated is when you try to do something more and a circuit breaks—when you try to install an air conditioner in the baby's bedroom, or try to run the kind of school that not only knows its students well but also manages to keep that knowledge alive across the years that they spend in school, or try to run the kind of school that makes an explicit commitment to educate students to a particular standard of quality. Of course, if you have built your house or school from scratch, you may never break a circuit, though some future occupant surely will (no wiring job stays good enough forever).

In the schools we studied, we found lots of broken circuits. The case study that follows is of a group of especially committed and energetic teachers who try again and again to plug in that extra air conditioner, microwave oven, refrigerator, and so on as the heat builds up in the old wires. I devote the bulk of this chapter to this case study because it captures what a number of stories told in less detail could not capture: the accelerating quality of the challenges facing schools in the wiring arena of school design. To rewire a school in the interest of making the school more accountable for teaching all its students to use their minds well is not to face a series of complex but discrete problems. It is rather to unleash a cascade of complex and interrelated problems. Moreover, as the case makes plain, the rewiring school must typically keep running even while it snips and pulls wires. Schools usually do not have the opportunity that some other industries have to shut down while they retool.

I include the case study too because its messiness seems a good corrective for the habit among some reformers, researchers, and policymakers to stand in relation to schools at too sanitary a distance. From such a distance, it is easy to assume that very difficult things are actually far less difficult. The school featured in this case is an exemplary one, unafraid of tough challenges and skillful in coping with them. Yet it has struggled with the challenge at the heart of this case for nearly a decade now. That is not the fault of the school, or evidence of a deficit of leadership or imagination. Rather it is evidence of how tough the job is, and how much of a long haul redesigning school will be.

A teacher, whom I will call Jennie, coauthored the case with me. Following the occasional tendency of our research to take the form of a seminar and the tendency of this book to draw on other voices than mine, the case is drawn first from Jennie's intimate and first-person account of her school's reform efforts. This is then augmented by parts of the actual transcript of a discussion among her and several others who had read the first-person account and wished to know more. This discussion took place at a Fall Forum, the annual meeting of the Coalition of Essential Schools. Thus the final part of the case is told in the form of a dialogue. I am among the parties to the dialogue, the one who occasionally tries to impose theory on the complex events narrated.

Following the case itself, I analyze an important piece of unfinished business in it. This unfinished business involves literal rewiring.

The Case of the Overheated Wires

The story begins with a move that is much advocated in the school reform literature today but that is also much attacked by some parents and others. A small junior-senior high school with well-developed beliefs about the process of education decides to pay attention to its ends. It dares to ask itself the question, What do we want all the graduates of the Henry B. Smith School to know and be able to do? Then it goes even further, and asks, How might we guarantee that they all get there?[1]

These are questions of school design. They begin in the arena of beliefs but lead quickly to wiring and tuning too. That is because they threaten the organizational norm among schools to be loosely coupled systems (Weick, 1976, 1982). Most schools are organized so that their espoused goals do not drive their core operations but remain instead within a loose appendage of belief. This design enables the school simultaneously to satisfy the diverse and conflicting interests that press on it and to hold them off. Schools that set out to take their goals more seriously than this, to turn the goals into actual outcomes, first have to figure out how to tighten up the connection between goal setting and actual teaching and learning. This involves a major feat of rewiring, as we will see in this case. But it also leads to a major tuning challenge. That is, as the school dares to define its goals more precisely and to dedicate itself to their achievement, it risks offending some set of constituents who would have preferred other goals—constituents who had previously found some satisfaction among the loosely coupled goals. Indeed, were more schools to become tightly coupled systems, it is

1. My wording in this paragraph suggests, impossibly, that a school has consciousness—that it can decide something and ask itself questions. Of course, the wording masks a complex and skillful exhibition of the leadership moves discussed in Chapter One. At the start of the events recounted here, the principal had been the head of the school for nearly a decade. When a thoughtful leader exercises leadership moves skillfully over a long period of time, what can result is what one teacher in the school described as a kind of generalized school leadership: "The wonderful thing about working at a school like Smith is that probably 50 percent of the staff get high off of sitting around working on this reform stuff, and the rest are willing to do it. That's why, despite what people say about aggravation and ulcers and even worse, it's definitely a labor of love."

likely that the larger system of public schooling as it has evolved in the twentieth century would have to undergo major redesign. There are signs of such redesign now in various states' experiments with charter schooling and choice plans, and the strain of it is visible in the political struggles of some schools that have declared themselves "outcomes based" (Davis and Felknor, 1994). Their efforts to tighten up their systems—to specify their beliefs, then make them count—have caused a rupture in their external relations. As a result of numerous instances of such rupture around the United States—and networking among the constituents who are feeling cut off—the very word *outcome* has recently become both religiously and politically supercharged (Burron, 1994; Kaplan, 1994). This has not happened yet at the Henry B. Smith School, although it may happen at some point.

Rewiring in an Alternating Pattern

At the beginning of what was to become a tortuous effort in rewiring, the Smith faculty conceived the task as "establishing a 'skills-based' diploma." According to Jennie, the school wished "to better clarify course and school expectations for students and parents and to give greater meaning to our diploma." Her description of the task suggests a less generous notion of outcomes than many outcomes-based reformers would advocate, and one calculated not to disturb the curricular status quo (Spady, 1988). To put this in context, however, the effort arose as a kind of countermarch to a long and successful effort to make the Smith School a place where teachers and students felt good about the quality of teaching and learning. A hallmark of this effort was to replace the curriculum that bored students and inclined many of them toward trouble with an engaging one. With that goal accomplished, the faculty next sought to articulate the fundamentals of the engaging curriculum it had managed to create—in other words, to lay out a rational basis for its intuitions. If the phrase it applied to this effort—"to establish a skills-based diploma"—seems reductive, the reduction is actually a strategy to bolster curricular experimentation with content. The principal, who was key to this effort, reasoned that a teacher would be more likely to plan an engaging pond study rather than a plodding coverage of Chapter Eight in the textbook, if he were backed by a schoolwide commitment to skills rather than content coverage.

The history of reform at the Smith School reveals an alternating pattern of emphasizing first the intuitive, then the rational. At the start of this case, the faculty seeks some rational shoring up, having just come off a long and satisfying binge of intuition. It envisions a "skills list" that might accompany the Smith diploma as a warranty, "with the dates of exhibition marked next to each skill." Such a thing would concretize and also validate the school's intuitive sense of its own quality. Over the course of a year and a half, the faculty undertook the first two steps of what it conceived as a rational three-step process: (1) to reflect on its teaching, (2) to abstract the "skills" implicitly targeted in it, and (3) to develop a means to certify achievement of the skills. Each teacher analyzed his or her courses, and each department compiled the results under the appropriate subject area headings. As the list grew, the school engaged in some tuning too, sharing drafts with parents, students, some local employers, and the teachers in the feeder elementary school. The final list of "guaranteed" skills—some 350 of them—was formally adopted at a public meeting of the school board.

Then, as happened in a number of other schools we studied, this final and heavy list pretty much dropped from sight for awhile. The work of assembling it had proved to be at once so time-consuming and so cathartic, and the product of the work so unwieldy, that the third step of the process—inventing mechanisms by which the school might be accountable for its guarantee—was postponed. It is likely too that while the final list had satisfied the faculty in a political sense, having distributed the skills across the existing subject areas in deference to the curricular status quo, it had also dissatisfied the faculty on a more fundamental level. Although the process was supposed to have distilled the school's values, some number of the values had clearly eluded distillation. The process had perhaps also stimulated reflection on the real gap between the school as it actually was and the school as a significant portion of the faculty wished it to be. In any case, the school suddenly paused from knocking on accountability's front door to seek an open back door.

Over the course of the next two years, without regard for the skills list and even at times in disregard of it, the school felt its way through some major rewiring. In the new wiring scheme it created, each grade of students (grades 7 through 12) was assigned three or four subject area teachers to share a common planning period and a daily four-hour block of teaching time. Within this time, they were to integrate their subjects to the furthest extent possible and accommodate the diversity of needs, interests, and abilities among the students at that grade level. This new wiring had built-in adaptability: the teams could regularly change the interior boundaries of their teaching time. If, for example, more time were needed this week for either a theater project or outdoor data collection, then the schedule would be redrawn to accommodate the emphasis.

The motivation behind this major rewiring job had more to do with the feel of teaching than with its ends. It followed a path first opened by the decision some years before to have an advisory system in the school, whereby every teacher meets daily with a small group of students and tries to know them well as students and people. Over time, this decision had created a more personalized environment for students, but it had also complicated the teachers' sense of who these students were. By creating teaching teams, the teachers decided in effect to pool their more complicated knowledge and to cooperate in the complex effort to accommodate their students' diversity. They did this despite the cost in terms of their own autonomy. One teacher told us, for example, "Sometimes teaming prevents me from doing something that I really want to do because it doesn't fit with what anyone else is doing." But this teacher and her colleagues preferred to pay this price rather than struggle against immense odds to teach well alone. It felt better to share responsibility for a task that seemed to them inappropriately complex for a solo. Shared responsibility is the heart of accountability, which is why I say that in experimenting with time and space, the school was searching for accountability's back door.

In due time, however, the rational (as opposed to the intuitive) reasserted itself. This happened when the eighth-grade team decided to build an exhibition system so it could know in some more definitive way how well it was preparing its students for high school. It developed an assessment consisting of a portfolio and some on-demand tests designed to assess—what else?—the writing and math skills of the skills list.

This exhibition system worked well insofar as it made part of the school's actual impact more manifest and enabled reflection. The reflection led to other changes. For example, the seventh-grade team of teachers decided to give its incoming students a diagnostic test in math and to collect writing samples from the sixth grade. Then the high school teams decided to pay explicit attention to accountability again and pulled out the list of 350 skills that it had tucked away. There was, however, a problem now with this list, as Jennie explains:

> Each team had been busy developing its own subject-integrated curriculum, and many of these skills and goals seemed to transcend the traditional subject area categories of the old skills list. It felt like a step backward, for example, to take skills such as "research" and "oral presentation," which were now guiding our integrated projects, and force them back under subject area headings.
>
> Thus began probably the most frustrating and confusing period of the whole process. Countless hours were spent recategorizing the skills into six "nonsubject" areas: literacy, expression, ethics/values, personal proficiency, problem solving, and cultural awareness. Teachers met again and again, sometimes with their teams, other times with their subject area departments, and even with a private consultant, to try to figure out new systems.

Tough questions arose during these meetings, some of them challenging basic premises of the school's existing wiring. Jennie explains:

> If we as a school selected competencies that every student should develop, then who would be responsible for assessing them? Moreover, do you assess them at the end of the senior year or in an ongoing manner? And if students are aware of these competencies early on, can they move at their own pace to prove to their assessors that they are competent? If so, what will happen to classrooms and curricula as we know them?

The first three questions that Jennie poses here are easy to answer only in a theoretical sense. In a practical sense, they are very difficult. And that is exactly the point of her fourth question. It acknowledges implicitly what is only rarely acknowledged amid all the rhetoric today about restructuring schools: that what must be restructured is fundamental—nothing less than what Tyack and Tobin (1994) call the "grammar of schooling." What must change are not just the basic relations of schooling, but even the assumptions that lie deeply and unconsciously beneath those relations—in a sense, the equivalent of what makes a noun a noun instead of a verb, and even of whether to have nouns and verbs in the language.

In her questions, Jennie describes a thickening plot, like all others subject to the temptation of a deus ex machina—an angel of resolution who might with a single gesture resolve it quickly and, of course, happily. In the recent drama of American educational reform, the deus ex machina has usually been played by the state. So it happened here. Into the Smith School's thickening plot one day dropped the Governor's Task Force on Education, with its own list of competencies for high school graduates. The list so resembled the Smith list that the school adopted it in place of its own. The school relished the tuning advantage—to be able to say that its list was now state sanctioned. And in an extravaganza of rational planning, the faculty began to parse the list across its new team-built curriculum. The idea was to create a report card "packet" in which students' progress in each subject would be pegged to a subset of the school's overall list. The faculty also tentatively decided at this time (the start of the 1991–92 school year) to introduce two additional exhibition systems: one for tenth graders and one for seniors. Although the tenth-grade exhibition was never instituted, the senior one took the form initially of a "portfolio class," in which each senior assembled a multimedia presentation of his or her best work. Later, it evolved further, as Jennie describes in the dialogue that follows shortly.

Then, predictably, in the middle of this process of finding the rational fit between the governor's three hundred or so skills and the school's curriculum, and in the face of the gargantuan task of "guaranteeing" every student's achievement of these skills, rationality yielded again to intuition. At the principal's behest especially, and over the quiet opposition of some who would have preferred to stay the rational course, the faculty diverted energy from its outcomes-based planning in order to build greater technological capacity. It felt right, particularly to the principal, for the school to acquire some tools that might be used to document achievement of the targeted skills. The fact that this seemed to involve more promise than prospect, that the school lacked a concrete plan for linking this capacity building with the accountability work, seemed to matter little. The principal sensed the traps that lay ahead in the effort to plan backward from outcomes, and he understood intuitively that he could only wire his way around these traps.

This time, literal wiring was involved. With the help of three foundations, the school made a major investment in computer and video technology. It added a large number of powerful new computers to its antiquated collection, then networked the building for both computers and video. It acquired a large number of notebook computers, counting on the strong community ethos of the school to keep them from disappearing. It built an elaborate video-processing facility and distance-learning studio, and hired a videographer with plans for teaching faculty and students how to use video to document their own work and the other work going on in their school, and to network with other schools. It acquired a large number of S-VHS camcorders, and installed video playback machines in every classroom. It installed the equipment it needed to experiment with some integration of its computer and video capabilities—not only CD-ROM players but equipment for digitizing video. And, finally, it began an association with IBM and with my colleagues in the Exhibitions Project, David Niguidula and Michelle Riconscente, to develop and pilot something called the Digital Portfolio. This is a tool for enabling students to present electronically work related to their school's goals. I say more about this tool later in the chapter.

Schools have frequently been criticized for investing in technology as if for its own sake, without a clear sense of its utility, without well-articulated plans for its integration (Cuban, 1986; Woronov, 1994). It is generally assumed that they do so because they have been led to believe through aggressive marketing that the presence of technology alone—quite apart from any plan for its use—will be transformative. Or it is presumed that they do so because external funds have become available that can only be used to do so; or that they do so because it feels right to the principal or superintendent to do so, in the same way that it may feel right to them in their private lives to buy a bigger car than they need, a food processor they will never use, and so on.

All of these explanations may have played a role in this case too. But there is one other explanation that seems to me more apt—one rooted in intuition. It runs as follows: (1) the heat is building up in this school's wiring as a result of its momentum in planning for accountability; (2) technology eventually must absorb some of this heat, even if no one now can say precisely how; (3) but technology takes slack—a lot of time to purchase, install, and integrate; (4) therefore it makes sense to invest in it early, particularly insofar as the investment is largely in infrastructure (networking the building, moveable machines, and so on) and particularly insofar as it comes at a rational ebb in the school's cycle of reform, when energy that might otherwise be devoted to plowing ahead is available for messing around.

This explanation, in contrast to the others, acknowledges an important subtext of the story. This school's intuition is well honed by belief, and therefore it is more trustworthy than that of many other schools. That is an important function of belief within the larger systems of a school: to keep things coherent even when dramatic change incapacitates people's immediate sense of coherence. At one point in writing about a particularly frustrating moment in the school's accountability planning, Jennie paused to exclaim, "Our work over the next few years is certainly cut out for us. On the other hand, if it can be done at all, we expect the Smith staff will do it." The tendency of policymakers in the face of this chronic uncertainty in educational reform is nearly always to trust the rational over the intuitive: to insist on a plan. One consequence of this tendency, however, is to disempower schools. It is deemed better to trust the district or state bureaucracies to test whether it can be done at all because they are better at planning. Schools, on the other hand, are less reliably rational entities. They are prone to sudden detours of intuition, as this case suggests. I think that is because they manage to arouse whatever future-mindedness they arouse from a necessarily incessant preoccupation with dailiness. Periodic detours of intuition offer a school the opportunity to ground its plans in that dailiness. Admittedly these detours sometimes thwart reform. But that is especially likely to happen, I would argue, when the school's reform beliefs are weak and maldistributed across the faculty, which is not the case here. I would argue further that real change becomes possible only when plans for it mix early and often with dailiness.

In the passage that follows, Jennie records the simultaneous enthusiasm and trepidation with which the Smith faculty ended the 1991–92 school year. She juxtaposes technology with another set of rising questions, capturing the delicate balance of that school year between the preoccupations of intuition and the demands of rational planning.

> With machines and parts still arriving every day, we have hardly begun the task of "technologizing" our assessment process. Our students, however, have descended on the equipment like vultures. Many have become quite skilled with the cameras and computers and are now helping the teachers figure them out! Many stumbling blocks remain. We have not ascertained which of the hundreds of skills in our packet should be required for graduation, assuming not all will be. We have much time still to spend on the topic of standards—how we know when a skill is mastered and on what level. And the heated debates have already begun over many of the skills such as cooperation, organization, and punctuality. Should an uncooperative but otherwise highly skilled student be refused a diploma? Must organization be demonstrated in all subjects to be considered mastered? Over what period of time must a student exhibit punctuality: a year, a quarter, a week?

Jennie is good with questions. These are practical derivatives of the theoretical questions, What are standards, anyway? and How can the school be accountable for maintaining them? The careful reader may discern a role for information technologies in answering some of Jennie's questions. The connection is not clear for Jennie, however, as she reveals during the dialogue that follows. In this regard, she reflects a prevalent dichotomy in the school's efforts at this time. Why does a school that is quickly filling up with technology on the one hand, and with difficult design questions on the other hand, not quickly connect the two developments?

First, there is the obvious explanation that technological capacity always takes longer to install than its enthusiasts project because technical problems always arise and also because nonenthusiasts resist the installation. But this lag time can be very productive. To force intuition to the surface too early, to cut out play in order to draw up plans before play has revealed what only play can reveal, is to put at risk all the wiring advantage of new technology. Every reader has at one point or another been victimized in this way, as when the computer application turns a twenty-minute job into a two-hour one. This happens when the new technology is simply wired on to the old—the videos hung on every classroom wall like hovering lecturers, the computer that is used to make already centralized decision making even more remote and arcane.

Back to the Rational: A Dialogue About Details

In the summer of 1992, a faculty committee at the Smith School, joined by the principal, faced up to a critical issue. The skills list, whether sanctioned by the governor or not, was just too long. One could not get one's teaching mind or learning mind around such a list. Still, the committee dared not simply scrap it, both because of the state's involvement and also because some number of teachers had invested in it as a planning guide. So the committee decided to call it that—a planning guide for courses—and then it cooked down the three hundred or so skills in this planning guide to just nineteen. It called these the school's "Graduation Skills." Among them were interpretation of graphical data, application of mathematics, and oral expression.

Jennie: Then we invented this elaborate filing system. George, the principal, ordered thirty file cabinets and thousands of folders, because we decided that each student now needed nineteen folders—one for each skill—so we had to start putting stuff in these files. If you go into my ninth-grade classroom, there are four file cabinets sitting there, and for each of the sixty-five ninth graders, there are nineteen folders in there—and this is true on every team now.

What we were really concerned about was how teachers and students get work into the files and how the decisions are made about what to keep, and how teachers grade them—because all of a sudden you're not grading the math test to see how well the students did in Chapter Twelve, but you are also having to grade it for how well they use technology, which in this case might be their calculator. So we had to discuss that too. At that point we were deciding that if a teacher or student had a piece that they felt should go into one of these folders, they needed to grade it for the skill, which might be different from the grade that was actually on the piece. Then if there was something else in the folder from that class previously, they were to compare the two and leave the better one. But they were not to replace any piece from another teacher.

The largest number of pieces you would have in a packet would be six, because a student has six teachers in a day. There would never be seven pieces in there, but there could be fewer than six.

Question: Why is the math teacher still worrying about teaching what's in Chapter Twelve? Why don't the nineteen skills drive what you are teaching? Isn't that supposed to be what happens?

Jennie: Because it was 1992, and we had just decided on the skills over the summer, and you can't retrain your staff that fast. That requires (and it's what we're working on now, in 1993) that you start changing the whole curriculum.

Joe: Rewiring.

Jennie: But really, when the teachers came back in 1992, they were teaching, for example, *A Tale of Two Cities,* and when they get the paper back, they're still trying to determine,"Did the kid understand the story?" But now maybe we want to also evaluate this piece for written expression, which means a regrading of it, because the written expression part of it might have only been a component of the paper's grade before.

That led to a lot of confusion, because if a student got an A paper, and said, "I want this in my folder," and then the teacher would say, "Well, I'll put it in there, but to tell you the truth, the written expression part of this is probably only 'at-grade level,'" this would leave the student confused. Many of the teachers were confused too, and still are.

Question: And I'm confused!

Jennie: See, one set of nineteen folders follows the student along, but we keep replacing things in them. You can replace things from previous years, but only if it's in your subject area. If the ninth-grade math teacher brings a test to the folder and sees an eighth-grade math piece, she could replace that one, but she couldn't replace an English piece. So there's always a maximum of six things in a folder because kids take six subjects. Even though many of these subjects are taught within the teams, we still think of ourselves as teaching different subjects.

Question: Why?

Jennie: Well, it's true that having the nineteen skills seems to free you from thinking exclusively within the different subjects, and I think that's what George, our principal, has in mind. I think he has decided that the only important things are these nineteen skills, but if you look at them, they're pretty content free. I don't think there are more than two teachers in the school who feel that's okay. The rest of us feel like, "I really think there's some valuable content in this course." Personally, I am not ready to say that I, as a math teacher, am really just focused on organization and oral skills and applying mathematics—whatever that is—without being able to specify what mathematics.

Question: So these nineteen skills are superimposed on top of course credits?

Jennie: Yes, the students still have requirements; they still get grades.

Question: So, they could earn all the grades, all the credits, but not graduate?

Jennie: And they could earn all A's and get twice as many credits as they need, and get the highest rating on every one of the nineteen skills except the one on cooperation—and theoretically they couldn't graduate.

Joe: There's a lot of old wiring showing here.

Jennie: Many teachers on the staff are saying, "I'm waiting to see George tell this very disagreeable kid we have—who never cooperates—that he can't graduate because of cooperation."

Anyway—back to the process—at the end of the year, we had a weeding process, where the student would pick one piece per subject to remain in the folders, so all that would transfer over from the previous year would be one for each of the nineteen skills, so there never would get to be more than six.

Question: What happens to those pieces that leave the folder?

Jennie: The kids would get to take them home. What the teams did—and this was a very important piece—was that, in order to do this fairly, we had to make sure that the kids were given opportunities to practice these skills, and if we went on teaching the way we were teaching, they might not necessarily have been able to practice them.

Joe: Some people call that "opportunity-to-learn" standards.

Jennie: Yeah, so we decided that would be the work of the teams primarily. The teams met over the summer, and took the nineteen skills and dished them out. In other words, they made sure that at least one teacher on the team was going to address each skill because it wouldn't be fair if you never got a chance to practice, and be assessed, on organization in the ninth grade and then suddenly be expected to know that skill in the tenth. So we sat around, as teams, and said, "Okay, as the math teacher I am going to work on skill numbers 7, 11, 12, 13, and 15."

And there was certainly overlap. I mean, problem solving is one of the skills, and all the teachers said, "Yeah, I'll do that." But there might have been a skill like using technology as a tool that maybe only the computer teacher said, "I'll do that." But we made sure that they were all covered somehow in the four or three classrooms on the team.

Question: To me, skills are everywhere, and they're in every class. I understand the need to make sure that students are getting them, but isn't reading or writing or expression something that should be part of everything rather than trying to break it down and putting it into folders?

Jennie: I mean, it wasn't that the science teacher was saying, "Well, I might not do any reading this year, so I'm not going to take that one." But the science teacher might not have felt as comfortable assessing a project just for reading, or just didn't want to have to assess that area of it. But one goal of Smith is to integrate, and every year we get a little more integrated. We find projects that cover all the subjects, and therefore the whole team can bring in these skills. We really had to make sure someone was going to assess these things each year. One of them is applying mathematics. So the English teacher didn't take that one, although the math teacher and the science teacher said, "Yeah, we'll assess that at some point."

Joe: Besides, even if this process seems a little cumbersome—you know, having the teams divvy up the skills—think of the innovation that it represents in terms of wiring. Here are teachers actually talking to each other during the day about what they intend to teach, and actually taking responsibility for teaching it.

Question: Jennie, is it possible that there would be copies of the same thing in different folders?

Jennie: Oh, absolutely, which is a completely different question.

Question: So, that means a kid could photocopy a piece?

Jennie: We just put notes in. If a kid writes a big term paper, and wants it for written expression, and organization, and starting and finishing a multi-faceted project, we just drop a note in the other two files that says, "See file 7." Where it really gets confusing is with cooperative projects where both kids might say, "I want this." Then you have to photocopy it or put another note in.

Question: Wait a minute now. Couldn't technology somehow help with that problem? I mean does it have to be sticky notes in manila files?

Jennie: Ultimately, the goal is to have a technological and electronic way to do this, but it's an ultimate goal. At this point only the computer teacher and a couple of outside consultants are working on it. They call it the Digital Portfolio. Most of the teachers at the school don't even know about it. Well, they probably know that it's happening, but nothing more than that. I don't think their fear right now is, "How am I going to get all this into the computer?" That's a hurdle that's way down the road. Right now, their fear is, "What is this system that we have now—the noncomputerized one—and how am I going to manage it?"

Question: And maybe technology would be a diversionary thing if you introduce it too soon. I think you're saying that you as a staff need to be focusing now on what those nineteen skills mean and how the content relates to them, and if you were to launch this Digital Portfolio thing, you could lose that focus. On the other hand, maybe launching it would better help the kids understand what the nineteen would mean.

Jennie: To me, this is just a filing issue. In some ways, the technology piece is not a bit important to me. It's just a way to do it electronically instead of on paper. It doesn't solve any of the problems that we're struggling with now. And, besides, the program is not even at a stage where the kids can use it.

Well, anyway, we started to come to terms with our new system when we put the nineteen skills on our progress reports, and when parents came in for parent conferences last year, we had each student pick out a piece—any piece—that they thought demonstrated one of the nineteen skills well. So, now, for about the first time, every parent came in and saw a piece of his or her kid's work in conjunction with a skill, and the adviser said, "Well, here's a paper that the student put in here for 'organization,' and here's what the teacher had to say about the organization." So, we slowly started to introduce parents to that.

But this meant that kids had to have a place to hunt for the right pieces. So this was the first filing experience for teachers, where, with very little direction, we were suddenly told, "We have to start getting things in these files," and this was just unbelievable. First of all, we realized that it meant we had to keep everything that the students did. So now each of us, on our own, realized we have to keep another file cabinet with the kids' names. I'm going to have to have one file for each of my sixty-five kids, and everything has to go in there, and then somehow I have to get it from there into the nineteen files and everybody started asking, "How can this happen?"

Everybody made up a different method. Some teachers decided, "I'm not going to do anything until the day before the parent conference, and then we'll have this massive sorting session, where all the kids will have dished out the classroom files, and we're going to go through them. And teachers did this! And they said, "Just pick one out for each of the graduation skills."

So, all of a sudden, the *student* was making the decision about what piece best fits what skill.

Question: Doesn't that make sense?

Jennie: Well, it's great because of the student input, but as far as I'm concerned, it's also rotten if we teachers are going to turn around and say later, "Oh, you can't graduate, because that piece doesn't satisfy the graduation requirement." We can't leave it up to the student to pick out the best piece. There might have been a better one in there in my opinion, and if I'm doing the grading, I'd better do the picking—or at least have something to say.

So that was one extreme: let it all pile up, and then start picking pieces at the last minute. The other extreme is that we kind of guarantee to these students that we're going to get the best piece in there somehow. We have to because if we're going to graduate them, or not graduate them, we have to make sure their best piece gets in there. Imagine the day when we say, "You can't graduate, because this piece doesn't show it." And the kid says, "I had a better one, but you didn't take it." And now that piece is gone, because the kid took it home. We're thinking legal battles! So the other extreme is that we really have to examine every single thing that every student does against every one of the nineteen skills. And we have to constantly be comparing back, because we have to make sure that we're getting the best piece in there at all times. So, we're sure that when we say to a kid, "You didn't master it," we know we've seen everything.

Question: Isn't one indication of mastery, though, knowing when you've done something well? So I would put the responsibility back on the student with coaching from the teachers and say, "You need to know when this is good." You could coach the students with that. You could flip it over and make the kids responsible.

Jennie: I would say, yes, a lot of coaching goes on. I would say, no, in the sense that this is going to be a graduation gate. Any student in his right mind would say in June of the senior year: "This is good enough!" I mean, what are they going to say, "This is NOT good enough. Don't graduate me"?

Question: But couldn't you have one mechanism where the students make a selection with some coaching on the side and another mechanism where the selection is assessed? That's what Central Park East Secondary School does or Alverno College.

Jennie: I think one difference between Smith and some of these other places is that they make a bigger deal about assessment. At Smith I think we're just looking at projects and assignments as they come in, and we're trying to catch the student doing something right.

Question: Yes, because when you catch the student doing something right, that's the difference between habit and an occurrence. In other words, if I hand you a paper that just happens to be excellent, it doesn't mean I really know how to do what you want; it just means that I did it this once.

Jennie: Well, that's the whole other issue that I haven't gotten into yet, which is how many times do you have to show one of the nineteen skills to prove that you've really got it?

Joe: But it's possible to have assessments—portfolios and so on—that assess habit. You have that senior portfolio class, right? The exhibition system in the senior year?

Jennie: Well, yes and no. In a sense, the portfolio class really expanded because now that we have this system, everybody was contributing to it, whereas before, it was really only this one teacher (who isn't even here anymore) who was given the whole job of putting things in files, and none of the rest of us was really doing it. So, at this point, everybody contributes to portfolios, and we don't really need a portfolio class.

Now there's a big senior exhibition at the end of the year—where they just fill the gym. Each student has a booth, and all their stuff is laid out, and much of the senior team time is devoted to getting that stuff together. So that's sort of what has become of that portfolio class.

Question: Is it like a country-fair exhibition—kids setting up their little booths as if they're exhibiting the pig they'd raised or something?

Jennie: It's really almost a coming out more than an exhibition. One kid brought his dirt bike in, because he raced dirt bikes, and this is what he was, and he brought that in there and was talking to people about it.

Joe: So townspeople visit the booths, and they talk to the kids about their work.

Question: But are these exhibitions evaluated?

Jennie: [*sighs*] Not yet. But all the pieces in it are.

Question: But if you don't have some overall evaluation, how can you be sure that you have the same standards for all students?

Jennie: First of all, the whole idea behind these nineteen graduation skills was to have the same standard for all students, except students with IEPs, who will be held to their IEPs.[2] But we were looking for minimum standards. We were really hoping

2. IEPs are individualized educational plans drawn up to guide the education of children with "educational handicaps" as defined by federal and state law.

students would go off with kind of a guarantee: if I graduate from Smith High School, I can do this, with some minimum level of competency, but we weren't trying to delineate exactly what this is.

We hadn't discussed any standards for them. All we did was write the list. The idea was that at some point soon, we'd sit down and define these skills. But our principal's idea was that they're going to be easier to define after we've worked with them awhile. George likes to just start things. So his idea was that we'll just have teachers and students start piling things into the folders, and then we'll have something to look at that will help us define it. Teachers, without a definition, were pretty much just throwing things in there or telling students to do it.

And some teachers just didn't do it. They just couldn't. They just hit the wall, and they couldn't do it.

Also, we were supposed to be grading them as at-grade level, below-grade level, and above-grade level. Teachers just didn't do that. When they said, "I don't know how to do that; we haven't discussed standards," George would say (and rightly so), "You've been grading them all along." I mean, every time you grade a paper, you have an idea in your head of what grade level is, and above and below it. That's how you decide what's an A and a B and a C."

But still, this was a different type of grading, and teachers just balked. So by the end of last school year, our timetable had slowed down so much. Still, we knew that at the end of the year, he'd say, "Bring folders, bring stuff," and teachers sheepishly went back to their rooms and looked, and they're (laughs) stuffing in things at the last minute. It was very discouraging, very disappointing.

Question: How discouraging? How disappointing? Enough that people were ready to abandon it all?

Jennie: I think that everybody knew that we were in the middle of something really important. And I think that everyone knew that we couldn't go back. But we also knew that we were just in this abyss, and it was like being in a dark hole, just walking around and banging into the walls. I mean, we were going to have to climb out. But people just felt like, "We just don't know," and, "How hard is George going to push this? Or how much are we going to have input? How much can we change at this point? It seems as if we've come so far. How much do we want to redo?" It was real tough, and I think people dealt with it by not dealing with it.

I think it was at the point where George wasn't making so many demands, so we were ignoring it. You know, he wasn't saying: "Do it, or you're out of here!" So it was either you do it or you don't do it. The staff has enough input that if there's enough foot dragging, George will know something's wrong, and we'll stop and try to fix it. I mean, we've been trying to fix it all along. So that's kind of where we were at the end of last year.

In the spring, we could sense that things weren't happening, and so finally, George decided that we had to devote a bunch of staff meetings to this. I feel that not enough staff meetings had been devoted to this, which just seemed so important. How could we, though, because there were so many other things going on?

Anyway, we started bringing in the pizzas, and looking and discussing. At least the conversations were good, but the more we talked about it, the deeper the hole got. I mean, you get a group together, and we'd say, "Let's try and figure out what 'using technology as a tool' is," and then it would just be a brawl, and people would leave feeling worse, as if to say, "I thought I could do this, but now I know I can't do this." It was just crazy.

But on the other hand, by going through that process, we had to ask ourselves the right questions. We knew using technology as a tool was important. And we knew it was more important than much of the content that we were currently teaching. We knew we had to get to the point where we could do this. And we just knew it was going to take a lot of conversation.

So this past summer, the committee had to get back together again. They tried to simplify the process a little bit, and one thing they did that helped was to decide that the team teachers were going to have to be the ones to coach this process. Before, we had said it would be the advisers, but it just turned out that on top of everything else, the advisers were going back to the teachers saying, "What was this assignment, really, because I don't understand it?"

Now every team teacher has a fourth or a third of the kids on her team, and those are her coachees. And at regular intervals during this year, George says, "Today is the day." They sit down, and they get the folders out, and everyone in the school is doing it at the same time, and the teacher sits there with the students and they go through, and they weed it out. They ask, "What's good and why?"

The other thing that they did is to create a cover sheet. It has the nineteen skills on it, and it's a grading sheet. And it's a process that the teacher, who is the coach, and the student both go through to decide, "Why does this show my organizational skills," and "What grade level is this at?" and "What needs to be improved about it?" They go through that process together, so they're not just throwing things together in a folder. Everything that goes in the folder now is accompanied by one of these cover sheets.

Question: So you have begun to wire the kids into this process.

Jennie: Also the curriculum. So teachers now realize that the nineteen skills are not going to go away. People are finally starting to say, "Okay, if I have to teach these skills, how am I going to do it?" Now when teams are planning their projects, they're not so much saying, "Well, I have to do *Moby Dick*, or similar triangles" as they are, "Let's design a project around these three skills. Let's design it so the kids have an opportunity to demonstrate them." Now that's the ideal, and some teams are finally starting to do that, but you're really talking about a big, big shift for teachers.

I don't think that teachers have entirely made that shift. None of us has. And maybe we shouldn't be making that shift without having some major, major discussion. Is there content that's really important? What do we need to hold on to? And that can't be done without a lot of conversation with colleges and employers and so on.

Joe: Tuning. Tuning.

Unfinished Business

The Smith School had done a lot of rewiring by the time this dialogue took place. Things that sound simple in the dialogue represent major feats of development from the point of view of the ordinary high school in the last decade of the twentieth century. Jennie says at one point, for example, "We started bringing in the pizzas, and looking, and discussing." In fact, most high schools today are too large, complex, and fractured to deal this way even with their major crises. And to the extent that Jennie means the word *looking* to suggest that the faculty spent some of this time actually examining student work, then the response is truly extraordinary.

Collective examination of student work is exceedingly rare in school at any level.

Nearly as extraordinary is what happens at the Smith School when the principal announces, "Today is the day," and teachers and students assemble for a ritual whose purpose is the discussion and illustration of the school's standards. And Jennie herself testifies to the great shift under way in the habits of teachers who in planning their teaching may think first about the school's goals and only second about engagement with a particular bit of curriculum, whether *Moby Dick* or similar triangles. This shift is from what I would call a narrative orientation in teaching to an instrumental one. Although I share Jennie's ambivalence about whether a complete shift of this sort is a good idea, she and I agree that some shift is crucial for genuine accountability.

Yet despite all the distance the Smith School has traveled in the direction of its own vision, much distance remains. The deepest wires still must be pulled and replaced. To trace these deepest wires, I find it helpful to consider the implications of the software tool that Jennie mentions in the dialogue, the Digital Portfolio, and in the process pose the following question: How must the Smith School be redesigned such that this promising tool might fulfill its promise? Note that I am not suggesting that any tool, however promising, can solve the design problems still facing the Smith School. But the virtue of this particular tool, as I suggest below, is that it may help the school understand what the rewiring is for. When I was a young child, my parents bought a clothes dryer that they could not use because the wiring in our old house could not support its use. For years, the dryer sat there mutely telling the family what it could do if we ever had enough money to rewire our house. At this point in the history of the Smith School's redesign, the Digital Portfolio is a little like our old clothes dryer.

The Digital Portfolio was created by my colleagues David Niguidula and Michelle Riconscente with the support of the IBM Corporation. A derivative of our research, it is as much provocation as tool. Unlike other tools with similar-sounding names, this one is not marketed for schools as they currently are, but it forecasts a future market. It implicitly challenges schools like Smith—schools with strong beliefs and still inadequate wiring—to press beyond the limits they ordinarily reach when they restructure. Specifically, it challenges them to take four radical steps:

1. To make the examination of actual student work the centerpiece of all the school's deliberations about standards, progress, and achievement
2. To let students themselves pilot these deliberations
3. To provide students access to all the other tools, as well as the space, time, and trust they need to be the pilots
4. To provide teachers some buffer between coaching students toward the highest standards and assessing whether the students meet these standards

This is an enormous provocation, involving a great shift of energy, information, and power, though the magnitude of the shift may not at first be apparent to the school interested in the Digital Portfolio. That is because it may see in the Digital Portfolio not a provocation to root out old wiring and replace it with new, but rather a technological deus ex machina, a tool to solve all its accountability problems. Were a school actually to install the thing on this basis, it would get a tool to do electronically what the Smith School does with filing cabinets, sorting sessions, sticky notes, and so on: keep track of its students' progress toward the goals it has set. But to do all of this electronically is not to do it better. In fact, as Jennie seems to suspect, the change would probably make hard work harder. Imagine the teachers at the Smith School having to do everything that Jennie reports they now do in tending their outcomes-based system, plus scan their students' work into computers and annotate it.

Design of the Digital Portfolio

The Digital Portfolio is a hypermedia environment for the display and annotation of student performance.[3] Like a home appliance, it works with almost any kind of house wiring, so teachers at the Smith School might use it in just the way that Jennie fears. They

3. The description of the Digital Portfolio here relies on a paper by David Niguidula (1994). It also assumes that certain design issues now being worked on—for example, those involving the storage and transmission of large multimedia databases—will be resolved.

might make all the choices of what performance samples to scan in, do all the scanning themselves, do all the annotating and updating, and so on—do everything they now do, but do it electronically. But that kind of use is neither what its inventors intended nor what interests me. If, on the other hand, the Smith School teachers respond to this tool's provocation to rewire their house in fundamental ways, they will instead use the Digital Portfolio to hand over to the students much of the business that is now turning the teachers into clerks. For the students, the business their teachers hand over involves much more than clerking; it is the means by which they may take responsibility for their own learning. It asks them to face their work literally, and to index it to the school's standards. In the process, it makes plain to them what was never made plain to Felicia in the story I told in Chapter Three: what is really expected.

The graphical environment of the Digital Portfolio is a set of screens (or pages, in the terminology of the software) that are linked by buttons. The user clicks the mouse to select buttons and thereby navigate among the pages. The pages may contain texts in any media—what the student has written, painted, performed on piano, and so forth. They may also contain annotations on these performances—by the student, the student's teacher, a peer, a parent, or someone else—and these annotations may be in print or voice.

Hypermedia environments are like books in which the pages have been released from ordinary linear sequence and allowed to form networks. Readers of the Digital Portfolio can easily jump around, browsing, so to speak, through the performances and annotations, or they can trace one particular line of interest in depth—for example, what the portfolio reveals about the student's achievements in science—and then reemerge to try still another route, say, the arts. In the process, the reader may discover links in the student's achievements where science and the arts intersect—her effort, for example, to sketch, as Audubon did, variations among bird species.

The initial screen a reader faces might, for example, provide a list of the Smith School's nineteen graduation skills. Each of these might then have a button beside it, inviting the reader to go more deeply. Does the reader want to know how the skills relate to the governor's task force recommendations? Does the reader wish to know more about how the school defines the nineteen skills or how it benchmarks them? And, of course, does the reader wish to see images of the performances that the student and her teachers judged by the light of these benchmarks? Does one of the skills involve oral presentation? Here is a video clip of an oral report the student delivered when she was fourteen, here is another that shows the student speaking at a school assembly last month, and here is a third in which the student characterizes the growth she perceives in the juxtaposition of the first two clips. Finally, here is what some assessors have said about her best oral performance to date.

That is how one reads the Digital Portfolio. Because the device sits on a local-area network (LAN), which might be connected to some wide-area network, like the information superhighway now being built, it may be read by a number of readers. These include the student herself, who benefits enormously from the opportunity to read the evidence of her own learning by the light of her school's and her teachers' expectations. And they may also include the student's parents, who—if they have to the kind of access now frequently touted as a likely feature of the information environment of the early twenty-first century—may read their daughter's work and her teachers' comments on their home computer or television. And readers may include college admissions officers who receive the portfolio via the next generation of the Internet. Finally, readers may include some who are less interested in the student's individual achievement and more interested in how that achievement reflects the efforts of her school to teach her well and to hold her work to the highest standards. In other words, the Digital Portfolio may enable such distant readers as the state's educational auditors to sample student work in a systematic way, suggesting a radically different state-level accountability system than the one operating today.

Depending on whether one emphasizes its write capacity or its read capacity, one sees the Digital Portfolio as a provocation for the wiring or the tuning arena of school design. The LAN on which it sits connects it to word and image processing tools that a student may use in her ordinary work, tools that digitize video or sound and scanners that digitize other inputs like sketches and photographs. This is the tool's write power. With this power, the student can manage her own record of progress relative to the school's goals. The Digital Portfolio is potentially far more than a personal filing cabinet. It is a user-friendly environment that combines filing cabinet, worktable, display case, and even coaching. It gives a student frequent and intimate access to her own performances as they appear in the light of her school's and her teachers' expectations. Most important, it invites the student to substitute new and improved performances, cultivating her own judgment in the process; and it enables her to make these substitutions easily. She and also her teachers, who have write access to her portfolio through the local network, annotate this record as it emerges and changes, with the teachers coaching on-line as well as in person. But the student retains the bulk of the power. In a sense, there is nothing unusual in this; students always retain the bulk of the power to decide what is learned, when, and how. The difference is that the rewired school in which the Digital Portfolio is used as intended—where the tool is a tool, not an ornament—acknowledges where the ultimate power lies and has arranged its constitution accordingly.

Conclusion

In this chapter I have presented a long and intricate case of rewiring and have examined the case from two very different perspectives. The first perspective is that of Jennie, an insider. My hope is that her perspective on rewiring an actual school—one that has to operate every day even while wires are being pulled, replaced, and rerouted—may help readers understand that rewiring is an inevitably messy business. I know that some readers will resist this message, however. I once shared a draft of the Case of the Overheated Wires with a group of educators, some of whose members thought that it was a little roman à clef. One told me that she was astounded that the teachers in this school had not yet become acquainted with *standards*—that standards would have solved their problem. I italicize the word to convey the emphasis she put on it in our conversation. She meant the package of levers I discussed in Chapter One. I listened politely but thought her analysis cheated Jennie's story of its most important meaning: that neither standards themselves nor the idea of standards can be plopped into a school, ready to use. Real standards—the ones that actually result in the school's taking responsibility for the intellectually powerful education of all its students—have to be constructed on-site. This is not to say that they have to be constructed from scratch. Schools need external partners in the process. Still, the meaning of whatever is constructed from whatever source has to be worked out on-site through a collective minding of the school community, and by the light of the actual performance of students. This is a necessarily arduous process.

In the last part of this chapter, I have also examined the circumstances of the Case of the Overheated Wires from an entirely different perspective than Jennie's. This is the perspective lent by the Digital Portfolio, a tool that does not yet fully exist. I have posed the question: What does its potential as a tool suggest about the issues at the heart of the case? My answer spans the boundary between the wiring and the tuning arenas of school design. Most of the talk today about accountability for the quality and depth of student learning focuses on how outsiders can gain inside influence on schooling by means of richer achievement tests, standards-based curriculum, teacher education, and so on. I think the real challenge, however —the one that the struggle for accountability in the Henry B. Smith School highlights for me—is how to have schools that want outside input and might actually use rather than deflect it. In my view, this requires a great boost in the read capability of insiders. It demands wiring on the inside designed to make student work central to the school's work, to keep it out in the open and readable by the light of the school's standards, and thereby to make these standards readable too. This is the promise of a tool like the Digital Portfolio. If the reading is reflective—if the wiring fosters a cycle of information, insight, and action on the insight—then what is readable by insiders can become readable by outsiders too. Moreover, reflection enables insiders to welcome outside readers in ways that they never otherwise could. Knowing their own work better, they can tolerate others' views of it and even assimilate them. Knowing their own work better, they can stay in charge of it too and can function as active clients of outside consultants.

I leave it to the reader to blend the two perspectives of this chapter—or, better, to hold them in tension, since both perspectives are crucial for successful redesigning. One urges patience and prepares us for difficult work. It cautions against depending on any simple solution to the dilemmas that confront us. The other urges us to take an imaginative leap, to make sure that we do not accept as givens precisely those assumptions about information, power, and energy that underlie the dilemmas that confront us. In the next chapter, I enumerate and discuss several challenges of the tuning arena of school design. But remember that the prior challenge for tuning lies here in the wiring arena. Outside input will never get in if the wiring inside cannot handle it.

Part Three

Tuning

As believing is not enough, neither is good wiring on the inside. The twenty-first-century school must have plenty of wires running to the outside too. These provide not only access to outside sources of knowledge but also a means by which values on the inside may be tuned to values on the outside, completing a cycle in which beliefs are tested and refreshed. After all, what is the point of rewiring the school if one intends it to operate as an intellectual terrarium, where learning is continuously exchanged within but never replenished from without?

The third arena of school design, which I call tuning, is all about resources for learning—teachers' learning and students' learning. The tuning arena invites schools to respond to their many stakeholders—not only parents, but local and remote cultural, economic, and political communities—and to learn from them. Redesigning school in the tuning arena is figuring out how to know, weigh, and arbitrate among many outside interests.

As in the previous sections of the book, the following chapters may be read in any order. Many readers will want to understand the challenges of the tuning arena from the perspectives of the schools the stories of which are told in Chapter Five. Others may prefer to move straight to Chapter Six, which offers some ideas about meeting these challenges.

Chapter Five

Tuning Challenges

We called them the suits from central office. Sometimes they descended en masse on our public alternative school, but mostly they came one at a time on a regular visitation cycle. These men were pleasant, and they respected our fierce independence. They said they just wanted to help, and they tried to enrich our vision and our practice with tales and materials culled from the district-wide curriculum they supervised. Sometimes they also tried to acquaint us with research findings or practical ideas they had picked up in professional meetings. They knew we ignored their curriculum utterly, but they did their job nonetheless. Although they may have been appalled occasionally by something we did, the attitude never surfaced visibly as far as I can remember. For our part, we treated them pleasantly in return, and never complained about the interruptions to our teaching that their visits caused, or what we took to be the generally poor quality of their contributions to our work. We were, of course, mindful that they signed off on our budgets and new staff and that they could cause us trouble with the superintendent if they chose to report finding something amiss in our school.

These central office supervisors were creatures of a tuning system installed over the course of the twentieth century in our district and most other school districts in the United States. It is overwhelmingly still the dominant tuning system of American education—that is, the principal way we ensure that teaching and learning within schools are informed by and accountable to the world outside. It discharges this responsibility by seeking faithfulness to a central plan, one that itself is informed by outside perspectives—as supplied, for example, by an elected school board and a state department of education. Sometimes, as in the case of our alternative school, the central plan allows for program variation. Those associated with the variation may believe that they are outside the system, though from the perspective of the system itself, they are part of the plan.

Today this tuning system includes nearly everywhere not only district-level supervision but also curriculum requirements and guidance at both the district and state levels, testing at the district and state levels, state or district textbook adoption policies, and college admissions requirements. The system depends on the articulation and dissemination of the best ideas conceived at the highest levels, on informed compliance at the delivery level, and on skillful supervision in between. It is characterized by what Linda Darling-Hammond calls the assumption of hierarchical intelligence—the idea that people are always smarter higher up in the hierarchy, which is to say further away from actual children (Darling-Hammond, 1994). It tends, whether deliberately or inadvertently, to treat children as objects: so many bodies counted and served, so many bundles of standards-based behavioral indicators (Clinchy, 1995). Naturally it tends to treat their teachers as objects too: the targets of policymaking and in-servicing, the curriculum delivery vehicles. The treatment is typically softened in myriad ways, but it is disempowering nonetheless.

If learning and teaching for real understanding were not such demanding activities, then the great effort this system expends might succeed. That is because it tends to engender passive compliance. This is the typical response of someone treated with whatever good intentions as an object—people asked, for example, to take a number at the delicatessen, or to board the airplane only when their row is called. But learning and teaching, at least as many have recently come to think of them, are more like playing well in an orchestra than like waiting well at the delicatessen, and one cannot make a better orchestra without the violinists' active participation.

As school redesigners of the early 1970s, my colleagues and I did not actively tune our work to the advice of our district supervisors. Although they gave us room to be different, they also implicitly regarded difference as deficit. They had to. It was their job. In a system based on the assumption of hierarchical intelligence and faithful compliance to central plans, delivery-level difference is deficit. For our part, we had to resist, albeit politely. Otherwise the stigma they implicitly attached to our alternative school would have stuck to our students. In their minds, the word *alternative* signified the state of our students: too different to be in a regular school. In our minds, the word signified the state of their system: too indifferent to all students to survive unchallenged.

I think the tension we felt toward the suits helped our school nurture the character or ethos, the sense of common purpose and self-confidence that some researchers today associate with higher student achievement (Lee and Smith, 1994; Bryk, Lee, and Holland, 1993). Yet, ultimately, the self-confidence could not sustain the school. Meanwhile, the suits felt a tension toward us, and they also had common sense on their side. Beneath a veneer of comity, they saw our school as a system-sanctioned aberration rather than our school. When a massive tax deficit hit the district in 1981, they felt no pain in recommending that the aberration be discontinued—notwithstanding its evident success, its parents' and students' strong support, and its considerable stash of political capital. To argue in those days for a kind of system in which our school would not be alien—a system based on the encouragement and support of productive difference, a suitless system—would have seemed absurd to most of our community. To argue that the crisis we were living through then might be an opportunity for redesign rather than retrenchment would have heightened the absurdity. Even we teachers, parents, and students who prized the school so much failed to make this argument or even imagine it. We closed our school with a whimper.

Today, in the same state where our school thrived for ten years and then died suddenly, a similarly threatened school can apply for charter status. Indeed, shortly after the conclusion of our study, two programs within one of the schools we studied seceded in just this way—one of many indications that the future of the suits may be up for grabs. In other words, the tuning arena of school design has recently become active after decades of being taken for granted. Still, old habits are deeply ingrained. I recall watching the principal of one of the schools we studied standing in the hallway outside a symposium on school restructuring sponsored by his district. He had been expected to participate. Indeed, the symposium on its surface seemed to offer him an opportunity to contribute his own considerable expertise. Yet he never actually made it into the seminar room where the symposium was held. Instead he managed in the hallway to find a string of people with whom to conduct some business. The form of his passive-aggressive engagement was symbolic. He was reacting, at least intuitively, to an unspoken assumption in his district that the real expertise of even the best principals has more to do with hallways than seminar rooms, that it is procedural rather than substantive. Good principals have a political knack, a sense of timing, and the courage to act on other people's big ideas, but they never have any big ideas themselves. The way this principal chose to confront the condescension ended up validating it instead. Meanwhile, he forfeited even the small voice he may have had in district policymaking. Moreover, since the state depended heavily on this district for advice in matters of school reform, he forfeited a voice in state policymaking too. He followed the same ineffectual course that we followed in our 1970s-era school redesigning: we too deluded ourselves into thinking that redesign was only about inside wiring, that we could always manage to marginalize the suits.

Alternative Tuning Designs

From the perspective of the tuning arena of school design, the schools we studied were no better off when they won small standoffs or achieved détente with their would-be supervisors or even when, on occasion, they forced them to withdraw. A central problem nonetheless remained for the school, one that can be framed by several related questions. How else can a school be tuned except by means of a supervisory superstructure? How else can the structures of educational policy be defined? What else is there between the suits and the inevitable parochialism of a nonsystem in which every school is utterly on its own? The supervisory tuning that the twentieth century installed was meant especially to protect against parochialism, and against the corruption that often grows in parochial settings. In most cases, it achieves this important but limited purpose. Children in many remote and insular communities in the United States do read textbooks consistent with their state's science framework, and they are marginally better off for it. The clerk who handles purchase orders within an otherwise ignored city school does expect an occasional audit, and the school's students are marginally better off as a result. But this is not enough tuning for the twenty-first-century school. It can at best result in only unengaged compliance—the crowd in the delicatessen waiting to order cold cuts, not the violinists. How can we do better?

For some of the schools we studied, this tuning question was the deliberate focus of some of their redesigning efforts and a spur for inventiveness. For other schools, however, the tuning issue was more a subconscious irritant than a source of active design. Nevertheless, all the schools we studied offered insight into the most important challenges of tuning the school, and these challenges are the focus of this chapter. Although they all involve policy issues, they cannot be met by ordinary policymaking. As matters of design, they cross the border between the inside and the outside of school. The result is that partnerships between insiders and outsiders are necessary in order to come to terms with them.

The three tales that follow highlight what I take to be the three key challenges of the tuning arena of school design: (1) balancing intimate perspectives with critical ones, (2) balancing the interests of professional educators with the interests of parents and other members of the immediate community, and (3) balancing the interests of the school community with the interests of the state and other remote stakeholders. For analytical purposes, I identify these challenges as discrete ones, but they frequently present themselves otherwise. We found them entangled with each other and embedded in complex circumstances. I believe that an appreciation of this messiness may be crucial to understanding them, which is why I choose to illustrate them in this chapter by means of stories. Each of what I call tuning tales has a major and a minor story in its structure. One wrestles with the theme in considerable detail, and the other offers a brief variation on it.

Tale 1: Warm and Cool

Meeting some seniors on the morning of their exhibition day, I feel lifted by their energy. It is my first visit to their school, but the energy melts my strangeness. I slip into this crazy, focused scene like any other backstage visitor just before curtain. One exhibitor searches frantically for a missing poster. Another scurries about recruiting substitute models for her fashion show (two of the models she trained last week are absent). A third goes over her note cards and secures last-minute encouragement from a teacher. Still another exhibitor sits tautly, calmly answering some questions I have.

The first of the senior exhibitions will begin in twenty minutes, completing a process that began formally a year ago. What I have come to observe today is an exhibition system as I use the term in Chapter One. Each senior has defined and pursued an interdisciplinary question, a pursuit involving library research and fieldwork. Each has met the deadline for a series of submissions: a list of research sources, an outline, note cards, an introduction, a whole draft, a finished paper. This is routine stuff for many high school seniors, although not usually required of all seniors as it is here. And here too, there is something else beyond routine: each senior has been allotted a half hour in one of the series of exhibition sessions starting today. During this time, the senior will present highlights from his or her inquiry, then stand for questions from teachers, other seniors, underclass students (all of whom will attend at least one session), some parents and other relatives invited by the day's exhibitors, and a handful of outside visitors like me.

Outsiders carry a special burden. The school has asked us to function as critical friends with regard to its exhibition initiative—to be at once appreciative of the school's courage and work in undertaking it, and also constructively critical of its process and products. Our burden is, of course, the school's burden too. To have invited us in the first place, however rare a gesture, is still the easier part. The school must also consider seriously what we have to say, yet avoid giving it more credence than it deserves.

When I get to the lecture hall where today's exhibitions will be held, I shake hands all around, amid the swirls of preparation. I try to appear confident that what I am about to witness will be interesting, novel, and worth my train ride. This is a gesture of connection to the proud and friendly company. Privately I am as skeptical as I am hopeful, the victim of many shoddy school drama productions, art exhibits, and science fairs. Such efforts become, I know, necessarily invested with a school's belief in itself. This belief is what carries everyone through the burdens of mounting the efforts outside the ordinary bounds of business. But it sometimes swamps critical judgment too.

I take my seat at the cue of the teacher who will introduce today's exhibitors. Now I ask myself, Can each one of the students sitting in these folding chairs fulfill the school's belief? This is the assessment question. In this case, it is a challenge interwoven with ceremony, rather like an intellectual senior prom. The challenge is real and difficult, which is why these seniors seem nervous, why they are wearing dresses and ties, why they have taken such evident care in the preparation of their graphic displays. Still, they have been well rehearsed and coached for the challenge. That is why parents, teachers, and principal sit confidently, why presenters step to the podium and speak confidently. "Good morning," each begins.

On the Warm Side

It is a scene primed for warm attachments—investments of belief in the performer that arise from a caring history. Even I, a stranger in this community, feel the warmth rising. Something about the mixture I hear of self-confidence and anxiety in their "good mornings," the seriousness I see in their dress and presentational materials, makes me instantly proud of these young men and women. I know, moreover, that warm attachments are crucial for authenticity in assessment, so I want to do my part. Without the benefit of warm attachments, most students will not perform at peak ability. They will fall short of peak to avoid the risk of disappointing themselves, or because they simply cannot care enough, absent a caring environment, to push for peak. On the other hand, I know that warm attachments can also smother authenticity by suppressing participants' critical perception. So I struggle to remember that I am a critical friend, who must be cool as well as warm. This is tough work at any time, but particularly in a ceremonial setting.

A number of teachers join me in trying hard nonetheless. We ask tough questions. Still, I sometimes find myself so pleased by the exhibitors' fortitude in handling the questions that I appreciate their answers too much. For example, I invite the senior who has just spoken about African American achievements in several fields, but who has omitted the arts, to correct the omission. "Who are the African American writers you admire?" I demand. "Maya Angelou, for one," he answers immediately, and goes on to say why in detail, though for my part he might well have stopped at the name alone, so impressed am I with his presence of mind. Similarly, I am so taken by the clarity and potential interdisciplinary sweep of another senior's exhibition question—"Is our water safe to drink?"—that I fail to recognize that only my own question moves his focus past chemistry and public health to an observation about water and images of purity.

Meanwhile, amid applause and the palpable pride of teachers, students, parents, and outsiders, another test is under way. What do these performances reveal about the school's systems? This is the evaluation question. Like the assessment question, it demands both warm attachments and cool repose.

I wonder, as I sit observing, whether the school will dare to face it. When emotions have subsided, for example, will the faculty view with a critical eye the videos it has made of these exhibitions? Video is, as Marshall McLuhan (1964) said, a cool medium. Will younger students watch them too? Will the portfolios that must accompany the exhibitions (documenting phases of the inquiry) inform the planning of next year's projects and coaching? How far back will the influence of these exhibitions and portfolios run? Will the experience of next year's ninth graders be different because of what this year's seniors have done? Will there be more time set aside from now on for project work and coaching groups? Will there be more practice speaking before strangers? Will the school's wiring be changed as a result? All these questions fly through my head, plus one more: will the faculty actually read and consider the comments the coordinator has asked me to write down?

On the Cool Side

A year later, I sit in my living room and watch the video of an exhibition session at the same school—not the session I attended but one that took place several days later. The video contains the school's selection of four exhibitions, chosen to explain itself to interested outsiders, to prepare this year's seniors to follow the lead of last year's pioneers, and perhaps to exercise its cool eye. But the tape was hard for me to obtain, despite the school's commitment to our research. On the one hand, the problem was logistical. Who has the time in the busy running of a reform-engaged school to copy a tape for a researcher? On the other hand, it was also emotional. Does this tape fairly represent the process it means to represent? Dare the school simply lend it out without the spin that the school ordinarily puts on its work when it makes a presentation—say, at a conference or to visitors? The teachers who made the tape know that when I watch it, I will be far in space and time from the warm attachments I felt a year before. I will be primed for cool judgment. Nevertheless, they send it to me, and, despite the risk to my own warm investment, I watch it.

The four exhibitions on the tape all deal with contemporary topics: substance abuse and fetal development; child abuse and the juvenile court system; recycling and the environment; cholesterol and the American diet. These are my characterizations of the topics, and I phrase them as I do—simple intersections of relatively broad subjects—in order to emphasize the immensity of the task the exhibitors faced, and also to say that each of their exhibitions might have benefited from more focus. This is the way with contemporary topics. They are difficult to delineate, which makes them unlike topics drawn from textbooks. Moreover, even when one has delineated a contemporary topic rather well, the delineation may slip away while one speaks. I notice this in the tape. It happens, for example, to the exhibitor whose topic is child abuse and the juvenile court system but who talks mostly about the court system. Only the first question, posed by the teacher who coached him, cues me that child abuse was indeed one emphasis of his nervous and rather muddled introduction. I think that I lost track of this side of his topic when I sensed his self-confidence surge back as he turned, pointer in hand, to his first exhibits: a flowchart description of the juvenile court system and a collection of document specimens from key junctures in the system. Pleased by his recovery from a nervous opening, he may have lost track of his whole topic then too.

From my cool living room, I also notice the liberties the exhibitors take in interpreting their findings. "Smoking causes low-weight babies," one exhibitor declares baldly, and "fetal alcohol syndrome leads to mental retardation" ("*can* lead to mental retardation," I want to add). "The three causes of retardation," he begins, and I wish I could interrupt coolly: "Only three?"

Finally, I notice that a strong presence frequently overwhelms substance. This may be a chronic problem in exhibitions generally: they require courage, and courage, being as rare in school as elsewhere, dazzles. So one exhibitor's demonstration of how to cook low-fat crab cakes, worthy in its flair of midmorning network television, seems to distract the exhibitor herself from attending to her main concern: the health impact of cholesterol-laden foods. It surely distracts the audience, too, which is promised the chance to eat the crab cakes. Another exhibitor's cleverness in presenting his own videotape of the city's Earth Day celebrations seems to relieve him in his own eyes—and perhaps in the eyes of the audience too—of having to tie this exhibit to his main point.

The faults I spy in the video would have been far less apparent to me, even struggling to stay the critical friend, if I had been in the audience for these exhibitions—anticipating crab cakes, seated behind the proud parents of the exhibitor showing his homemade videotape. Nor do I think there is much the school can do to correct these faults within the warm setting. Oral exhibitions like this nearly always tip the balance of attention from substance to presence. One reason is that contemporary students, enveloped by pop culture, have enormously more access to models of presence than to models of substance, but few opportunities to emulate them in school. Given the chance, they often take it. For their part, however, schools can and must ensure that the assessment system, of which the public exhibition is merely one part, builds in plenty of substance checks along the way and plenty of substantive models. This is partly a wiring challenge and partly a tuning one.

Risking Contact with the Outside

The school where I played critical friend on my first visit requires a portfolio as well as an exhibition. The portfolio documents the exhibitor's process of inquiry. It is supposed to include note cards, interview transcripts, drafts, and a finished paper. The trick in the use of such a device is to make it count as much as the presentation does. Any teacher who has ever collected a novice researcher's note cards knows how easily such an exercise can become one of assessing form alone and how impossible it is to know—without taking the time to interview the student—what the cards really represent of the process under way. On the simplest level, this requires rewiring: the school must provide time for such coaching. But when it does provide time, the provision creates a need for still more adjustment. The teacher who manages to get very close to the actual process of a sustained student inquiry discovers that it is an exceedingly messy process, and matches only very roughly the kind of template he ordinarily uses to marshal a roomful of students through a research paper production. Indeed, he learns that one cannot coach genuine inquiry well in the context of teaching a course. It is not enough to pause from lectures and discussions every few days to meet with one or two students at a time, while everyone else in the room does seat work—not enough, that is, if the goal is to prepare students to be committed, skillful, and intellectually powerful inquirers and to make deep and serious inquiries.

It begins as a significant rewiring challenge—how to organize school on some other basis than allotting all the time and energy of school to classroom-based teaching and learning—but it ends up a tuning challenge of how to link resources on the inside with resources on the outside. To inquire deeply and well into such areas of interest as substance abuse and fetal development, or recycling and the environment, students must have access to expertise beyond that of their teachers. Even teachers working in teams cannot know enough about all the possible fields of interest that intellectually active high school seniors may propose to study. As Ron Berger (1996) has suggested, the same limitation may apply to teachers even at the elementary school level. In general, teachers cannot be the sole suppliers of question-generating experience and inquiry tools, the only coaches through the inevitable snags and near-disasters of serious inquiry, and the only prescribers and guardians of standards. Students must also dig for substance in the gardens of mentors who can show them in various ways what excellence means (Gardner, 1989).

Of course, teachers can and must model inquiry in general, but good student inquiry has more than generic quality. It has the whiff as well of incipient expertise. This is what we are used to sensing in some extracurricular pursuits of teenagers: the knowledge of cars or music or even retail merchandising that already exceeds what we may know about these things, and which we sense is headed for real depth. Even preteenagers can impress us in this way—for example, by the way they use complex information technology, the commitment they show to their hobbies, or their care of pets. We seldom expect, however, to be as impressed by their schoolwork. One reason, I think, is that we tacitly limit schoolwork to school grounds.

Most of the schools we studied, including the one I visited for the first time on exhibition day, try to give their students much broader rein for their inquiries than is usual. But this takes great resourcefulness and courage. There are, first, the safety and legal concerns: Should a student be allowed to take the subway to the public library or field site? Should a seventeen-year-old be able to drive herself ? Can she drive her friend too? What if the library is in a neighborhood regarded as dangerous by the student's parents? What if the field site is a remote and lonely spot, or a potentially hazardous workplace? These questions are enough to cause the average principal or superintendent to confine all official learning to school property.

Then there are the pedagogical problems, and these may apply whether students do their digging in actual outside sites or in virtually outside ones by means of telecommunications and CD-ROM. When they are not directly supervising the dig, how do teachers ensure that the digging time is productive and that the students dig hard? And how do teachers teach when the material students work with is material the teachers do not control, and when they know very little themselves about how to negotiate its intricacies? It has become routine today to talk about the information explosion and the challenge it presents to school curricula, but to understand the real thing, take any of the four topics explored by the exhibitors in the videotape I watched—let's say substance abuse and fetal development—into a well-equipped library. See for yourself what the on-line catalog, electronic databases and searching services, and periodical indexes provide. Unless you are highly focused in your inquiry and comfortable with all the odd discourse of data in the fields this topic touches, you will surely feel overwhelmed—and perhaps even yearn for the comforting information vacuum of the average high school library with its out-of-date books and its incomplete collections of *Time* and *Science News*. Imagine then the problem the teacher faces who knows that her students are about to be overwhelmed in this way. What kinds of scaffolding can she rig up by remote control such that the experience somehow accelerates rather than chokes off learning? What supports can she offer back at school, provided the school is sufficiently rewired so that she can provide any meaningful support at all to students digging in outside gardens? What if she is at heart intimidated by the student's topic and by the libraries or field sites where it takes her?

Balancing Warm and Cool

Tuning a school is not just about mixing inside perspectives with outside ones. All of the problems I have cited—from dealing with the outsiders' feedback on exhibition day, to finding the courage to give the outsider a videotape meant for insiders' eyes, to handling the structural and emotional challenges of letting one's students go digging on their own on the outside—involve a more fundamental tension than the one between inside and outside. This is the one between warm and cool. Outsiders can supply either perspective, as I illustrate above: first, I was a warm visitor on exhibition day; later I wrote a cooler reaction. Insiders can supply either perspective also if they design for both—if, for example, they bother to videotape exhibition day and also sit down to view the tapes and discuss them once the day's glow has faded. Indeed, questions of whether to invite outsiders in or whether to allow students outside always depend on the current temperature outside, and on how much the school or the students need either warming or cooling at that moment. They require therefore that the school has come to terms with the difference between warm and cool, and the purpose and value of each.

Like so many other challenges of schoolkeeping that involve balance, the challenge of balancing warm and cool is a chronic one. Managing it involves learning to alternate impulses. So the school I describe above first hesitated to give me the "cool" videotape, then readily handed it over. On the other hand, no one there ever asked me what I thought of it. Nor did I hear anything back when I sent the principal a copy of the article I wrote based partly on my viewing it (McDonald, 1993). Still, I was invited back year after year to watch more exhibitions. Does this mean the school was ambivalent about outside input? Probably so, and properly so. Does it mean that it was ambivalent as well about cool input? Not necessarily. Schools need not listen to any tune that comes along, so long as they listen to some and act on what they hear, and so long as the ones they attend to are not just the warm ones. Schools need lots of warmth to keep going, but they also need enough coolness to avoid complacency and parochialism. It is crucial, however, that the school itself have the power to adjust the balance between warm and cool. This means that the outsider's contribution—whether warm or cool—may sometimes be rejected. The second story in this tale elaborates on this idea.

Outsiders and Insiders

Throughout our study, my colleagues and I played two roles with respect to the schools we studied. As researchers, we sought insights from their struggles that might help us illuminate important issues in the redesign of schooling. To gain such insights, we had to bother the schools with requests to send us the videotapes they made of themselves, to share copies of internal documents, to let us eavesdrop on countless meetings (some of them tense), and to let us visit frequently and wander around whenever we did. At the same time, whenever asked, we played the role of critical friend to the schools. So I went to the exhibition day I described earlier and dutifully filled out my feedback sheet before heading back to the train station. Whenever the principal of another school invited me at the conclusion of every visit to share my candid assessment of the school's progress in reform, I complied. When, as I report in the next chapter, I was invited to participate in a day-long critical friends' review at a school, I accepted the invitation. And even when I was asked at still another school to call a local newspaper reporter to provide a researcher's view of the school's progress, I agreed to do it. In the earliest days of the study, I worried that I would not be able to keep separate my roles as researcher and critical friend. What I did not know then, however, but learned quickly, was that the schools also had a deep interest in my maintaining this separation. It turned out that I could count on their enforcing the difference even when, on occasion, I let it wear very thin—whether out of vanity or misguided helpfulness.

Consider, for example, the occasion I describe in the following field note:

> I observed a humanities team meeting in the morning. Janet, the team leader, had asked me to join the meeting, so I figured that the team wanted to draw on my expertise—such as it is. Actually, no. When I offered one brief comment near the end, I was cut off and not returned to. I was only a guest, which meant apparently that I was just to listen. Meanwhile, the conversation alluded to several sources of other outside expertise: the New Standards Project portfolio training, the Bard Writing Institute, and a talk by some people involved with the Vermont portfolio project.

The field note suggests that at the time I found it ironic that my outsider's expertise should be ignored. Now I think the only irony is that in the face of the researcher's willingness to compromise valuable distance, the subjects of the research preserved it for him. In fact, these insiders cared very much about outside perspectives, but preferred for very good reason to keep them outside their weekly planning meeting. This was insiders' time. They chose not to have an outsider present who was anything more, in this instance, than researcher. Over the course of two hours, the team talked about a great variety of things, including the proper role of telling in teaching; whether a teacher ought to worry about behavioral objectives; how prominent the school's overriding goals should be in daily lesson planning; who should lead the team the following year, and what the leader's responsibilities should be; how to spend the remaining dollars in the team's budget; whether they were somehow cheating their students by sacrificing coverage to depth ("My kids don't know who Andrew Jackson is"); and what recent outside professional development experiences they valued. They talked about these things with great animation and purpose, and with a candor and openness characteristic of only the warmest settings—where people trust each other, where no one need fear that another will think less of one for asking, "What is a behavioral objective?" The team that invites an outsider to such a meeting takes a great risk.

Why then did Janet invite me? The best answer, I think, is that she invited me because I am a researcher. She thought the meeting might be useful to me in accomplishing what she took to be the purpose of my being in her school in the first place. From the school's point of view, and from Janet's, I was there to learn as much as I could about this school so as to help represent it to other outsiders. The school would also use my representation to reflect on itself, but in its own time and in its own way. Meanwhile, I should shut up, and let the insiders talk at their own meeting.

Tale 2: A Democratic Dilemma

On an early winter evening, sixty or so citizens gather in a brightly lit high school cafeteria. This is a good turnout for the fourth of a series of community dialogues in this town of eight thousand people. Most of those gathered are parents of children in one of the town's three schools. The dialogues have been hosted by the new superintendent of schools, who has acted partly in response to a statewide initiative. In the grip of a lingering recession, the state aims to improve the quality of its workforce as a way to stem further economic erosion. Historically, this workforce has been conditioned by an economy of plentiful low-skilled jobs. In the 1990s, however, the jobs are vanishing fast. Attracting new jobs to replace the lost ones will depend, says the state, on a transformation in citizens' attitudes toward education. Throughout much of the state, this means encouraging children to be academically ambitious instead of ambivalent, and to prepare for work quite unlike the work their mothers and fathers do.

To support such a difficult turnaround, with its perils of class and community betrayal, the state has authored a set of goals based on high expectations for all the state's children, and it has invited communities to use the set as the basis of community dialogues like this one. Here, though, the issues are different than they are almost everywhere else in the state. This community has one of the state's highest per capita incomes. It is full of professionals who work in a nearby city and moved here from elsewhere because of this work. They already push their children to be academically ambitious. They need not warn them against depending on vanishing factory jobs. Most parents in this community (though not all) expect their children to leave home after school in order to attend good colleges. And once there, they expect them never to return, to live after college wherever they can find the best work, though in towns like the one their parents chose—namely, those with the "best schools"—the ones that reliably get their graduates into the best colleges, typically defined as elite private colleges or land-grant universities in other states.

The astute superintendent who is chairing the community dialogue tonight knows well that the issues are not the same here as in most of the state's other towns. Not only is the ordinary motivation attached to getting an education different here, but so is the motivation for change. It is strong, though also quite complex. There is little complacency here among three key constituencies: parents, the district administration, and the high school faculty. Insofar as one can characterize their respective views in any common way, these three groups all believe that the town's schools are not quite so good as they ought to be, despite their reputation among real estate brokers and college admissions counselors. That is not to say, however, that the three groups agree among themselves on the nature of the problem or on how to handle it.

Most parents seem to think the problem is a slippage of standards. Their perception in this regard has been fueled by several current and recent controversies. One involved a fight at the elementary school between advocates of a whole language approach to the teaching of reading and advocates of a phonics approach. There were parents and teachers on both sides, and rigidity on both sides. It was ultimately settled by a pledge on the part of the superintendent and school board to focus curricular decision making on children's developmental needs and differences rather than on ideology. However, it left scars, one in the form of a political lesson. Some parents, whose children are now heading toward high school, learned that only their own political action at the district level saved their children from what they took to be a threatening innovation. A second recent controversy with a residual impact involved an effort by the relatively new principal of the high school to end a number of long-standing faculty baronies there. The principal wanted a more collegial and reform-minded faculty, and encouraged the retirement or departure of several teachers widely regarded by students and parents as faculty stars—the sort of teacher one would want to have writing one's recommendation to college. Finally, a third controversy, still simmering, involves a faculty merit pay system adopted more than six years before by an earlier superintendent, school board, and teacher association leadership. The point was to reward the best teachers with extra pay and to put the worst teachers on notice. At this point, virtually all the teachers involved in the merit pay plan are receiving merit pay, and recently the town manager's office reported that the added cost of the plan is approaching $1 million a year.

In the superintendent's view, as expressed to me in an interview some days after the community dialogue, these controversies exacerbated a basic relational problem between the parents and the faculty of all three schools. Many parents in the community bring elitist assumptions to their relations with their children's teachers, she told me. They regard themselves as smarter than the teachers for having earned their degrees at nonlocal and more prestigious colleges and universities. For their part, many teachers, she added, fail to honor parental priorities in academic matters. Families in this community already do for their children on weekends what some teachers want to do on field trips and in some class projects. The parents want the schools to do other, more rigorous things. Although many parents may equate higher standards with more demanding teaching, the superintendent worries especially about the quality of the demands. Quoting David Perkins (1992), she told me in the interview that she thinks the schools could do more to encourage genuinely intellectual rather than merely academic ambition in their students. She would like all three schools in the district to start early and work in common to disturb children's naive interpretations of experience, to promote knowledge that can survive translation to contexts outside school, to prize the application of knowledge over its ritual recall. She thinks parental complaints about standards would evaporate given some evidence of genuine thoughtfulness in the work that students take home.

The superintendent knows well, however, that she must wield her diagnosis very gingerly. In the process of encouraging thoughtfulness in her schools, she must not discourage the community's moral and financial investment in them. For one thing, she wants desperately to pass a bond issue to rebuild two schools and upgrade the third one's technological capacity. Essentially, as she sees her work, she must redirect the community's educational commitment without deflating it. This is a somewhat different challenge from that facing the state, which must stimulate educational commitment in the first place. However, it is a comparably delicate challenge politically.

In her opening address to the fourth community dialogue, the superintendent mentions the Total Quality Management (TQM) strategies pursued in the workplaces of many of the parents present, and she suggests that the economic challenges that have stimulated profound changes in industrial and business management are making demands of schools too (Deming, 1986, 1994). Schools need a new definition of productivity, she claims, one geared to a higher absolute standard, with near-zero tolerance for anything less, and quality built in rather than inspected for. This is the state's message—high expectations for all students—though subtly repackaged to suit this particular audience. It fails, however, to appeal to at least one of the audience members, a middle-level executive at one of the region's TQM-focused corporations. During the small-group dialogue that follows the superintendent's address, he tells me that he thinks the main problem with the town's high school is that it has watered down its honors classes with too many students who belong in the lower college prep track. The next day, several high school students I talk with echo his complaint. They also add that the school has driven out its best teachers—a reference to the barons. Although they do not say so, some may also have heard the complaints about town that the remaining teachers are paid extra for being good.

The High School's Reform Agenda

In reaction to its own discontent with the state of the community's schools, the newly collegial high school faculty has been reevaluating its goals. For over a year, it has been meeting in departments to specify subject by subject what it thinks all students should know and be able to do before graduating. The result has been a series of outcome statements, plus some new wiring: the adoption of a spiral math curriculum, the greater integration of special education and classroom teaching, more investment in and reliance on the library–media center, and some experimentation with performance assessment. But the exercise has also engendered a vague anxiety on the part of some influential faculty members. This is reform anxiety—the sense that alert teachers pick up as if from the wind, but which actually derives from a thousand small encounters with dissatisfied customers: the parent of a ninth grader obsessively concerned about the girl's college prospects, the boy who slumps in his seat and will not engage, the talk show host who rails against the state of schools, the education monthly that prints a picture of the sinking *Titanic* on its cover. One teacher can only describe this anxiety to me indirectly: "I thought the problem was curricular, but when I work on curriculum, I find myself just dancing harder. Something else is wrong."

Spurred on by the principal, the faculty has recently begun to deal with its reform anxiety through an exploration of the ideas of the Coalition of Essential Schools. By means of a small grant obtained from a corporate philanthropy, a number of faculty members have attended a regional meeting of the Coalition and visited some Coalition-affiliated schools in the region. The principal, who describes himself to me as an aggressive and at times impatient reformer, not only promotes the Coalition connection, but also a Coalition-like wiring innovation: revamping the schedule to create longer teaching blocks. Many teachers are quietly supportive of the principal's plan, but many students and parents are wary. One student tells me that some of his teachers are boring enough in forty-two minutes; he can only imagine how they will be in eighty minutes. The superintendent, sensing another controversy that may distract the community-wide conversation she believes is needed to improve the town's schools (and get the bond issues passed), is also urging caution on the schedule change. She is worried that the principal's wish to get a new schedule in place may outpace his ability to work out the bugs ahead of time.

Just before the community dialogue I attend, the principal tells me that he has not had much time to bring parents and students into the discussion about the Coalition, but he will use my appearance at the dialogue as an opening in this regard. Although the people I talk with there and elsewhere in the next several days—the superintendent, parents, students, and faculty—understand my interests as a researcher, the principal's introduction has its impact: most also regard me as a missionary from the Coalition. They seem nonetheless comfortable with me. The superintendent makes it clear to me that she respects the research base of the Coalition.

Some parents I meet at the community dialogue make it clear to me that they respect the fact that the Coalition is associated with Brown University. And the faculty makes it clear to me that a missionary is just what they need now, since they plan to spend the next year engaged in a struggle whose quasi-religious nuance is unavoidable: the struggle to understand and assume the Coalition's beliefs.

A Tuning Strategy

The principal's scheduling proposal goes nowhere. The superintendent thinks that both the school and the community are ill prepared for the change, and the board nixes it. The principal takes the setback well. He had wanted to lead the school through a wiring innovation, but he turns the faculty's attention to tuning instead. Having nearly completed its curricular introspection, the faculty especially needs an outside perspective now, he suggests—some framework of understanding that it can use to assess what its introspection has turned up. Here is where the Coalition connection seems to him especially valuable. Over the course of the next six months, he leads the entire faculty through a systematic reflection on its work by the light of the nine principles of the Coalition of Essential Schools. At successive afternoon meetings, they meet to consider the principles in turn, posing the same questions of each:

- What does the principle mean?
- What would it look like if it were in effect?
- How do we look in comparison?
- What changes does the comparison suggest are needed?
- What are the obstacles to making such changes?
- What are the disadvantages of making such changes?

The school preserves the record of each discussion and sometimes revisits it during the next discussion. The tone of these meetings (judging by the one I observed) is deliberative and not at all anxious, as if the motivating anxiety had been dispelled by the method of the inquiry, by a sense of tuning progress. The transcripts portray a conversation over time that is more diagnostic than prescriptive. It is full of questions. It records no decisions reached or even contemplated. It seems to open up the programmatic possibilities of the Coalition's principles rather than to settle on any. Of course, the parents who are not privy to these discussions do not know this.

Membership Vote

When word begins to get out that the faculty is considering full membership in the Coalition of Essential Schools, parental concerns surface. The principal argues at two public meetings held on the subject that the Coalition is not a franchise and that parents need not worry that membership means the wholesale adoption of a program or curriculum. In effect, he downplays the Coalition's wiring ideas and emphasizes its tuning powers. In a briefing paper prepared for one meeting, he writes,

> The Coalition is an association of secondary schools and an increasing number of elementary schools whose major goal is to ensure that students learn to use their minds well. It is a group of schools having a conversation about what education should be, based on a set of common ideas. The ideas and answers about what ought to be are as varied as the participants in the conversation.

The teachers who speak at this meeting, and at the faculty meeting where 81 percent vote in favor of Coalition membership, also emphasize tuning. One talks about the impact on her practice of the Coalition aphorism, "student as worker/teacher as coach." She used to be a "chalk and talk teacher," she says, but now she organizes class time around activities. Another highlights the influence on her practice of the Coalition's emphasis on the exhibition of student learning. Still another says that the conversations about Coalition ideas have reinforced her efforts to become a science teacher who teaches students how to use science, not just know it in an inert way. These three and others speak of reform ideas that are not exclusive to the Coalition, but their claim is that the Coalition has given them access to these ideas and a network within which to explore them. There is an important subtext to this claim: that the intellectual resources and supports of a single three-school district—even an affluent, well-respected one—are insufficient to sustain a lively teaching practice.

With few exceptions, the parents either do not understand this argument or do not accept it. The following sampling of comments captures the tenor of their response:

"I see nothing that the staff can't do on its own."

"Can't you still work on Coalition ideas even if you don't join the Coalition?"

"Teachers have always had the chance to be creative. What do they need the Coalition for?"

In her memo to the board on the subject of Coalition membership, the superintendent implicitly echoes these parental sentiments. She begins with a quotation from a reform-minded teacher of 1909, who advocates that schools be reorganized so that children think and do most of the talking, and she also quotes William James, an early-twentieth-century Harvard psychologist, and David Perkins, a contemporary one. She acknowledges the value of the Coalition's ideas, but the subtext of her acknowledgment is that the same ideas are also available from other sources.

A number of board members are sympathetic to the teachers' argument, some of them having attended Coalition meetings. "The Coalition is like a think tank," says one. "It could be good to be affiliated with a think tank. It's good to know about other schools and to talk with other teachers." But the dominant perception of the board is that Coalition membership is not just about teachers and their tuning needs. Indeed, as the superintendent reminds board members in her memo, the Coalition itself requests a school board vote on all membership applications, thus acknowledging the importance of a good fit between the Coalition and a school's community. And in the matter of fit, this board is clearly dubious. The chairman voices his reservations thus:

> The Coalition does provide an opportunity to network nationally, yet we don't want to be an experimental school. We are successful in getting 90 percent of our graduates into college. We need to

> look carefully before joining any national group. Inner-city schools in the Coalition seem to be doing better, but what about suburban schools? Before we join, we must have consensus.

The *we* of his statement runs to the heart of the policy questions in this story. Who owns the schools? Who should be in charge of deciding how they are tuned, and to what end? The superintendent is unequivocal on this point. The schools belong to the community, she tells me.

Meanwhile, the parents' concerns about Coalition membership have little to do with tuning. Their minds are on wiring issues. Despite the faculty's deemphasis of the point, they understand that Coalition membership implies rewiring of a particular kind:

"My daughter is an individual perfectionist and dislikes groups. How would this kind of student and her teachers cope with the requirement of more group work?"

"What is the connection between the Coalition and the proposed change in schedule to longer periods?"

"How have you involved students in the discussions about the Coalition and the transition to their being workers?"

"How do you measure mastery? Only by performance and exhibition? I don't see references to other forms of assessment in Coalition literature."

"We want teachers to have the support they need, but we have to blend that with the reality that kids have to take achievement tests to get into college, and they can't refer to material there that they haven't memorized."

"I would like to see the current curriculum goals and what they would be like under the Coalition."

The Wiring at Stake

Although it is at times convenient—whether politically or tactically—to distinguish among the arenas of school design, one must ultimately design across them all in order to have a coherent design in the end. The parents whom I quote above understood this intuitively. While the school may have been right to emphasize tuning when it did—to gain strength following the reaction to the scheduling proposal—it would have had to turn to wiring again before long. When I got close enough to this school to form an opinion on the source of its latent discontent, I found a wiring problem. The school's wish to become a more unified community, expressed first in the believing arena by its work on goal clarification, and then in the tuning arena by its exploration of the Coalition, was blocked by a strong attachment to tracking. Although the school was relatively small—under five hundred students in four grades—its curricular offerings were divided into three or four levels—for example, junior English, college prep junior English, honors junior English, and advanced placement junior English. In the way teachers, students, and parents talked about these levels, they seemed to regard them as given, natural, and unproblematic. In my visits to classrooms, I was frequently advised that I would find a particular group "rowdy" or "bright"—with the label affixed as if identifying a found condition rather than a created one. What I actually encountered always seemed to me a responsive adaptation: the low-track class that had bargained down its teacher's already low expectations, affecting a dumb camaraderie in the process; the high-track class that liked to engage in intellectually conscious though not intellectually serious talk, and whose teacher clearly enjoyed and so spurred on the banter.

The principal was right: the Coalition offers no program to supplant this or any other features of a school that joins it. But the framework of its principles—urging that a school's goals apply to all its students but that the school treat each of its students as a unique individual—moves schools away from tracking schemes like this. The parents who feared another whole language debacle, and the one who said, "I would like to see us not get into a major upheaval," may have sensed this direction, and probably feared it. Surely the superintendent did too, though for a different reason. She would have liked to address the same problem in another way. It was not that she disliked the Coalition; quite the contrary, she told me later: the Coalition offered her a networking opportunity too. However, she wanted to rely initially on community-wide dialogue rather than dialogue only among teachers, and she wanted to tune this dialogue to state rhetoric and new industrial theory rather than to the Coalition's principles. She believed that parents must be won over first. Indeed, from where she sat, there seemed no other way, so fragile had the town's trust in its schools become. Nor, she reasoned, could this be accomplished school by school, a process that she thought would first confuse and then polarize the community.

Meanwhile, the faculty and its principal put their trust in professional networking. To redesign the school to work well for all its students, they believed that the professionals who staff it must acquire a richer stock of design ideas and tools. A good way to do this, they argued, is through an association with a national school reform network like the Coalition of Essential Schools. The Coalition was particularly appealing to them because it did not advocate a single design. It did not, for example, tell them that they had to solve their tracking problem by simply integrating all their classes, making every one heterogeneous in its composition. Ted Sizer is fond of saying, in fact, that he is all for tracking, so long as every student gets his or her own track. The Coalition offers instead a paradox: the school must have universal goals for all students, but it must also personalize each student's pursuit of these goals. The faculty liked the idea of spending a year working on the solution of this paradox and on similar problems of design. Students and parents could be brought along later, they thought, once the teachers began to see their own work more clearly and to understand what alternatives were possible.

Both the superintendent and the high school faculty made sensible arguments, and they proposed reasonable tuning strategies. At first, the strategies seemed to coexist compatibly; then they collided. The reasons for the collision are complex, the chemistry of particular circumstances: the relational problem the superintendent identified between the district's faculty and its parents; the particular personalities involved and their political instincts; the steep learning curve involved for both parents and teachers, particularly with regard to tracking and the issue of the possible impact of reform on college admissions; the presence of certain opportunities, like the corporate grant and the state's initiative, and the fact that they tugged in somewhat different directions.

A year after the board's decision to table the question of whether the high school should join the Coalition of Essential

Schools, I asked both the superintendent and the (by then) former principal to consider what had happened. "The organization was not strong enough," the superintendent told me, "to handle the discontent that I felt was building in the community. I couldn't put good people in a situation where they would be the lightning rod for that discontent. The Coalition would have been an early casualty in a disaster."

"I can't believe the organization wasn't strong enough," the principal retorted in a separate interview. "The real story is that the Coalition was too dangerous, given the fragility of support for the bond issues. A lot of people on the faculty thought she sold us out—maybe she did —but a superintendent has other pressures. This one may have said to herself, 'What I can do here is rebuild the buildings and clean up some messes I inherited. If the curriculum is not what I would have chosen, and if high school reform is a casualty, well, then, so be it.'"

Indeed, the superintendent, contemplating retirement, told me that she is likely to regard her tenure in the district "as an intervention at a time of great crisis. My job was to stabilize the system, so that change will be possible later." The key to this stabilization for her was trust between the schools and the community. "Relationships are far more important than any of us once thought," she told me, "all kinds of relationships within and outside the school."

Policy Reflections

Particular as the circumstances of this story are, the dilemma they provoked is hardly unique. It underlies some major policy questions facing all designers of the twenty-first-century school. Can community-controlled and community-wide public schooling be counted on to provide the highest standards of teaching for all the children of the community? Can it move fast enough to provide the changes needed? Should we continue to rely on school districts as the fulcrum of democratic schooling, or should we fashion a different kind of system?

One way to think about this problem is to situate this second story in a policy context quite unlike its own, though conceivable in a hypothetical sense. Imagine the faculty, or some portion of it, taking advantage of state law to create a charter school—in effect, seceding from the existing school to form another in the same town. Imagine the designers of this charter school, however, competing for parent and student customers from other towns and the nearby city, thereby skirting smugness about what kind of education is for the suburbs and what kind for the inner city. Then, as proposed in some policy schemes, imagine such a charter school joining a charter district—one formed on the basis of ideological commitment and with a tuning purpose at its core (Hill, 1995). Imagine, for example, that the other Coalition member schools in the region had organized themselves so as to have the capacity necessary to hold each other accountable by means of visits to each other and the auditing of student work. Imagine further that they had honed their beliefs in common to such an extent that they were able to market them—that they had formed the equivalent of such networks in the independent sector as Montessori or Waldorf or Sacred Heart schools.

But could such a system be democratic? Should it be eligible to receive public funds, including funds taken away from the public schools its students would otherwise attend? At the heart of these questions are several deeper ones that put great demands on the designers of twenty-first-century schooling. They are questions that are currently without answers, which is to say, questions that beg for thoughtful experimentation. The first set of them concerns the nature of democratic participation. Which vote is more powerful: the one I give in a school board election, or the one I give when I choose my son's or daughter's school? And what about parents unaccustomed to choosing? Is a democracy where some significant number of potential voters do not vote, or even conceive of themselves as voters despite their technical right to vote, an actual democracy? The second set of questions concerns the problem of recognizing and accommodating other stakeholders of schooling besides parents and professionals: How can citizens who do not have children in school have a genuine voice in a market-based schooling system? What if the ideological bases that drive both the demand and supply sides of that market create rifts that affect the community in other ways, that make the community's people even less inclined to regard themselves as members of the community?

A Southern Variation

At the same time that the events I report above were unfolding, another school in our study group was experiencing similar tensions.[1] Both schools were situated in affluent suburbs of regionally important cities—bedroom communities for the executives of regional corporate headquarters. Both had also engaged in a good deal of work in the believing arena, and in the process had discovered the Coalition of Essential Schools. In fact, as a result of this network connection, the schools became acquainted with each other and exchanged faculty visits.

In some other respects, however, the two schools were very different, and the differences are provocative from the perspective of the tuning arena. For purposes of comparison, I will call the school I wrote about above Northern High School and the other one Southern High School.

One important difference is that Southern was not the only high school in its town, but one of three. This meant that at every point in the evolution of its design, students and parents had another option. They could always vote with their feet. Indeed, the school might not have survived an eventual crisis, except that the school board was able to permit and encourage this option as an outlet for dissatisfaction. The fact that few exercised the option was irrelevant; the safety valve was there, and everyone knew it.

A second very important difference is that Southern High School did not simply contemplate or propose an untraditional wiring design, as did Northern High School. It actually opened with one in place. It was a new school, founded quite deliberately on principles different from the other two in town—most notably on the principle that although it would dutifully follow the district-wide curriculum (heavily influenced by the state), it would not carve it up into levels. It declared that it would be an untracked high school. The advantage of the declaration, and of the fact that it acted on it, is that the problems it eventually faced in terms of parental concerns could be resolved through accumulating evidence. Would the

1. For important details of this story, I rely on research conducted by my colleagues Bethany Rogers and Lisa Lasky.

students be better off in the new wiring or not? This was an empirical question at Southern in a way that it could not be at Northern, since all change there was speculative. Of course, it would take time for the evidence to accumulate—state assessment scores, satisfaction surveys, college board scores, and college admissions—but eventually it did. Meanwhile, the principal boldly called attention to the question, and when the data came in by and large the way he hoped they would, the community was prepared to accept his validation claim.

Before the data came in, however, he needed political cover. He got it from several sources, including the state, school reform networks, and the press. Like the northern state, the southern state was also interested in figuring out how to educate all its children to a standard commensurate with the emerging demands of industrial productivity. Yet Southern High School was its only untracked high school. The principal brought this to the state's attention, and then worked a deal. Southern High School was declared a demonstration school for high school restructuring, and thereby given easy access to waivers of state requirements in exchange for its willingness to entertain frequent visitors from around the state, especially educators interested in learning how an untracked high school might operate.

Like the principal of Northern High School, this principal also cultivated connections to regional and national school reform groups. Unlike his faraway colleague in reform, however, he seemed at least as interested in how these groups might provide additional political cover as in how they might provide new ideas and other resources. He made sure not only that his school's faculty took advantage of the partnership the school formed with the reform network headquartered at the state university—read the literature, attended meetings, and so forth—but that the network's leaders knew the school well and could be called on to testify as to the value of its innovations. Similarly, after the school became a member of the Coalition of Essential Schools, the principal not only arranged for the school to take advantage of the Coalition's professional development opportunities, but he also formed a close relationship with the Coalition's communications office. He wanted to be able to call on it for public relations assistance if needed.

Finally, the principal cultivated some press cover. He made sure that the editors of the local newspapers, as well as the education and editorial writers of the nearby metropolitan daily, were aware of the school and its different design. He was always open to their inquiries and never defensive. In his communications with them, as with the school's parents, the school board, and outside visitors to the school, he always highlighted rather than downplayed the school's beliefs and the consequent differences in its wiring. He was also forthcoming with all data that might reveal the impact on students of these differences. So, for example, when the first set of scores from the Preliminary Scholastic Aptitude Test showed the school's average performance to be slightly below the national average in the verbal area (though higher in mathematics), these data were displayed prominently on the front page of a newsletter published by the school for the community, along with other standardized test scores, the average daily attendance for the year, the numbers of suspensions, the numbers of students on the honor roll, the numbers studying fine arts, and so on. In the same issue was an article on the Coalition of Essential Schools and why the school joined it. Again, the fact that the school was not the only high school in town played a role in this communications strategy. The principal knew that his habit of producing and revealing such data would exert pressure on the other schools—perhaps through the press—to do the same, and he suspected that his numbers would look better—a suspicion that proved true in many instances. I emphasize this factor throughout this brief story to suggest that some choice in the system may be essential to effective redesign within a democratic context.

Meanwhile, in first accentuating the differences in his school and providing many data by which to consider them, the principal was following a smart press strategy, which also ultimately fostered democracy in this case. He was validating the emerging sense among the members of the press who visited or called that there was a story in this school. They obliged by getting the story out. The people who followed it were then able to make informed decisions about the fate of the school and its redesign.

Predictably, the school's wiring was controversial despite all the effective communication—almost as controversial as it would have been if tried at Northern High School. Near the end of the new school's first year, the local newspaper, reporting on an upcoming vote by the school board, headlined its report, "Supporters cheer, critics deplore new program":

> There's a battle under way concerning the county's new high school, and it has nothing to do with dollars. Instead, it's about the way the school's teachers teach and its students learn. Many of these students, and even some parents and state education officials, think the school has achieved a brilliant feat of reform. But the same feat has left another group of students and parents complaining that this first year of the school has been an entire waste for the students who might have learned the most, namely the brightest ones.
>
> Fifteen parents recently demanded of the school board—which will vote on the proposal tonight—that it scrap the whole experiment and turn the school into a regular one. What has them so concerned is that though the school uses the same curriculum as the town's other two high schools, this one does so without benefit of bells and textbooks, and without tracking students into slow, average, and advanced classes.[2]

The next day, the article reporting on the results of this board meeting was headlined, "High school survives having book thrown at it." By contrast, the counterpart headline for Northern High School—the headline in its local paper following the board meeting at which the question of Coalition membership was tabled, read, "Board rejects school reform."

Tale 3: Between Bottom-Up and Top-Down

I had gone wandering in search of a coffee one February morning, and in search too of some chance encounter that might help me better understand the school I was visiting. Entering the cafeteria, I found a scene I understood intuitively as a result of my own experiences in school. The whole senior class was assembled, though in

2. I paraphrase this excerpt and offer no citation in order not to breach confidentiality.

an unnatural state: silent, spread around the room, two or three persons to a table.

"What's the test?" I asked the teacher in charge, a man I had interviewed the previous day.

"The new state assessment."

"Oh."

I had heard about this. The state was piloting a substitute for its ordinary reliance on norm-referenced, multiple-choice tests. The effort was part of its systemic initiative, combining statewide curricular expectations with criterion-referenced, performance-based assessments. These assessments were still paper-and-pencil tests, however, so a wanderer encountering one as I did this morning could not mistake the scene. What seemed so familiar to me was familiar also to the assembled seniors, since they had acted in such scenes many times before.

Yet for all the familiarity, something was also different, and the difference was sparking more than the usual anxiety. I detected this when I overheard one student's exasperated complaint to the teacher in charge. She had approached him carrying her copy of the test booklet, and waving it before his eyes, she whispered to him angrily that she had never seen such questions before. "Just do your best, Lakesha," the teacher told her, and she glumly returned to her seat. I felt her pain, imagining that she was in the habit of caring how she performed on tests but had been too surprised by this one.

Unlike others she had encountered in settings like this—or, indeed, in most of the classes she took—this test asked open-ended questions, for example, "Write an essay accounting for the persuasive techniques employed in the following newspaper ad." It also included some questions about the school that may have seemed nearly as difficult to answer: "How many times in the last month have you been required in English class to write a persuasive essay?" This test was a tuning tool, devised by state authorities who suspected that many of the state's students would be stumped by the first question and that their answer to the second would help to reveal why.

"Can I see the test booklet?" I asked the teacher who had just told Lakesha to do her best. "Sure, but I can't let you take a copy." He knew my instincts as a researcher, though he need not have worried in this instance. I knew the protocol. Standardized testing in the United States, even when performance based, typically depends on keeping its questions secret (Schwartz, 1990). Test givers try to catch test takers by surprise. Naturally they want to make sure that all are equally surprised—that the senior who takes the test in one school on Tuesday does not slip the questions to his friend who takes it in another school on Friday, and that neither school prepares its students for the specific questions. Nor do they usually release their test questions even after an entire test administration is complete. Test development is expensive, and they like to use questions in more than one test. Indeed, they must, if they intend to claim that the tests are comparable.

The surprise and secrecy in American testing habits has an impact on the test takers. Lakesha had evidently been surprised past caring. The test makers had no way of knowing this would happen in her case. Nor could the test scorers, who later examined the blanks in her test booklet, have known why she gave up. Meanwhile, the results of her test, arriving back at school some three months later, failed to include any record of the questions that so surprised her. Even if she or her teachers had by then come to care about the results of this test, they would have lacked the means to treat her surprise, and her response to it, as a learning opportunity.

Certainly the state has both a constitutional and moral responsibility to ensure that students its schools are about to graduate are not surprised by questions about persuasive techniques, or by other questions on the test I examined that morning: one requiring the test taker to write out his or her sense of the main idea of a political cartoon, another asking for a narrative based on information supplied by a map and a graph. But in this case, the state reached down too far with its own hand. Naturally the grasp proved clumsy. Lakesha and many of her peers felt the surprise of this test as an indignity, and indignity is not a good motivational device. And the school felt it as a disrespectful intrusion—one that utterly ignored the school's own efforts to become more accountable, to create a culture of higher standards for learning and teaching.

On the other hand, the school might have managed the intrusion so as to learn something from it. Instead, it tried to dodge it, as it dodged most accountability gestures by the state or district. As a city school serving mostly minority students, it was used to being treated badly by both state and district—having all its resources squeezed even while being attacked for low test scores, and having its own accountability efforts discounted or even subverted. For example, at the time of my visit, this school and every other school in its medium-sized city were reeling from the impact of an $8 million budget cut in the middle of the year. And at the same time, the school's principal was struggling—unsuccessfully, as it turned out—to get the superintendent and school board to acknowledge the legitimacy of the school's own homegrown performance assessment system. District officials worried that it imposed an unfair graduation burden on the schools' students, one that other students in the city did not have to bear.

Qualities of a Good Assessment

A good assessment does three things in an interrelated way. First, it faces outward to reveal to a school's stakeholders what the school's students can do—or not do—now that the school has taught them. The inertia in any school's operations is very powerful. Redesigning them in the interest of teaching all students to use their minds well depends at least initially on knowing how well the students are doing now. Theoretically, that was what the state was up to the morning I spied its work in the cafeteria. It was asking Lakesha to face outward and show whether she had learned some things it regarded as important to learn. The problem was that it had not managed to enlist Lakesha in the effort—being too interested in surprising her, and being too remote to know her. Ironically, the school itself was at more or less the same time making more or less the same inquiry. But knowing Lakesha, and also being determined not to surprise her, the school stood a better chance of enlisting her in the effort. Another way of saying this is that, on its face, the school's assessment was more valid that the state's. Once I bought a silly book about the IQ of dogs and administered the test it included to my West Highland white terrier, Basil. I remember one particular prompt: roll your dog in a blanket, call the dog, and, using a stopwatch, determine how long the dog takes to undo the blanket. The problem was that Basil liked being rolled up in blankets, and so he was exceedingly slow to respond to my call. The test taker has to want to face outward for the test to have even minimal validity. On the morning I met her, Lakesha certainly did not want to face outward, at least not on the terms required.

Having a legitimate need to know about Lakesha, the state came one morning to her school's cafeteria to find out about her. But in addition to failing to let her know beforehand what it was up to so as to enlist her support, it also failed to inquire beforehand what the school already knew about her or was in the process of finding out. In the end, what does it matter that state-level authorities or any other outsiders find out that Lakesha is not faring well, if the process does not empower insiders to do something about it? So, in addition to facing outward, a good assessment points inward too, causing a school to pause from its ordinary running in order to consider what the assessment reveals about the school's systems. That is why I asked the proctoring teacher that morning what would happen when the test results came out. Would the faculty discuss them, act on them, at least dispute them?

"We'll be the bottom of the heap, again," he said.

"What?" I asked.

"When the results come out, the newspaper will say that our school is at the bottom again. Different test. Same result. That is not a good incentive for discussing."

It is not even a good incentive for disputing. In most cases, it is only an incentive for disregarding.

The third quality of a good assessment is that it presses deeper to make knowledge more vibrant and stable, even as it tests for it. We know already how the assessment I witnessed that morning seemed to affect Lakesha: it shut down her learning rather than deepened it. Exactly the same thing happened to the school. There are complex reasons that this happened here, and why it happens to many students and many schools even in this era of systemic reform. For example, there are all the things I complain about: the surprise and secrecy, the lack of access even later to the questions, the failure to enlist students or really to treat them respectfully, the arrogance in the assumption that any distant authority can learn much of consequence about an institution by simply sweeping in one morning with a dipstick assessment. And there is one other thing too: the basic orientation of a tuning effort in which one set of stakeholders is considered on top and the other on the bottom. David Conley (1994) captures this orientation well in a road map for systemic reform, recently promoted in a U.S. Department of Education publication:

> In the changing relationship among some states, school districts, and school sites, the state establishes standards and encourages innovation and experimentation. It creates accountability for the achievement of standards but allows schools considerable freedom to decide how best to meet the standards. Enhanced accountability through reporting of school-by-school performance is likely to cause schools to demand greater flexibility so that they can adapt their program to the unique needs of their constituency and achieve greater success [p. 13].

So the state establishes standards and creates accountability, and these exertions of power cause schools to demand greater flexibility. In other words, the initiative is presumed to come from the state—the top—and to engender responsiveness from the schools—the bottom.

Lakesha's school was not the only one in our sample where this presumption proved faulty. The failure to achieve any balance of power here, however, was especially ironic.

An Ironic Detachment of Wiring and Tuning

Lakesha's school was involved at the time of my visit in significant rewiring work based on the introduction of an exhibition system. The principal had begun this work as a result of what I call a sighting. At graduation one year, he had found himself handing a diploma to a young man who he knew could not read or write beyond a rudimentary level. That night, the principal vowed not to repeat the experience. Within a month, he and key members of the faculty had designed and installed the first element of what was to grow into a complex system. This first element required that all seniors write and defend orally a persuasive essay, called a senior exhibition paper. The paper was to focus on a controversial subject of social importance—one the student chose. To pass muster, the paper had to be well written according to standards developed by the English department and had to have at least three supporting arguments and three citations. Two English teachers, reading all the papers blindly, judged the results. Contributing to each student's score too was the quality of an oral defense, made before fellow seniors and the author's own English teacher.

Recall that I met Lakesha in the cafeteria while she was taking the state's test. That is where I saw her give up the struggle to get past a gut feeling that the persuasive techniques the state was asking her to identify and write about were things she had once been taught but had since forgotten or else had been absent for. Instead, I might have met her on another day in the library, struggling to learn and apply analytical and persuasive techniques in the process of completing her senior exhibition paper. If so, I would likely have found her in a more hopeful mood, and supported by more than a proctor's last-minute encouragement to do her best. She might have been working with the senior tutor whose office was in the library and who frequently coached seniors in the development of their papers. The tutor had been hired as part of the rewiring associated with the school's accountability efforts.

The tutor described for me one day her central tactic in working with seniors on their papers: "to pull them into the confusion of the subjects they express an interest in." The point of "getting the kid inside the controversy," she added, is that they might emerge on the other side really owning the argument they make, and really feeling the justification of their grounding. In the process, she helped them immerse themselves in print and other materials related to the subject they had chosen; that was why her office was in the library. She also provided them opportunities there to meet with other seniors and share drafts as well as accounts of their process and problems. Finally, she offered them access to models of how others had solved the thinking and writing problems involved.

Moreover, this coach did not confine her coaching to the seniors. When she visited senior classes, she also chatted informally with senior teachers about what they might do in their teaching to give students practice in fashioning and supporting arguments. Simply providing a senior tutor was a remarkable act of rewiring on the part of this school, given the ordinary reluctance of most high schools to fund teaching positions that do not absorb a specific teaching load; but hiring one who could also manage to connect outside tutoring with teaching and learning inside classrooms was a provocative act of rewiring. It forecast, however dimly, a future design for teaching and learning in this school that would not depend on isolated cells.

I was with the senior tutor one day while she visited a still functioning cell: the classroom of a veteran English teacher. She was in the habit of visiting this classroom once a week and functioning there as an assistant teacher. After each class, she and the teacher would discuss, by the light of the demands of the senior exhibition paper, the teaching and learning they had just observed while working together. This was a properly bounded discussion in the tutor's view, one based on mutual respect. She was acutely aware, she told me, that the exhibition paper was an imposition on this teacher's ordinary practice. In such circumstances, one had to negotiate change, not try to force it. "I don't want to be a link in that kind of system," she told me, meaning the coercive kind. She helped the teacher not as a ploy to gain his confidence, but as an obligation to support his efforts to collaborate with her. The point of their collaboration was to get the seniors they both taught to produce good exhibition papers.

As sheer performance this particular morning, the teacher's teaching was brilliant. He was entertaining, informative, clever in what he chose to focus on and in the links he made to other topics, and very engaged with the students. They laughed, and scribbled away, and punctuated his lecture with the one-word answers he asked for. By the light of the demands of the exhibition paper, however, the teacher's teaching was dreadful. He gave students absolutely no opportunity during this class to engage in elaborated discourse or to initiate their own ideas. Their only discourse opportunities involved responding to his cues with single-phrase responses. Yet in speaking with me later, he pronounced himself sick at the incapacity of his students to write complete, coherent statements or to make cohesive arguments. The new exhibition requirement had helped him to see this deficit, he explained. Just as important, it seemed to me, the requirement had also begun to cause him to reflect on his own deficits.

"Is it *my* problem?" he told me he asks himself. The question echoed not only against my image of his teaching, but against what I knew was a long history in this school of thinking about academic deficit as the students' problem. They do not work hard enough. They do not care. Their parents do not care. They are not cut out for learning such things. And so on. But in the conversation between this teacher and his teaching colleague, the senior tutor, I heard him reject this logic. No, it was neither the students' problem, he seemed to understand, nor his alone. It was instead their problem —a problem for a teaching and learning team, that of teacher and tutor and students. With the knowledge and cooperation of the students, and eventually their investment, he and the tutor could solve the problem slowly by planning together, talking together about the teaching and learning they observed, and making painful adjustments. He surely knew that the pain would be mostly his. He confessed to me, in fact, that as he approached what he called the assessment issue—that is, the issue of the real impact of his teaching on student learning—he became nervous enough to shake. He clearly had the real problem in focus. Although he could not at the time of my visit yet frame a coherent answer, any more than many of his students could then frame a coherent argument, he understood that the emerging answer somehow entailed his giving up a large part of his acknowledged strength as a teacher and a great source of personal satisfaction. The truth was that he liked having the attention on himself; he liked contributing most of the discourse. The truth too was that his students also liked these things. The adjustment would be painful for them as well.

Meanwhile, the senior tutor was clearly a crucial catalyst. No number of outside visitors like me, or outside consultants and in-service providers, could possibly have as powerful an impact on this teacher's teaching as she was having. That is not to say, however, that her power derived from her being an insider who just happened to have time to collaborate. As I talked with her and sensed her values, I learned that she was really an outsider working on the inside, one who was managing a delicate task: to be at once deeply empathetic with regard to the plight and the values of insiders in this school, and to be devoted also to changing both. She told me one day that she viewed the school as a family that has the same fight over and over, and only some days moves on. She was enough outsider to see the pattern, enough insider to recognize and cherish the days when the pattern failed to hold.

The senior tutor's salary was paid by outside dollars rather than district ones. At the time of my visit, with major district layoffs looming (recall the $8 million shortfall), the union was demanding that these dollars be diverted to fund regular teachers. Again, as in so many other instances across the schools we studied, a vitally important new bit of wiring, this position of senior tutor, had been introduced as shunt rather than integrated wiring. The definition of regular teaching as invariably carrying a load of particular classes full of students had remain unchallenged. Another vital kind of teaching—one crucial to genuine accountability—had been introduced, but allowed to be considered irregular. Then, as they inevitably do, the regularities asserted themselves. The position of senior tutor was very easy to cut in a crisis, and shortly after the conclusion of our study, it was.

Meanwhile, the state was then spending, and continues to spend, millions on its systemic initiative, apparently oblivious to the failure of its grasp to come anywhere near the ambition of its reach. Certainly the state was oblivious to the fact that Lakesha had a real chance to master persuasive writing in her school, and that the students who followed her have had less of a chance—the state's new assessment notwithstanding.

How might things have turned out otherwise here? Long before the crisis that cost the senior tutor her job—and the school a large measure of its accountability for the genuine achievement of students like Lakesha—the district ought to have negotiated a contract with the union that put learners first. I do not mean only learners like Lakesha, but also learners like her English teacher whose teaching I observed. When the senior tutor left, he was thrown back into solitary teaching, and a key source of his learning was shut off. The district should also have honored the accountability system the school installed rather than try to subvert it at every turn, or force it into disguise (The senior exhibition paper is not really a graduation requirement, the school was forced to tell the superintendent at one point. It is just part of the senior-year English course).

Meanwhile, the state should have constructed its systemic reform initiative so as to build local capacity for the negotiation of learner-centered labor contracts, and the design of school-based accountability systems. Then, instead of coming to Lakesha's school in order to assess her, it ought to have come in order to assess the school's attention to her and all her peers, and its willingness to be accountable for their learning. This would have required an investment in other things than mass performance assessment.

Tuning Together

Ultimately, the best tuning design for a twenty-first-century school system will reorient the map we use now in terms of where its top and bottom really are. Meanwhile, however, stuck with the old orientation, we must experiment with attempts to meet in the middle, between the top and the bottom. What we now call bottom-up school reform strategies—despite passionate leadership, compelling beliefs, and even the most innovative interior wiring—inevitably encounter ceilings. These are the policies that constrain a school's innovations, intrude on them, or effectively cancel them out. Similarly, what we now call top-down strategies—despite all rhetorical sympathy for the school's perspective, the best intentions, and the cleverest and most systemic designs—inevitably encounter floors. These are the limits imposed by commitment withheld.

It is exceedingly difficult to meet in the middle, between ceiling and floor. But I saw it happen at least once during the course of our research, in conjunction with a regional conference devoted to the use of a tool described in the next chapter: the Tuning Protocol. Several schools—networked as a result of their membership in the Coalition of Essential Schools—were gathered in a conference space donated for the day by a major corporation. They had spent most of the day presenting some of their students' work to each other, and tuning their standards by giving and receiving both warm and cool feedback on this work. Because all the schools were from the same state, they had a common interest in ensuring that their efforts to tune and raise standards were not blocked by the state's own initiatives in this regard. So they invited some representatives of the state to observe their conference, and to stay afterward for some discussion.

This context is important. One great problem that both schools and higher-ups face as they try to get past ceiling or floor is that long-standing inequities in the distribution of power take their psychological toll. When the state holds a conference and invites reform-minded schools to discuss reform, the burden of these inequities is obvious in the very context, and often subverts the undertaking. When the schools hold the conference instead, there is a great and beneficial psychological difference.

This state was not the same one that had tried to assess Lakesha with more authentic techniques, though it too was involved in the pilot phase of a systemic reform initiative. But its initiative was much more interesting. Instead of redesigning just tests themselves, it also intended to turn over much of the testing responsibility to schools. This was at least rhetorically its intention. The point of the meeting I happened to observe was to ensure that more than rhetoric was involved. Old habits die hard, and the particular habits of interest here are protected by a gap of experience and culture that is quite formidable.

Naturally the meeting was tense. The school people wanted to know why their waivers for the state's ordinary testing were always held up so long, indeed why they needed waivers anyway, given what the state was proclaiming as its policy direction. One superintendent declared flatly, "My district will no longer apply for waivers in these matters. We will take the state's statements at face value, and exercise the powers they give us."

For their part, the representatives of the state were conciliatory, though not condescending. They could hardly be condescending in the circumstances; they were being grilled, and by people who knew their stuff. These school people had read the relevant policies. Many had spoken directly with the state's commissioner of education. Some had testified at meetings of the state board. They were not naive dabblers in policy matters. The state people pleaded for patience, spoke about how hard it is to move a vast bureaucracy, pledged their ombudsmanship, and so on. They were doubtlessly affected by what they had observed in the conference that preceded this meeting. They had examined actual student work, had heard schools dare to offer each other criticism on the basis of these observations, had seen the standards issue up close rather than from the ordinarily remote perspective of state policymaking. It was as if they had had to give a test to Lakesha herself, and to coach her through it.

On the other hand, they were merely three people—indeed, small cogs in a vast apparatus of state supervision. Turning it into an apparatus that does its tuning in other ways is an immense undertaking. One of the people who grilled these three while I observed spoke privately of her frustration at the prospect of the number of such grillings necessary to form a genuine partnership in the middle:

> What I say to the state—because they really do care deeply about this—is that if it takes me all the energy that I have to expend to continue to move ahead on the kinds of assessment measures that we're doing, there's no other superintendent who'd be crazy enough to do it. Why would you? For example, I hand delivered this math variance to the state in September. I still haven't got a formal okay to do it.

Meanwhile, however, this same superintendent—head of a district whose schools participated in our study—continued to push teachers in her schools to act as if the state department of education really meant what it promised, as if it were not staffed nearly entirely by people who did not understand what it had promised, as if it really had the capacity to deliver on the promise. "Go for broke," she told them. Initially startled by the challenge, they responded powerfully in the end, creating a new accountability system for the district based on substitutions for nearly all the parts of the state's highly intrusive and detailed system. Slowly—certainly at a rate that infuriated the superintendent but failed to deter her—the waivers and variances arrived.

The state had drilled down through the floor with its rhetoric; this district drilled up through the ceiling with its assertiveness and inventiveness. In the end, they had both produced a small but valuable peephole on the educational policy needs of the twenty-first century.

Conclusion

The challenges of school design embedded in the three tales in this chapter inhere in the general problem of ensuring that the school stays responsive to all its stakeholders and that it avoids complacency and parochialism. The first tale highlights the most basic of the three challenges, one that turns up below the surface of the other two tales as well. This is the challenge of designing for both warm and cool perspectives. Warm perspectives are empathetic, informed by personal connection and personal history. They highlight the best qualities and most promising characteristics of whatever they reveal. They are crucial for even minimally successful schoolkeeping and learning because they enable schools, educators, and children to believe in the power of their best intentions and efforts. Cool perspectives are comparative, informed by standards rooted in other contexts. They highlight needs for development or improvement. They are crucial to the kind of schoolkeeping and learning advocated in this book because they enable both schools and learners to step outside the glow of their best intentions and efforts.

I suggest in the first tale that outsiders can play an important role in helping a school acquire a capacity for warm and cool reflection by making themselves available for consultations. However, insiders must arrange things so that such consultations are productive. Outsiders can at best be catalysts. Ultimately the tuner is the school itself rather than the outsider, who may supply merely a particular sound on a particular frequency.

This idea of tuning reverses the power emphasis of the supervisory model of schooling. In the supervisory model, the tuner is presumed to be the central planner, whose plans are typically sanctioned by various democratic bodies, like school boards and state bureaus. Supervisory agents try to ensure that the school carries out the plan, stays tuned to the correct frequency. As the second and third tales in this chapter suggest, the supervisory model is still both prevalent and powerful. Yet even in the most benign circumstances—for example, with a smart and reform-minded superintendent in charge, or a thoughtful state systemic reform under way—the supervisory model interferes with the development of reflective capacity in schools.

The second and third tales highlight an important condition of most American public schools at the end of the twentieth century: in crucial matters of schoolkeeping, they are not independent. They may not decide on their own what to teach and how. They may not set policies except within narrow constraints. They may not decide on their own reform agenda. They may not design their own accountability system. Their dependence with regard to these matters is a hallmark of democratic schooling as that is commonly defined. We have arranged the system to ensure that professional judgment remains subservient to the will of the larger community—insofar as this may be expressed by a school board or a state board. Similarly, we have arranged the system so that the inclinations of one school's faculty may not outweigh the interests of parents whose children attend more than one of the community's schools, and so that the inclinations of one community may not outweigh the interests of an entire state in the education of all its citizens. In theory, the American tradition of democratic schooling affords a voice to all stakeholders—including the state, the local community, parents, students themselves, and the professionals who teach them (Gutmann, 1987; Apple and Beane, 1995). In practice, however, as the tales suggest, such a broad inclusion of voices is very difficult to manage without compromising each party's vital interests.

By examining difficult questions about tuning through complex cases, I have tried to suggest problems with the status quo without imposing simplistic solutions to these problems. As with so many other matters discussed in this book, it will take time to evolve a better external governance system for schools. Yet I would like to draw two explicit lessons from the tales with regard to the direction for change. The first lesson is that schools need a greater degree of independence than most have now, and parents need a greater degree of choice. Both are crucial to ensure that there is the greatest possible chance that intelligent decisions will be made where they count most. It is a necessary but insufficient condition for intelligent decision making that it be located as close as possible to the children. The added condition that makes for sufficiency is a capacity at this same level for reflective conversation—one informed by outside stakeholders, and by cool as well as warm perspectives. The second lesson therefore is that the states and districts must invest in the development of such capacity in schools. That is, they must put their efforts and their money not into tuning schools but into helping schools to tune themselves. This means they must abandon the behaviorist assumption implicit in the strategy that victimized Lakesha: that a school can be made to align its teaching to a new assessment like so many iron filings to a magnet. Instead, they must figure out how to work on the actual problem. The next chapter presents some ideas in this regard.

Chapter Six

A Tuning Protocol

In my first year of teaching, I met my last class of the day during the tenth period. It started at about 3 P.M. and ended an hour later. The seventh graders I taught then were on the school's staggered schedule, one designed to ameliorate overcrowding. By 3 P.M., they had already had six other classes, a lunch that came too late, and no recess. They were unfit for sitting still. However, like most other beginning teachers, I had only a few teaching strategies in my repertoire, and most of them required students to sit still. It was obvious to me at the end of the first day of school that I had a problem. Adding to the problem, I thought, was the fact that the tenth period was about ten minutes longer than the other nine, a by-product of the bus schedule. I had to think fast.

While packing up my papers that first day, it occurred to me suddenly that I could never force these students to sit still and that I should not even try. The thought induced both panic and relief. Somehow, torn between these feelings, I managed to think about theater. I had done some work in theater—too little to have acquired much expertise, but then I did not have much expertise in anything else either. If I focused this class on theater, I realized that I could make a virtue of movement. In a tumbling nonsequence of fast thinking, I settled on theater for my curriculum and recognized simultaneously that the extra ten minutes was now slack rather than burden. I also noticed other available slack all around me, important since theater needs lots of slack. For example, the classroom next door was empty during the tenth period, as was the little conference room on the other side. This meant I could open a flimsy room divider to make my little room into a great big one and have a breakaway space as well. Since tenth period was the last one of the day, I would not face a next-period class tumbling into this big room each day, demanding a furniture arrangement consistent with its seating plan. My students and I could arrange the furniture any way we wanted, or we could push it aside if it suited us and take full advantage of the floor. And the floor was carpeted, a crucial detail.

Just as the perception of slack and the idea of what to do with it occurred to me simultaneously, the same thing happened to my students too. They streamed delightedly the next afternoon into the renovated space, and threw themselves onto the floor to play. In what was for me in these days a rare instance of good timing, I managed to capture their attention almost immediately with an announcement: "That's exactly what we're going to do this year: make plays."

Over the next weeks, through trial and error and in full collaboration, my class and I invented a protocol for making plays, one that we used nearly every day throughout the rest of the year. Although drama was officially only one-fourth of the seventh-grade curriculum, I made it four-fourths. I got away with the adjustment by using other kinds of literature as grist for the plays and by engaging the students in many kinds of writing focused on the plays: plans for the plays, reviews of the plays, stories of the plays' construction, stories to be turned into plays, reflections on playwriting, and so on. Mysteriously to me at the time, these students never tired of this work. In retrospect, I think it was because it was, indeed, always play for them as well as work, because they felt themselves growing in verbal facility and self-confidence as a result of what was essentially a year-long inquiry, and because the protocol that guided the play and the inquiry proved reassuring in an otherwise turbulent time in their lives. In the same way, supper with the family or a bedtime ritual may prove reassuring in an otherwise turbulent day.

At the heart of the protocol were the plays themselves, written and acted by the students and performed on special days regularly set aside for performance. Initially the plays were brief and constrained in their use of space and physical materials. As the year progressed, however, they became more elaborate, with levels of space introduced by clearing the surface of two teacher's desks and yoking them together to form a back or central platform. Initially, they were performed in a proscenium created by the partial restoration of the room divider, but later they were most often produced in the round, taking greater advantage of the space available. Costumes and props of various complexity were also introduced, and the conference room was soon turned into a dressing room, as well as private precurtain gathering spot for actors.

The students created the plays in an earlier part of the protocol that we called a play conference. Here, small groups of students wrestled with some raw material for playwriting: a given theme, a story they had read, an idea gleaned from some other medium like a song or a television show, and so on. I fashioned this material from ideas that bubbled up in class through conversation and reading, and I offered it to the small groups as a challenge in imitation of an ancient Greek playwriting competition. We called the full set of plays produced in response to a particular challenge a "cycle of plays."

One rule of the play conference was that the group had to play, not just talk. Typically, this meant that they moved about on the floor, improvising scenes. They almost never used their desks, which we ritually piled against one wall almost every day. There were other conference rules too, concerning participation, documentation, and other matters. Each conference, which typically lasted for days, ended with the assignment of preparation tasks: writing the official script, gathering costumes and props, preparing the director's notes. It was always followed by at least a day's rehearsal, and then the cycle's performances, one after another.

Another part of the protocol followed each performance, when the audience members (everybody but the actors and director of the particular performance, plus some occasional visitors to the class) were asked to react to what they had just witnessed. First, they were required to say what they admired about the play, and then they also had to say what they thought might have been improved. Today, I would call this "warm and cool feedback." The group's director (students took turns playing director) was designated to respond first to the audience's critique, though the performers usually had some things to say as well. We finished each cycle of performances and performance critiques with a class discussion about the cycle as a whole and what we had learned from it. This discussion was intended to serve as grist for a reflective essay, which closed the protocol.

My recollection of what I am calling here a *protocol* is doubtlessly much neater than the actual experience could have been, given the nature of seventh graders and beginning teachers. In this regard, some readers who are familiar with both may think *protocol* a pretentious word in such a context. But I like the word here for the same reason that I like it in the context in which I use it throughout this chapter: its two principal meanings reflect some deep dynamics of these contexts. First, there is the diplomatic meaning: the circumstances my seventh graders and I found ourselves in—they with their end-of-a-long-day restlessness, I with my inexperience—needed more lubricant than ordinary middle school civility can supply. Diplomatic protocol provides a way for people with different interests, even deeply antagonistic interests, to interact productively and respectfully while protecting those interests. A protocol in the diplomatic sense is a kind of treaty governing a particular realm of interactions. Importing this diplomatic usage into their world, contemporary computer scientists speak of protocols as sets of rules by which one computer manages to talk with another. Importing it into our analysis of the tuning arena of school design, my colleagues and I refer to mechanisms whereby different stakeholders of schooling can talk with each other despite their different operating systems. Without our protocol, my seventh-grade students and I would not have been able to talk with each other. In fact, we would have had to fight each other, though the way they pitched themselves happily onto the floor on our second day together, but also looked up at me for direction, showed that they did not want to fight me. I knew for sure that *I* did not want to fight them. It was just that the situation was inherently contentious. It is also inherently contentious whenever schools seriously solicit the viewpoints of interested outsiders. Tuning needs extra lubricant too.

Second, there is the scientific meaning: a protocol in science or social science is a plan for an inquiry. Our seventh-grade protocol was also a plan for an inquiry, and so is the protocol that I focus on in this chapter. The truth, as I acknowledge above, was that I did not know enough about anything in my first teaching days to teach my students through telling, even if telling were an effective pedagogical strategy. It was lucky for both of us that the circumstances early and quite obviously discouraged telling. So we structured the time and space to inquire into the drama through constructing it over and over, puzzling together over the constructions, and with the help of some outside resources, especially other authors' plays, making generalizations. The same strategy is required for tuning schools to the highest possible standards. No one on either the inside or the outside of schools can tell what these standards ought to be. They must be groped for steadily through a process of inquiry, one in which both inside and outside perspectives are crucial. Another way to say this is that they must be continuously negotiated.

Negotiation requires a lot: willing partners, status equality, and the right mixture of toughness and hope. It also requires diplomacy and inquiry. In Chapter Five I laid out what I take to be the key challenges of tuning: balancing warm and cool perspectives, balancing professional and lay interests, and balancing top-down and bottom-up power. Each involves negotiation. In this chapter, I describe a tool that aids negotiation, called the *tuning protocol.* My purpose is not to offer it as an answer to the problems I am posing in these two chapters. Indeed, it cannot supply answers at all, though it is a useful source of diplomacy and inquiry. Rather, my purpose is to stimulate readers' interest in finding and fashioning still other tools like this one.

The Tuning Protocol as a Work in Progress

It was my first visit to one of the schools we would study for the next three years, and I was lucky enough to have arranged it on the day of a special faculty meeting. The first difference I spotted between this faculty meeting and the kind I was used to is that this one required unusual preparation. During the morning, I was handed three student papers and a rating sheet, and was asked to make time during my day of interviews and classroom observations to read and rate the papers. The rating sheet, or rubric, described particular traits—for example, observation of writing conventions—at four specific rating levels. Referring to the matrix formed by the intersection of the traits and the levels, everyone in this school spoke of gridding papers. The papers I had been handed had all been previously gridded, but each faculty member was asked now to treat them as new papers. Since I would be an observer at this meeting, my hosts thought it made sense for me to do this too.

Three Features of the Meeting

Three features of the faculty meeting I observed that day my colleagues and I later borrowed for the tuning protocol. The first was that it was designed around actual student work, which is why those attending had to read and rate the papers. No one could participate or even sensibly observe without this preparation. Designing a faculty meeting around student work may seem as if it should be a logical occurrence given the mission of schools, but it is in fact a highly unconventional move for most schools. Most school faculty meetings, whether focused on policy, students, curriculum, standards, or anything else, typically proceed without benefit of the most obvious evidence: how actual student work reflects the issue under discussion. Do we need a new policy on spelling? Let us examine a random sample of student work to see what is going on in our school now with regard to spelling. Is a particular group of ninth graders headed for real trouble? Let us see what their work can tell us about them. The rarity of such logic in school is the product of several regularities of wiring, especially the tendency to define both the production and the judging of student work as private rather than public phenomena. To treat as public what is assumed to be private is to engage in a culturally wrenching act.

A second feature of the meeting that we later borrowed for the tuning protocol was the insulation it provided between rehearsal and actual performance. The student work that was the focus of the meeting's deliberations had already been rated. But the meeting's participants understood that this previous rating was neither under suspicion nor in dispute. In fact, some of the students whose work was discussed at this meeting had already graduated on the basis of this work, and no regrets in this regard were to be countenanced at the meeting. Indeed, the old ratings were not even available at the meeting for discussion, though some of those who had originally gridded the papers volunteered their old judgments as contributions to the discussion. Nor was the meeting aimed in the narrow sense at gaining better inter-rater reliability. That is, it was not a benchmarking exercise designed to elicit agreement among the raters of these papers such that the papers might inform judgments of other papers. Rather, the members of this faculty wished to gain the benefit of each other's diverse perspectives absent the pressure to agree. In effect, this session was designed to elicit and explore disagreement.

The third feature of the meeting that my research colleagues and I later borrowed for the tuning protocol was apparent to me only after I stepped into the room where the meeting was about to begin. Although I was asked to read and rate the papers, it was only so that my role as observer might be enhanced. At no time that day was I ever asked to share my ratings. I was an outsider at this faculty meeting, and the protocol of the meeting required that I keep my judgments about the papers to myself. Yet good protocol in the diplomatic sense does more than rely on tacit understanding. It reinforces tacit understanding through a manipulation of place. I understood, of course, that I was a visitor to this school and could not participate freely in one of its faculty meetings. Still, I might have been tempted to speak once or twice, prefacing my remarks by a deferential, "Now I am only an observer, but. . . ." That is why the facilitator of the meeting asked me not to sit in the chair I had originally chosen in the large circle of chairs she had arranged but rather in one of the chairs at the periphery of the room. The use of protocol sometimes clashes with the informal etiquette of school life, so this designation of place felt awkward to me at first. It felt awkward as well to a faculty member who entered just after me, and who, seeing me off in a corner, invited me up into one of the empty seats. Having gotten over my own awkwardness by then, however, I declined with a simple, "No, this is fine back here. I'm just observing." With no offense intended, the facilitator had merely wished me to have a continuous reminder (in the form of a place) to just observe.

Several years later, I was invited to participate in an entirely different kind of tuning event at this same school. This time, the express purpose was to hear outsiders' perspectives. As outsider, I was joined by several other researchers, principals, and teachers from other schools, as well as some district and state officials. We were asked to interview publicly two recent graduates, examine privately three full portfolios compiled by still other recent graduates, and then share our reactions frankly. This second meeting also had its protocol: except for two hosts, the faculty stayed at the periphery and spoke only to answer informational questions. Protocol in the first meeting guarded against the possible arrogance of outsiders, while protocol in the second meeting guarded against the possible defensiveness of insiders.

Meanwhile, in my place at the first meeting, I scribbled furiously to keep up with the pace of the conversation, since tape recording in this setting would have been indiscreet. The meeting got down to business in a straightforward ritual. The three papers were brought up in turn, and volunteers solicited to discuss their ratings. When people wished to speak, they raised their hands, and a monitor added their names to a speakers' list. The facilitator used this list to call on participants, but was also permitted to ignore it if she thought a productive colloquy had developed about a particular issue. Some speakers spoke only about the papers themselves, while others introduced information about the papers' authors. This was how the warm entered an otherwise cool environment.

One person recalled that the author of one paper read a draft of it to his advisory group, which found the issues compelling. "The effect was spectacular," she reported to the meeting, "and when that happened, I lost all objectivity on this paper."

"The kid worked so long on the paper," another teacher remembered, "two months at least. And it clearly meant a lot to him. That, as everybody in this room knows, would get him a passing grade anywhere else."

"But," another teacher countered, "I also think everyone in this room thinks this isn't a passable paper. By focusing on the process, we just describe our own dilemma of how to teach this kid to write."

"Then are you saying that we penalize the kid because the teachers haven't gotten it together? I say that this is a minimally passable paper, and that we could encourage the kid to defend it, as is, before the graduation committee, where he would also get to call on other strengths than writing."

"Besides," added another teacher, "I don't think telling Jorge now that this is no good would be a productive move. It wouldn't crush him, but it wouldn't help him either."

"But I think it helps a lot whenever we acknowledge to a kid how hard something really is. It's not a bad thing to learn that you aren't quite there yet because getting there is very hard."

Each of the three papers sparked a similar exchange of disagreement. The facilitator allowed for a full exploration of this disagreement but made no attempt to work it toward resolution. After all, the fate of these papers was not in doubt. This was merely practice judging, a safe arena in which to explore disagreement that might then be worked out over time by means of many negotiations. It also provided an excellent opportunity for learning the discourse of disagreement and for gaining what my colleague Pat Wasley and her research associates (1995) call the habit of "civil discourse," and which they regard as crucial to successful school reform.

Emerging from this meeting that afternoon, I wondered whether what I had just seen—a discussion of teaching and learning focused on student work, insulated from the ordinary wiring of the school, and marked by protocol—might serve accountability functions beyond the school itself. Although I had not yet adopted the term, I wondered about its general powers as a tuning tool. My wonder had been stimulated by something else I had learned that afternoon: this school had recently engaged in something like the same ritual, but with a group of outsiders. It had invited a group of local college professors, all instructors of freshman writing courses, to evaluate a small set of papers written by the school's students. The professors had been asked to read the papers ahead of time, to evaluate them using the same standards they would apply if the papers had been written by their own students, and then to gather in a circle to discuss the papers with each other. Using fishbowl protocol, the school's faculty simply watched the discussion. Later, they privately discussed with each other what they had learned from watching. The administrator who told me about this experience said that the school was also contemplating repeating it with other groups of outsiders. Much later, I was a member of such a group.

Meanwhile, in the months following this visit, my colleagues and I came slowly to understand accountability from a school perspective. Eventually we began to express this understanding by suggesting a third arena of school design, beyond the ones that we then called vision and restructuring, and to explore the challenges I described in Chapter Five. About two years after my visit recounted above, my colleagues and I felt ready to host a special seminar on tuning. With special assistance from IBM, we convened that seminar in May 1992.

Boston: The Protocol's Debut

We invited five of the ten schools we were studying to come together in a conference hotel in Boston in order to share and discuss examples of student work. We asked that they bring work generated by their exhibition systems and to use the work as the focus of a presentation of the features of the system. We asked them in their presentations to attend to what our research had inferred to be the dimensions of an exhibition: vision, prompt, coaching context, performance, standards, and reflection. We told the schools that we understood the difficulties of presenting their students' work to relative strangers and of capturing in such presentations the subtleties of circumstance that properly matter a great deal to teachers, but we asked them to put aside all of their concerns in this regard. Indeed, we asked them to provide only the minimally necessary information about the circumstances under which the student work was produced: the assignment itself and a brief summary of the instructional context. We told them that we were also inviting a number of interested people from IBM, and a small number of other researchers too. Finally, we told them that we planned to videotape the event.

We were well aware that what we were asking the schools to do was hard. Most teachers and principals are not used to talking about such matters as the vision of performance that prompted the design of their assessments, the standards they use in evaluating performance, or the mechanisms they employ to reflect on their assessment systems. Moreover, we had prepared what must have struck them as a very cool setting, one full of researchers and people from IBM. Most educators are used to presenting their students' work, if at all, only in warm settings, where the respondents know the students, know the school, and share the school's appreciative frame of reference. Or at least they are used to situations in which they are permitted to try to warm up the otherwise cool setting with a lot of explanatory preface.

Meanwhile, we had our own planning to do. We had to figure out a format for this seminar that ensured it would be indeed a seminar. Borrowing from the experience I mention above, as well as from others, my colleagues and I invented what we called for the first time a tuning protocol, a term that denoted a concern with both inquiry and diplomacy.

We thought of tuning itself as a kind of inquiry—that schools might best tune up their standards and tune into others' values by engaging in joint investigations of the qualities of actual student performance. We also presumed that the focus on exhibition design would spur inquiry. Indeed, it did, though not as we expected. In fact, I suspect now that our real intention in this regard was didactic. Luckily, the schools did not let us get away with that, as I explain below.

As a tool of diplomacy, we hoped that the protocol would make the seminar safe for honesty and risk taking, so we designed it to provide buffer between the presentations and the responses to the presentations. The presenters and critical friends (two from each of the nonpresenting schools, plus two others drawn from either the researchers or the people from IBM) would take turns: twenty-five minutes for the presentation, fifteen minutes for the response, and finally fifteen minutes of open conversation (see Figure 6.1). These turns, we decided, could not be interrupted by a comment or question from the other side. Respondents might well ask questions during their turn, but the presenters would have to delay their answers until their own turn came around again. The presenters shared a large conference table with the critical friends and a moderator. Everybody else was asked to observe silently from a ring of chairs at the room's periphery, to take notes on the process, and to share these notes as well as any other observations at the conclusion of the protocol.

We also planned five minutes of silent reflection between presentation and response. During this time, presenters and respondents were to use a form we provided to help them focus their thoughts on the dimensions of an exhibition, and sort their reac-

Figure 6.1. A Schedule for Tuning Protocols.

I. Teacher Presentation (25 mins.)
Participants briefly introduce themselves (name, school/organization). Teacher presents: *context information* (e.g., Exhibition vision, coaching, scoring rubric, etc.); *samples* of student work (e.g., photocopies of written work, video clips).

II. Pause to Reflect on Warm and Cool Feedback (5 mins.)
Participants may choose to write down feedback items they'd like to share.

III. Warm and Cool Feedback (15 mins.)
Participants share feedback; teacher-presenter is silent.

IV. Open Conversation (15 mins.)
Teacher-presenters respond to whatever comments/questions they choose. All may participate, but teacher-presenters begin conversation.

tions to the presentation into warm and cool categories (see Figure 6.2). During the response turn, we asked for balance between warm and cool comments but without blending. That is, we asked respondents not to follow the common pattern of starting off warm then turning cool. We wanted both warm and cool to have their place. Recall what I said above about the function of protocol in assigning place. We were mindful of Peter Elbow's (1986) quip that only Jesus and Socrates were able to be at once fiercely critical and immensely supportive; the rest of us have to practice alternating. As moderator, I would be allowed to participate in the response time also and would use this license to keep the balance, offering either a warm response or a cool one as needed.

Although we built in a lot of artifice, we were also wary of artificiality. We knew that both our school colleagues and our visitors from IBM and other research organizations would intuitively prefer a more informal format. I remembered how awkward I had initially felt with the protocol of the faculty meeting I described above. But we decided to ask all invitees to try our strict format through at least one round, trusting our hunch that it would

Figure 6.2. Tuning Standards.

May 18–19, 1992
Exhibitions Conference
Coalition of Essential Schools/IBM

During and after each presentation, you will be asked to write down your perspectives on each of the five dimensions of the exhibition system. You can decide whether to share these comments with the presenters; your thoughts here should help you organize some ideas for the reflection phase of the exercise.

School: ______________________________

Phases	*Reflections*	
	Warm (taken from a believing, supportive, appreciative perspective)	*Cool* (taken from a constructively critical, doubting, discerning perspective)
Vision		
Images of competence		
Orienting the exhibition		
Call for Exhibition		
The prompt or assignment		
Setting		
The support and coaching		
Logistics of time/space		
Samples		
Glimpses of student work		
Benchmark performances		
Standards		
Criteria for judging the exhibition		
Tuning mechanisms		

relieve rather than elevate anxiety. Privately, we also decided to soften all the edges of the protocol by means of generous moderation. As moderator, I would watch the time with my gut as well as my watch, forgive any presenters who had not prepared as expected or who failed to touch on one or another dimension, and in general relax all other rules as needed.

Now, after many runs of the tuning protocol in various versions and after observing both strict and generous moderating styles, I still prefer the generous side. However, I learned very early that one can also moderate too generously. Trying out the protocol for the first time among some of our Brown University colleagues, for example, we discovered that relaxing rules on the spot can create great anxiety. Although the presenter in this test run made only a mock presentation, she reported feeling grilled when I violated the rules at one point to allow critical friends to ask questions during the presentation.

This was a lesson I had to learn twice, however. When we did the real thing for the first time, one of the presenting schools brought some students to help in the presentation. During the response time, a responder posed a direct question of one of these students. "I'm going to allow a violation of our protocol here," I interjected quickly, "since we have two live students here, and I'm going to allow them to answer direct questions directly." I meant to be solicitous, but the gesture was condescending, and as one of the student's teachers quickly pointed out, unfair too. "Wait a minute," he said. "The students are expecting the same format as the rest of us. We reviewed the format with them, and they know how it works. They know that hard questions are going to be coming at them, but they want the same time to think about their answers that the rest of us get."

I apologized and went back to following the rules. Indeed, the teacher had clearly expressed one of the two reasons that everyone participating in this first protocol session opted after the first round to keep the no-interruptions rule (there had been grumblings at the beginning that it felt too artificial). The other reason was that it enabled the respondents to build up a well-modulated response—to get a lot of issues out on the table, and with sensitivity to the roundness of the whole package, particularly its balance of warm and cool. "This was great in terms of the flow of the criticism," one of the first-round respondents said. "We were able to get so many topics on the table, but if we let them answer any one of them along the way, we'd probably be off in Nebraska somewhere."

"Okay," relented an earlier proponent of allowing interruption so as to ease awkwardness, "but let's appoint a recorder for the questions so that they don't get lost." In fact, though we tried this suggestion in the next round, we discovered that losing some questions was not so bad. The presenters themselves recorded the questions, then as a group sifted through them to set priorities. In the process, they deliberately lost some that they regarded as less important, or that they needed more time to think about. Some in the latter category turned up again in the open conversation that closed each of the rounds.

These open conversations tended to be very rich, but I believe that this was so because of what had led up to them and because of the freedom lent by turn-taking without interruption to ask, think, and prioritize responses. Years later, a principal who uses an adaptation of the protocol in running some faculty meetings told me that although it feels at first like an utter violation of communication norms to take turns and avoid direct responses, it can end up making genuine communication possible in circumstances otherwise prone to either avoidance of communication or miscommunication.

The conversations at the session were also rich because we had some interesting questions to talk about. The main one, threading the day and a half of protocols, concerned the value of exhibitions in redesigning school. One of the first presenting schools challenged the givenness of this idea in our conference planning. In asking the schools to organize their presentation of student work around the dimensions of an exhibition system, I admit that we intended to instruct these schools in our theory. We thought that such instruction might help them make their exhibition systems stronger. We also knew that one of the presenting schools did not have an exhibition system, but we asked it to present as if it did—to shoehorn some elements of its own design into our design. Naturally, this was the school that took us on.

We asked all the schools to bring to the meeting both paper and video depictions of their exhibition systems, including a range of student performance samples. We got variable compliance on this. One school brought the timelines and guidelines for the senior exhibition plus a video sampler of exhibitions held just a week earlier, though with no range apparent within the sampler and no writing included. Another school brought a list of readings and questions for its upcoming senior seminar, as well as a video of a practice seminar, but again no writing. One school brought not only actual senior exhibition papers and the video of a paper defense, but also two seniors who had recently defended. And one school seemed to ignore our preparation instructions completely. It brought lots of video, none of it about what we took to be the school's budding exhibition system, and it also brought a question that it posed to the seminar: Do exhibition systems emphasize product over process and thereby misdirect teaching?

I recall being annoyed by the question. I had assumed that the main purpose of our seminar was to examine and discuss student work. The question seemed to me to invite digression. Still, I followed our plan of generous moderation and refrained from interference or disapproval. The result is that this question helped enable the schools to take ownership of a process that might otherwise have belonged to the researchers. The question not only dominated the round that followed its introduction but appeared in subsequent rounds as well. It turned out that at least three of the five schools were deeply interested in it. The question—or at least its substratum, the dilemma of whether to emphasize product or process—was at the time haunting the redesign of the school that introduced it. Meanwhile, two of the other schools had deliberately put the question aside in order to proceed with their redesigning. This is an important question, they had agreed tacitly, but we cannot let it stop us from finding out what our students can do. Now, however, in this reflective setting, they were interested in taking it up again, and interested in arguing it.

It is a valuable question because it encourages an examination of core beliefs. We who planned the debut of the tuning protocol planned a simple inquiry into the qualities of student work. But at least some of the participants understood intuitively that this is not enough for tuning. One must plan a more elaborate inquiry, one for which the simpler one is merely means. In short, one must be prepared to use the student work as an occasion for a sighting—in effect, to inquire into the values that underpin the production of the work. A good way to do this is to ask presenters to pose an important question that they hope to answer at least partly through the examination of student work. We did this inadvertently during the protocol's debut, by stepping aside as one of the schools insisted on making this change in the format we had planned. During the years of our subsequent experiments with the tuning protocol, however, my colleague David Allen, who has managed most of this experimentation, has insisted on building in the larger inquiry from the start. In planning their presentation, schools are now asked to pose an important question that they want help in answering and to orient their presentation of student work around this question. Of course, their critical friends take the opportunity to answer unasked questions too.

In Chapter Three I described the third-grade girl who managed her own digital portfolio, and I surmise there that she invested energy in this management because she wanted to, because she was interested in monitoring her own progress. She would never have done so, I claim, just because her school, district, or state was interested in monitoring her progress. It is the same for schools' tuning. If we outsiders want them to tune up, and to tune into the values of outsiders like us, then we have to offer some other reason than simply that we want it. We have to construct an opportunity for them to get some answers to their own most important questions.

A final point to note about the protocol's debut in Boston is that the participating schools, though all members of the Coalition of Essential Schools and of the Exhibitions Project, felt no particular obligation to hold each other accountable or even to provide each other continuing support. For one thing, they were all from different parts of the country. Only very recently has the Coalition begun to experiment with lateral accountability and support, and then typically within regions where schools share a common policy context, and are close enough to visit each other without incurring great expense (see Futures Committee, 1995). By lateral accountability, I mean an effort to reroute the ordinary structures of accountability in American education. Now, they run mostly up and down, a matter of regulation and compliance. Lateral accountability schemes introduce back-and-forth patterns—both across schools, and between schools and visiting stakeholders. In effect, we anticipated the emergence of lateral accountability in the Coalition of Essential Schools and elsewhere with our Boston invitation. Our previous investigations into the tuning arena had surfaced a dilemma that we meant to address at least theoretically in Boston, and that might be stated as follows:

> Schools cannot by themselves be accountable for teaching all students to use their minds well. They need help defining the objective and also understanding the actual impact of their work. This is not because they are recalcitrant or stupid. It is because the knowing that lies at the heart of genuine accountability cannot occur except through relation. Yet the mechanisms now available for providing help through relation—namely the mechanisms of hierarchical accountability—do not, in fact, provide it. These mechanisms are frequently clumsy, condescending, disempowering, and tangential. As such, they are often irrelevant to genuine accountability—that is, irrelevant to the actual work of ensuring that every child learns well and no child falls between the cracks of the system. On occasion, they seriously interfere with genuine accountability.

How else, then, to get the necessary relational help? We planned the Boston meeting with the thought that schools might help each other if they are given the right protocol, the right incentives, and just enough (though not too much) participation by other stakeholders (the university-based researchers and representatives of a major corporation).

Of course, the Boston meeting was an abstract exercise in this regard; we were merely researching the dynamics of a ritual. Later that year, however, our research encountered a policy opportunity. At the annual Fall Forum of the Coalition of Essential Schools, my colleagues and I held a second protocol session, involving two other schools we had been studying intensively, and we invited observers to this session. Two who accepted the invitation, Maggie Szabo and Steve Jubb of the California Center for School Restructuring, were then in the process of creating a network of schools whose mission was explicitly to combine support and accountability. Our tuning protocol appealed to them in the same way that the faculty meeting protocol I once observed had appealed to me.

To California and Back

The California Center for School Restructuring (CCSR) is a creature of California Senate Bill 1274, A Demonstration of Restructuring in Public Education, one systemic reform initiative in a state full of them. The original intent of this one was to furnish the existence proofs for the cumulative impact of all the others. What does it actually look like when a school understands and uses the perspectives of the California statewide curriculum frameworks; when it knows how to construct and use performance assessment; when its teachers manage to integrate what they have learned in the California Writing Projects and Math Projects, and so on; and when it takes seriously the state's exhortation to educate all its diverse children to high standards? The idea was to identify and support a number of lead schools of California school reform—approximately 150 of them located throughout the state—that they might leaven the efforts of all the other schools.

Szabo, Jubb, Joel Shawn, Meryl Vargo, and others entrusted with this legislative intent approached their work with several premises in mind. The first was that they were going to have to help nurture a large number of these lead schools, given the immensity of what the schools were being asked to demonstrate. The $25 million the legislature had appropriated would be helpful in this regard, though prior commitment and active engagement on the part of the funded schools would be even more important. The second premise was that the system of interest in systemic reform is at least as complex and dynamic within schools as it is without. Another way to say this is that schools are themselves systems, not just the nodes of one. Finally, the third premise was that the part of the system that lies within schools is at least as susceptible to the influence of peer networking as to hierarchical intervention. The American schools of the late twentieth century are so much alike not because of the massive implementation of a common design, but because of the cumulative impact of copycat designing up and down the system. In short, lateral influence is already considerable in American education. Why not, then, harness it for accountability?

Acting on all these premises, the leaders of the CCSR tried to fashion a network of schools dedicated to continuous internal inquiry and reflection—particularly, reflection by the light of the state's goals of educating all children to high standards. And they tried to endow this network with a capacity to engage in periodic lateral exchanges of insight and critique. It was in connection with the latter objective that our tuning protocol caught their eye.

The CCSR network of schools was born in early 1993 as a result of a series of regional conversations involving teams from schools selected for funding. These conversations led also to the adoption of the California protocol. Fashioned from bits of the Boston protocol as well as other inputs, the tool is intended, according to guidelines issued in November 1993, to help the CCSR network schools do four things:

1. Ensure that restructuring and change efforts continuously focus on the real, specific learning needs of students
2. Glean lessons to guide future action
3. Share what they have learned with the statewide community of restructuring schools
4. Make an accounting of their lessons for interested external stakeholders [California Center for School Restructuring, November 1993, p. 15]

Like a high mass sung in a cathedral, the California protocol is an elegant manifestation of a ritual intended to be pervasive and generally much simpler. Like the high mass also, it is meant to inspire lower efforts—that is, to be picked up and modified for local and even internal use. The CCSR network was to be founded on inquiry. Its assumption was that if the money it had been entrusted was to be well spent, if the connections across schools it encouraged were to be productive, if the overall goals of the project were to be met, then every participating school would have to become practiced in reflecting on its own operations and in taking action on the basis of these reflections. Moreover, these reflections would have to be principled, disciplined, and honest. The principles would have to involve a commitment to provide a powerfully intellectual education for all the children the schools served, and a commitment to disaggregate all achievement data so as to understand any variability by race, ethnicity, class, or gender. The discipline would have to involve an orientation to explicit student outcomes—consistent with the California curriculum frameworks, but also emerging from the schools' own beliefs about their duty to children, and it would have to involve a willingness to look for evidence of these outcomes in actual student work. Finally, the honesty would have to involve efforts to submit this evidence to hard scrutiny and to solicit and respond to both warm and cool feedback.

The problem facing the designers of the network was that capacity for this kind of reflection is exceedingly rare in schools, even in ambitious restructuring schools. That is because it depends on wiring that is typically not present: time for teachers to meet with each other, a habit of examining student work together, rituals for doing so, and so on. Thus CCSR had to encourage massive rewiring. But how? It could not, for example, simply require such rewiring in exchange for funding. Principled, disciplined, and honest reflective capacity cannot be commanded by state agencies no matter how well intentioned or well funded. One has to learn to distinguish between certain kinds of school reform objectives in this regard. Some—the ones akin to orderliness while waiting at the delicatessen counter or boarding the airplane—are susceptible to compliance mandates; others—akin to playing the violin beautifully in an orchestra—are not. So, what then can a state do? One answer, and the one that CCSR chose, is to work on beliefs: to create a ritual that crystallizes the beliefs desired, to train schools in the ritual, and to hope that the new religion might trickle down in a way that mandates never can. This was the purpose of the California protocol.

I first saw it performed at a gathering of all 148 CCSR-funded schools at Anaheim's Disneyland Hotel in May 1994. Like many of the other attendees, I could not resist the symbolic qualities of the setting. Would we see Tomorrowland or Fantasyland? Although the protocol was the centerpiece of the three-day gathering, with each school partnered with one other school for a three-hour "protocol analysis," there were other rituals in evidence here too. For example, there were a number of inquiry sessions, each framed to address one of the conference's overall questions from a specific perspective: (1) How do restructuring schools meet the learning needs of all students, and (2) How do we become more thoughtful, powerful, and reflective learning communities? There was also the craft fair, in which representatives from these demonstration schools demonstrated their innovations for each other through posters, videos, exhibits of student work, and conversation. Finally, there were core seminars in which teams from three different schools wrestled together with themes provided by several keynote addresses. Two of the keynoters played with what they worried might be faulty assumptions lurking within the name of the new network: the California Center for Restructuring Schools. Michael Fullan warned that there is a difference between restructuring and re-culturing, and that the sequence of going from re-culturing to restructuring may be easier than the other way around. Carlos Cortes also urged the schools to take on cultural work. Otherwise, he claimed, all their restructuring would come to nothing. They must build school cultures that value the uniqueness of each child, he said, that help those functioning outside mainstream culture to get into it, that empower all students multiculturally, and that help them develop intergroup bonding.

I place the protocol sessions I observed within the larger context of this conference in order to suggest that lateral accountability is highly dependent on a context infused with belief. There seems to me little point in having schools share their perspectives on actual student work if they do not also share some attitudes with regard to the purpose of schooling and the nature of children and children's development. This was true of the schools we gathered together in Boston, and of the schools in the Bronx whose protocol session I describe below. By means of their choice of schools, their design of this conference, and the emphases of their protocol design, the leaders of CCSR hoped to make it true of the schools in their network too. This was harder for them, however, than for us in Boston or for the schools in the Bronx. That is because the CCSR schools were not previously members of the same belief-based network, because California is so vast and diverse and their schools came from every corner of it, because the network was founded by the state, and because some number of schools might have joined it largely for the money. Still, I found much more Tomorrowland than Fantasyland in Anaheim.

The California protocol was designed to summarize what a school community has learned from more in-depth examinations of student work among a broad number of people at the school site (CCSR, 1993, p. 3). This design makes it, in some sense, a metaprotocol. That is, the inquiry on the spot points backward toward earlier inquiry. Four presenters, having previously prepared a preview of two to five pages read by four reflectors (the other presenting team), open the protocol with a three-minute oral introduction (see Figure 6.3). In this introduction, they identify the student outcomes that undergird their restructuring efforts and provide any contextual information necessary to understand these efforts. They may refer as well to the critical questions they listed in their preview—ones their "school community had identified *recently as a result of examining student work*" (CCSR, November 1993, p. 4, emphasis in original). These are questions they especially wish the reflectors to address. Next, the reflectors have an opportunity to ask clarifying questions, which the presenters may answer briefly (five minutes). Then begins the team's analysis (thirty minutes). Here they share a set of student work previously examined within their school community, consider the work by the light of the school's standards, and discuss the ways in which the work does or does not reflect the qualities of work that all students in the school are in the habit of producing. In meta-analytical fashion, the team is also asked here to say how typical an analysis this is, how many members of their school community typically participate, and how such analysis contributes to the school's ongoing restructuring.

All this is, of course, a lot for thirty minutes. In the four presentations I observed, the student work itself got less airtime as a result. In other words, the analysis tended to overwhelm the evidence. Of course, the time crunch was likely not the only reason for this. The direct examination of student work is a countercultural act for most schools and easily avoided under any pretense. Still, all the teams I observed did present student work, sometimes in more than one dimension—for example, physical artifacts of project work, writing, and videotape of oral performances. The quality of the analysis of this work depended, in my view, on the quality of the critical questions the teams posed. One team asked about variations in learning outcomes across the different instructional units or families into which the school was divided. This is a tough and important question, and it has great meta-analytical appeal. That is, the school could answer it in thirty minutes only by referring to and providing evidence of more in-depth inquiry back home. By contrast, another school spent its thirty minutes on what seemed to me a self-congratulatory analysis of how it had confronted student apathy.

The analysis section of the California protocol is followed by another five minutes of clarifying questions from the reflectors and brief responses to these questions. Then the reflectors take the floor. In contrast to the Boston protocol, however, they do not aim

Figure 6.3. Time Format for the California Protocol.

Welcome

5 min. Moderator welcomes participants and reviews the purpose, roles and guidelines for the Protocol.

Analysis

3 min. Team A provides an Introduction, perhaps referring to one or two highlights of the written Preview.

5 min. Team B and other reflectors ask brief questions for clarification. Team A responds succinctly with clarifying information about the preview and introduction.

30 min. Team A gives its analysis to Team B and other Reflectors following the content expectations for Team Members.

5 min. Team B and other Reflectors ask brief questions for clarification. Team A responds succinctly with clarifying information about the analysis.

Feedback

15 min. Team B and other Reflectors respond to Team A's analysis with warm, cool, and hard perspectives in order to help the members of Team A reflect on their work. Team A listens and does not respond.

Reflection

2 min. Team A members individually reflect, perhaps using a journal, on the perspectives captured during the last 15 minutes. Moderator reinforces the need for quiet time.

10 min. Team A members engage in reflection, planning, discussion *with one another* (rather than in direct response to the Reflectors). This is a time for everyone else in the room to be privy to a discussion among members of Team A in which they reveal how they reflect, think, plan, adjust.

Break and Repeat for Team B

15 min. BREAK; Team B sets up.

70 min. The process is repeated for Team B's analysis, feedback, and reflection.

Discussion and Debriefing

15 min. Moderator facilitates a discussion among Observers about what was learned from listening. The purpose of the Protocol is to get an honest look at the school's work, so the criteria serve to elicit constructive comments from a common frame.

15 min. Moderator facilitates an open discussion and debriefing of the experience among all participants.

TOTAL TIME: 190 minutes = 3 hours & 10 minutes (including break) their warm, cool, and hard feedback (defined in the guidelines as concerned with issues of standards, validity, reliability, and equity) directly at the presenters. Instead, they form a fishbowl with the presenters looking in, and they discuss among themselves what they have just seen and heard. I found the format awkward, though I reminded myself that protocol always feels awkward, and that, indeed, this is exactly the point: to use awkwardness to remind one of one's place.

Following the feedback, the presenters also form a fishbowl, this time with the reflectors looking in, and here they discuss among themselves what they have just heard, following two minutes of silent reflection. This segment provided the most extraordinary moments in all four of the protocol sessions I observed. Here the awkwardness of the indirect discourse proved especially helpful in generating meta-analysis. That is, the presenters used some of the reflectors' comments to identify fault lines in their ongoing analyses back home, giving the observers present a rare opportunity to peer into the complexities of a school without actually visiting it. For example, one parent member of a presenting team, prompted by a reflector's comment and supported in her view by a teacher member of the team, dared to open up what was clearly a chronic back-home dispute. The school's heavy emphasis on research projects, she said, diverts her daughter from the "creative" pursuits in which she takes greater interest. For the next several minutes, the team enacted in this public arena an ongoing argument of considerable importance, one that neither this nor any school can settle without benefit of good tuning from outside stakeholders. What does a school do when the values of rigor and creativity seem in conflict? How much should it press children beyond their interests, and how much should it encourage them to pursue those interests in depth? Indeed, the tuning agents in this particular protocol session—the reflectors, and also the observers whose comments close out the ritual—had much advice to offer with respect to these questions. Much later in the day, I passed a team member from this school who told me that the team and a good number of observers had retired to a suite following their morning session, and had discussed this issue for hours more.

In a report to the member schools following the Anaheim conference, the CCSR leaders acknowledged unevenness in the quality of the protocols performed there and in their level of meta-analysis. But they were heartened, they said, by the evidence they found both in Anaheim and in their visits to schools that the protocol, and many variations of it, were finding a place in the ordinary conduct of school business. As I might have put it, the protocol was beginning to work its way into the wiring.

At the same time, it was beginning to work its way back east too. A few months after Anaheim, the Coalition of Essential Schools, which had shown little interest in it before, made the tuning protocol—with some California rules mixed in among the Boston rules—the centerpiece of its 1994 Fall Forum preconference gathering. Since many of the Coalition's lead schools participate in this annual preconference, the protocol thereby infected the whole network. Before long it was turning up everywhere, including the Bronx. That is the way things go in America: nothing gets passed along in the culture that has not first passed muster in California.

In the Bronx

Just before Christmas in 1994, Ambassador Walter Annenberg announced the largest philanthropic initiative in the history of public education. With a half billion dollars of his personal fortune, he pledged to match other philanthropy aimed at ensuring the survival of the American public school system. He hoped especially to benefit children going to school in the nation's largest cities.

The first city to respond to his challenge was New York. There a remarkable consensus developed around a radical policy scheme. It involves opening new small schools (up to five hundred students), many of them carved out of the resources now devoted to large failing schools. These new schools are to join together in small networks (four or five schools per network), with each of the networks under the initial tutelage of one of four ideologically diverse school reform groups.[1] The plan is as follows: The reform

1. The reform groups are the Center for Collaborative Education, an affiliate of the Coalition of Essential Schools; the Center for Educational Innovation, an offshoot of the Manhattan Institute, a conservative think tank; the New Visions Project of the Fund for Public Education; and ACORN, a grassroots community organization.

groups launch the schools and support them at the city level with ideas, political clout, and an effort to match the Annenberg dollars, but the schools support each other at the network level to ensure high qualities of teaching and learning. Moreover, they are expected to hold each other accountable for results. Regular, external audits of the networks undertaken by the district and state will seek to ensure the genuineness of this accountability.

It is intended that the schools in these networks will eventually enroll up to 5 percent of the total school population of New York City—a representative 5 percent in terms of ethnic and class diversity. In the massiveness of New York, percentages can be deceiving, however: this mere 5 percent is nearly the equivalent of the public school enrollment in Boston, and somewhat more than that of Seattle. Thus the scale of this new school design is remarkable, as is the fact that it is sponsored by groups with distinct if different ideological profiles, a major departure from the twentieth-century habit of nonideological public school design. Another noteworthy aspect of the initiative is that the participating schools are to be granted a significant degree of autonomy with respect to district regulation, in exchange for their demonstration of accountability. As the recent history of school-based management initiatives suggests, such grants of autonomy are often more sweeping in the promise than in the reality. Nonetheless, the planners are hopeful. As one planner, Deborah Meier, reported in a memo to her colleagues, this plan "puts the shoe on the other foot. It doesn't start off by asking what waivers we want. It places all power and funding in the hands of the schools and their networks, and then takes it away as some public interest requires." In the process, the policy orientation of the initiative splits the difference between neoconservative and neoliberal school reform strategies, as Meier further explains:

> It's an act of enormous chutzpah, and requires the greatest sense of self-responsibility. We're betting that we can invent a better system of schooling than those who would abandon the public enterprise entirely for one or another form of privatization. We're also betting we can do better than those who would tinker with the existing system in the hopes that with greater decentralization of management along with a tightening of top-down curriculum and improved forms of bureaucratic accountability mechanisms, they can preserve the familiar system of public schooling.

So, this is not just a matter of dumping the suits and of holding the individual school responsible for the achievement of its students through a market mechanism, as in charter school schemes. Nor is it a matter of holding the individual school responsible in the ordinary hierarchical sense for outcomes, while allowing wide latitude for means, as in most other contemporary systemic reform initiatives. It is about creating a very different kind of policy system, one where sideways glances bear the burden that hierarchical supervision is supposed to bear in the current one, or that the market is supposed to bear in privatization schemes.

Yet how can one recondition even 5 percent of a system such that actual lateral accountability replaces spurious hierarchical accountability? How can one prevent both the best and the worst teachers from burrowing for cover, screening out interference, and hoarding slack? How can one ensure that the bureaucrats and the politicians butt out but still keep sufficient resources flowing? How can one ensure that the city, state, and union—all supportive of the original plan—stay supportive through successive changes in leadership? Where are the schools going to find the time for networking? How can they be persuaded not only to struggle to know themselves, but to share that knowledge with outsiders? How can the professionals who work in these schools come to think of professionalism as engaged public performance rather than private practice? What can persuade them to exhibit actual student work and so risk the questions, "You think this is good? This is as good as your students can do?"

As Meier wrote, taking on such questions as these is "an act of enormous chutzpah, and requires the greatest sense of self-responsibility." True to the enormity in both respects, the work will take some time to develop. And like most other reform enterprises, it is unlikely to develop exactly as planned. In any case, one feature of development will be the invention of tuning tools. Meanwhile, at least one network of schools in the Bronx, has experimented with one we invented.

In early June 1995, Paul Allison, of University Heights High School, organized a two-day conference for his school and the other high schools in its network, and he planned it around tuning protocol sessions. Allison knew the protocol well because his school had earlier adapted it as a mechanism for the evaluation of

Figure 6.4. Schedule for Tuning Protocols.

I.	Introduction Facilitator briefly introduces protocol goals, norms, and agenda Participants briefly introduce themselves (name, school)	10 mins.
II.	Teacher Presentation Context for student work (describing assignment, scoring rubric, etc.) Focusing question for feedback *Participants are silent*	20 mins.
III.	Clarifying Questions (Facilitator will judge which questions more properly belong in warm/cool feedback)	5 mins. max.
IV.	Examination of Student Work Samples Samples of student work (these might be original or photocopied pieces of written work and/or video clips)	15 mins.
V.	Pause to reflect on warm and cool feedback	2–3 mins. max.
VI.	Warm and Cool Feedback Participants share feedback while *teacher-presenter is silent* Facilitator may try to give some focus by reminding participants of an area of emphasis supplied by teacher-presenter	15 mins.
VII.	Reflection Teacher-presenter speaks to those comments/questions he or she chooses to, *while participants are silent* Facilitator may intervene to give response focus, clarify, etc.	15 mins.
VIII.	Debrief Open discussion of the tuning protocol	10 mins.

seniors' graduation portfolios, and even as a mechanism of teachers' peer review.

For this conference, Allison and David Allen of the Annenberg Institute devised a Bronx protocol that borrowed features from both its Boston and California cousins (see Figure 6.4). Participants included teachers and administrators from four Bronx schools, parents, students, and outsiders recruited from several community-based educational agencies—for example, the Literacy Institute at Lehman College, the Center for Children and Technology, and the

Educational Video Center. As in California, the protocol sessions were embedded in other activities too: structured conversations, get-acquainted activities, and so on. This was both a working session and a ceremonial one, with both aspects focused on forging a real network. It clearly had another purpose too, one similar to California's meta-analytical purpose: it was designed to foster leadership in the schools. The responsibilities of the presenters were presumed to extend well beyond their presentations. They had been empowered to lead their schools' effort to define an inquiry on which to hang the presentation, to collect student work and other materials relevant to that inquiry, and later to lead postprotocol reflection back in school.

Such deliberate cultivation of leadership opportunities seems crucial to the lateral accountability hopes of the New York networks. After all, schools cannot network; only the people who work in them can. If network connections remain only at the level of the schools' formal leadership, there is likely to be no lateral accountability in the end. There are two reasons for this. The first is the most obvious one: genuine accountability is felt and exercised by teachers and, in time, by their students who assume responsibility for their own learning. The principal who tries to teacher-proof accountability—say, by mandating test-based drills—may boost test scores, but the scores will be puffery. They will not reflect an actual boost in learning. The second reason is more subtle. Genuinely lateral accountability involves a two-way dynamic. It is partly about bringing peer and other outside perspectives to bear in order to press teachers to ensure that their students are learning the right things and as deeply as possible. But it is equally about bringing knowledge of the complexities and uncertainties inherent in the craft of teaching to bear on questions of learning. I call this raising a teacher's voice in policy matters (McDonald, 1992c). One reason that hierarchical accountability systems usually fail is that they leave too little room for the consideration of teachers' intimate knowledge of teaching. Indeed, most hierarchical accountability systems seem to dismiss this crucial knowledge, regarding it as ignorance or resistance. By contrast, a smart tuning system leaves room for it and engages it in dialogue. Another way to say this is that a smart tuning system honors *being there*—the experience and the feelings that only true insiders can acquire—even while pressing these insiders to bring their intuitions to the surface so as to examine them critically.

There was an excellent illustration of the two-way dynamic of lateral accountability in one of the Bronx protocol sessions. One teacher, who presented student portfolios, posed the following question for the respondents to consider: What do these portfolios reveal about how language is used and taught in the school? True to the spirit of the protocol, his question generated both warm and cool feedback. One of the cool comments clearly moved the presenter to rethink an important aspect of the school's practice and to pledge his leadership in ensuring consideration by his colleagues. Then, a second cool comment, illustrating the other half of lateral accountability's two-way dynamic, enabled him to help the outsider who made it rethink how teaching and learning really work.

In his presentation, the teacher had described the language background of his students as one-third Spanish speaking, one-third English speaking, and one-third bilingual; and he had stated that an important goal of his school is to graduate students who are capable of using language powerfully, who are articulate, and who can sway people. The first cool comment referred to this goal, and came in the form of a gentle admonition to remember that language has an expressive as well as a pragmatic function. In his response time, the presenter said that this admonition made a great deal of sense and that he and his colleagues back at school would need to consider its implications. He mentioned it again later at the end of the conference, when he said that the comment had awakened an important issue for him, focusing on how much his school's goals for its students must involve their capacity to use language to reflect as well as to interact successfully and to overcome oppression.

The second cool comment referred to feedback on student work. A respondent said that he noticed in the portfolios presented that the students did not typically take much account of teachers' extensive comments on first drafts. "Sometimes there were no changes," he said, "except the handwriting was neater the next time. It made me wonder about follow-up. How much attention are the teachers really giving to revision? Are they really insisting on it?" In his response time, the teacher took up this point too, speaking in a voice devoid of either defensiveness or resignation, but a teacher's voice, one seeped in the knowledge of *being there*:

> This observation about the drafts. Part of what you had to say was stuff that I thought about, and part of it was new. You know, it was a war sometimes. Because we would get pieces of student work, particularly work on their final exhibitions, and we would mark it up—we might say that certain observations were unsupported, or unconnected to others. We'd ask questions about things that just seemed thrown in, like Where is this coming from? Where's your evidence? Things like that. And of course, spelling and grammatical corrections that we wanted. And, just as one of you said, the work would then come back and it would have no changes, except that the grammatical and spelling errors were corrected. I can think of students that I really went nuts with, saying, "Well, what about this?" And they'd just absolutely refuse to engage with these questions. One student, whose work was presented here, I was just noodging her for weeks about this stuff, and she was just getting angrier and angrier. And she just finally took her work from me and took it to another teacher, José. Of course, she gave him a brand new computer printout that didn't have any of my comments on it. José made the same observations, and asked the same questions that I had. Then, she just threw up her hands and said, "Okay, I'm going to go home and think about this," and in that case, she did eventually do real revision. But other kids never did, never did.

Often, for want of intimate contact with school life, outsiders assume that the connection between teaching and learning is less complex and less mysterious than it is in fact. As in this case, they may take evidence of a learning gap as evidence also of a teaching shortfall. Sometimes they are right. Sometimes, as in this case, they are wrong. But whether right or wrong, their perspective is limited and properly regarded as valuable, even crucial, input rather than definitive judgment. Because they know how limited an outsider's perspective really is, teachers often find it very hard to attend thoughtfully to what it may reveal. "If only you knew a tenth of what I know," the teacher may think, "you would not presume what you do." But, faulty presumptions aside, what the outsider notices is precious because it is often noticeable only from the outside. What the protocol offers at its best is an opportunity for the teacher to gain the benefit of this precious noticing without having to give it undue weight. I mentioned above that the presenting Bronx teacher was neither defensive nor resigned in his answer to his critical friend's cool comment. I believe that this was because he was not forced to answer it quickly or directly or deferentially, and because the protocol implicitly afforded his own perspective—what he had been able to notice on the inside—equal attention and respect. The consequence is that he seemed really to listen to what the respondent said and to ponder its implications. This is what I mean by saying he answered in an unresigned way, as if he regarded the problem they were both noticing as not dismissable and ultimately resolvable. For her part, she seemed to listen intently to his rejoinder, and she may have learned in the process as much as he. In general, this has been our experience with tuning protocols: that both parties to the process walk away richer in insight.

Other Tuning Tools

The tuning protocol was only one of several tuning tools we fashioned during the Exhibitions Project, all of them predicated on external perspectives as spurs for reflection and knowledge in action. Two of these tuning tools are still under development at the Annenberg Institute today under the direction of David Allen, with the additional support of the IBM Corporation and the State of New York. I close this chapter with brief accounts of that development as a way to signify my sense that the tuning arena of school design, perhaps more than the other two arenas at present, is especially ripe for invention.

These other tools seek to keep tuning energies focused on student work, and they create texts whereby one can read this work in the context of a school's goals, teaching efforts, and reflection. But they lie at very different points along a continuum, defined on one end by virtual contact with outsiders and on the other end by actual contact. This is a deliberate distribution. Those of us involved in thinking through the development of these tools felt that for various reasons—including, on the one hand, the indispensability but expense and disruption of the most intense tuning experiences, and, on the other hand, the need for schools to consider the viewpoints and practices of very remote others—that we should design along the entire continuum. The tuning protocol is in the middle of this continuum: the presenters face their critical friends across an actual table, but the table may be in a conference hall far from school, or, if in a school, may represent a pause in the school's ordinary conduct of business. In this setting, the images of teaching and learning around which tuning proceeds constitute a text that has been removed from the ordinary entanglements of context and bracketed for close attention. Within the brackets, one may be better able to read and discuss it, though at a cost. In bracketing it, one may also distort it, for example by considering it more representative than it actually is.

An Assessment Collection

On the virtual side of the continuum is a tool we call the New York Assessment Collection. It uses hypermedia to facilitate tuning from a distance. Like the California and Bronx protocols, its purpose is to encourage lateral accountability as well as build capacity for reform, though the relationships involved are less formal and sometimes one-sided. A middle school in Rochester, New York, may have an important impact on a middle school in Hicksville or Yonkers, but without knowing that it has had that impact and without feeling any impact in return.

The prototype version of the New York Assessment Collection, developed by David Allen, presents case studies of exemplary local assessment design in New York, each in a hypermedia format defined by the dimensions of an exhibition discussed in Chapter One: vision, prompt, evaluation, student work, coaching context, and reflection. So, the Frederick Douglass Middle School in Rochester not only presents the prompts and coaching context for its elaborate assessment involving the construction of scale model bridges, but also explains how this assessment fits into its overall goals for student development, and the standards it uses to evaluate the results. Moreover, it presents results for the distant reader to examine and with benchmarks attached. That is, the school dares to say publicly exactly how it evaluated particular pieces of student work and why it thinks the evaluation is appropriate. Finally, it reflects on the design by means of teachers' and students' comments on its strengths and weaknesses. But the reader need not read through all of this detail. By flicking the mouse on his or her computer, the reader can jump easily from one dimension to another, or from the Frederick Douglass school case to the Jefferson school case, Jefferson being another Rochester middle school.

Users access the collection by means of a CD-ROM available at cost from the Annenberg Institute, or by downloading a version of it from a World Wide Web page. The plan is that users will also be able to engage in an asynchronous conversation on the Web with the teachers who developed the assessments and with other users. There they may offer warm and cool feedback, discuss possible adaptations, or talk about any other matters that seem appropriate.

A School Portfolio

Of course, being in an electronic chat room with teachers or students from the Frederick Douglass Middle School is hardly the same thing as meeting them face to face in a tuning protocol, or—on the other end of the continuum of intensity in tuning—meeting them in their own school, and in the presence of their own daily work. The state of Illinois is currently experimenting with a method that provides this most intense level of tuning opportunity. It is called School Quality Review, and is modeled loosely on the school visitation practices of the HMI, the band of Her Majesty's Inspectors of schools that has been visiting schools in England for over 150 years (Wilson, 1995). A former HMI, David Green, was a consultant to New York State in the design of its School Quality Review process, and is now consulting with Illinois. As a visiting fellow at the Annenberg Institute, he also worked with my colleagues Michelle Riconscente and David Allen, as well as with Jan Hawkins of the Education Development Center, to imagine an electronic tool to be used in conjunction with the process—or, indeed, with any other serious effort to know a school from an intimate perspective, and to account for its qualities with images of its teaching and learning. They call the tool that they imagined, and are now busy developing, the Digital School Portfolio.

To understand how it works, one must know something about the School Quality Review process. Lynn Olsen, a reporter for *Edu-*

cation Week, participated in a review of a New York City elementary school in early 1994, and wrote a day-by-day account of the adventure. The account begins Sunday night, far from the school in a midtown Manhattan hotel, where the principal of the school offers the reviewers a two-and-a-half-hour explanation with wall charts of what her school is all about. Following this opening, Olsen pauses the narrative to preview the story to come:

> Over the next five days, the state's "school quality review team," of which I am a part, will camp out in [this principal's] school. We will visit classes; interview students, parents, faculty members, and community representatives; and attend schoolwide meetings and activities in an effort to understand the school's mission and how it is being met. Our goal is to act as "critical friends," holding up a mirror to the school that will reflect the quality of teaching and learning in the building. In the end, we will produce an oral and written report that the school can use as it sees fit. The report will remain confidential. But the expectation is that it will encourage a culture of self-examination in the school that will continue long after we depart [Olsen, 1994, p. 21].

Olsen is one of her team's partnership reviewers, that is, someone who is neither an educator nor a staff member from the state education department. Each team has at least two such reviewers. The majority of any review team's members, however, are teachers—an emphasis intended to bolster the review's attention to teaching and learning. The team reviews teaching and learning through two sets of lenses. One highlights particular dimensions of teaching and learning: how they are organized, the breadth of repertoire they reveal, their relation to a curricular entitlement, the influence on them of a professional culture in the school, and several others. The second set of lenses highlights particular contextual factors: availability of financial and other resources, impact of socioeconomic factors, influence of policy actions, and evidence of community partnerships and collaboration. The lenses do not constitute a checklist of standards. The accountability they are meant to induce is not particular in that way. As Olsen puts it, "After years of exhorting, regulating, and monitoring public schools," the School Quality Review represents "a different approach: What happens if schools are encouraged to engage in a process of self-reflection and continuous improvement, with the support of outside observers?" (p. 21). As one principal who had been through a review told Olsen, "No one was criticizing. They were saying, 'This is what you are doing. Is this what you want?'" (p. 27).

Such questions are unremitting, however, which makes them more powerful than they may seem. That is, the School Quality Review process, as designed, is not a week of external review, but a continuous cycle of self-review punctuated once every five years by an external review. If the process works, the school trains the lenses on itself, creating a collective sense of what it sees when it does, and it takes responsibility for whatever gap may appear between what it sees and the highest qualities of teaching and learning.

But how does a school represent itself to itself, using the lenses of the School Quality Review? How does it keep track of its progress in achieving higher qualities of teaching and learning? This is where the Digital School Portfolio comes in. Recall that the principal of the school reviewed by Olsen and her team colleagues brought wall charts to represent her school. They were the product of the school's own internal review. In an important sense, they are also the inspiration for the School Portfolio. What if they and other artifacts of self-review, along with images of actual teaching and learning, could be incorporated in a user-friendly, computer-based multimedia presentation? What if this were the text that reviewers tended across the whole five-year cycle of the review process—the one the internal team prepared and updated, the one the external team examined and annotated? What if this text with its external annotation were available to parents, prospective parents, and others interested in knowing about a school—say, by means of a computer kiosk in the school's front hallway, or in the public library, or through home access via an information superhighway? Olsen notes the advantage in this regard of having the report of an external review team: "What strikes me is the difference between what parents typically learn about schools from test scores and what they could learn from something like the School Quality Review Initiative" (p. 26). How much more might they learn from the school's externally annotated self-report, illustrated in a hypermedia format by student writing, photos of student artwork, video of student exhibitions and other performances, and by any other data including test scores that the school decided to include or that the reviewers mention?

My colleagues' ambition as developers of the Digital School Portfolio must overcome many obstacles, not the least of which is the ordinarily antiquated wiring of schools. Nor do I mean to seem enthusiastic about a technological solution to a deeply complex problem of school and policy design. I know that technology cannot by itself redistribute energy, information, and power; foster a coherent belief system where none is already evident; make a school reflective; or transform hierarchical policy structures. Nonetheless, I am always enthusiastic about efforts to work on what seem to me to be the right problems, in what seem to me to be the right ways. And in this case, I think my colleagues have the right problem: the problem of knowing a school. Moreover, I think that my colleagues have chosen the right way to work on this problem: through a resolute focus on student work, the examination of this work by the light of the school's beliefs, the dependence of this examination on collaborative perspectives and multiple forms of data, and the effort to ensure that the entire inquiry is accessible to a wide array of stakeholders. Still, neither they nor I think their work will be easy. In a conversation with me, David Green suggested what they are up against. "Very few people know what's happening in schools," he said. "A lot of people infer it, suspect it, believe that they know, but few really know. And that includes teachers and principals."

Conclusion

In this chapter, I have focused at great length on one method of knowing a school, a method that brings together the perspectives of insiders and outsiders in a spirit of inquiry, and with plenty of lubricant available to ease the difficult meshing of these perspectives. I have also examined two other methods in less detail, and have suggested that all three lie along a continuum defined on one end by knowing and tuning on a virtual basis, and on the other end by knowing and tuning on an intimate basis. I have suggested that we need tools and protocols across the entire continuum so that schools of the twenty-first century may have access to the perspectives of both their closest stakeholders and also very remote ones.

Schools are complex and culturally dense phenomena that resist facile attempts to tune them. It is perhaps inconvenient that a cleverly conceived and worded performance standard in mathematics is distorted by one teacher, spurs another teacher to inventive heights, strangles another teacher's inventiveness, and fails to affect still another teacher in any way whatsoever. But that is what may really happen. Similarly, it is perhaps inconvenient that a cleverly conceived and executed charter school policy prods one school threatened with a loss of customers to make significant reforms, while it siphons off all the reform spirit of another. But, again, that is what may happen. Meanwhile, it is certainly inconvenient that a particular school may elude the ordinary efforts of its principal and teachers to hold it in mind, to know it in any genuine sense, but that is almost always what happens. That is why tuning requires extraordinary measures. Ordinary policy operations and ordinary schoolkeeping are not enough.

The problem of tuning schools—holding them accountable to standards of practice and performance rooted in larger perspectives—is the problem of knowing them. This is the most important of all school design problems. And it is everybody's problem—one for insiders as well as outsiders, for students as well as teachers, for parents as well as policymakers.

The problem also happens to be the problem that my colleagues and I, as researchers, wrestled with throughout the research this book reports. We intended to be what John Ralston Saul (1992) calls faithful witnesses to serious redesign efforts. We believed that this is the only authentic way for anyone to know something as complex and volatile as a school. The faithful witness, as Saul puts it, "is at his best when he concentrates on questioning and clarifying, and avoids the specialist's obsession with solutions"(p. 576). However, it is very difficult to be a witness to a tortuous and passionate activity without imagining solutions and without seeking somehow to impose them—that is, without, on occasion, feeling smarter than the people doing the real work. That is because the witness, unlike the doer, can rise above uncertainty. From the researcher's point of view, therefore, the problem of knowing schools is a problem of understanding them in some other way than by imposing on them one's smarter and more certain frame of reference. This involves honoring the realities of being there and of respecting the firsthand knowledge of insiders who are so much there as to be sometimes lost there. On the other hand, the researcher must avoid becoming lost him- or herself. This is a delicate balance to strike.

My purpose here is not to call attention to researchers' problems, however, but rather to point out that our problem mirrors the school's problem. Indeed, this mirroring is the central dynamic of the tuning arena of school design. A school enters into relationships with outsiders like researchers, representative stakeholders, visiting teams, or colleagues in a network because the school finds its most trustworthy reflection in the struggle of these outsiders to know the school. With this reflection as its guide, the school can then adjust its behavior so as to be more accountable for children's learning, and for the quality of that learning.

Some who are passionate about introducing more accountability into American schooling ignore this learning loop, as if a complex institution like a school could simply be told to be accountable or be pushed into accountability with the help of the right lever. Others who are passionate reformers of American schooling presume that they can skip this cycle of reflection wherein the object of change comes to understand why change is needed. By contrast, one participant in the first trials of the Bronx protocol showed far more insight into the actual change process, when he said that the point of the protocol seemed to be to allow important issues to be surfaced and named. Once named, he continued, the issues can then be taken back into the school and worked on openly. That is, they can be worked on knowingly. The external perspective gained through participation in a protocol session is crucial to the naming, and to the sensing that precedes naming, but the real accountability begins in the knowing.

Indeed, we cannot have schools of the twenty-first century that actually teach all children to use their minds well unless we strive for better knowing as a pervasive condition of these schools. Children have to be able to count on being well known, so that they can go on to know themselves as intellectually powerful people. Teachers have to practice knowing their own work and the children's by the light of a larger world, and parents and others who care have to know that this is the teachers' practice. In this knowing, I believe that we all can find the energy we need to take action. If we fight for the resources too, then we will have a chance.

Conclusion

Scaling Up by Scaling Down

Shortly before finishing this book, I found myself standing in a luncheon line just in front of an old teacher of mine. We were inching our way toward cold cuts, and he asked me what I was working on. I told him about the book. "What do you call it?" he asked at once. "*Redesigning School,*" I answered. "Wrong image," he chided.

"What do you mean?"

"Sounds like blueprints, and you're the one drawing them."

"No," I protested. "The book redefines redesign."

But I did not have time to explain, because by then we had reached the cold cuts, and our conversation trailed off. But he got me thinking. How exactly does this book redefine redesign?

To answer this question, I first have to ask and answer another one. It is the one I raised in the Introduction, alluding to Langston Hughes. What happens to a dream deferred? In the twenty-first century, will we have schools at last that provide all American children with a powerful education? I have tried throughout the book to be hopeful but not utopian with regard to this question. Maintaining the attitude to the end, I offer the following answer: We can have schools in the twenty-first century that teach all children to use their minds well, but only if we really want such schools, and then only if we reorient our common sense about how to get them.

The first necessary but not sufficient condition—to want an intellectually powerful education for all children—requires renouncing a deep and sometimes unacknowledged attachment to the idea that only certain children deserve or can benefit from an intellectually powerful education. Rhetorically, most Americans support equal opportunity for all children, but many implicitly invest in the continuation of structures that make the rhetoric meaningless: giant factory schools for the urban poor, access rights defined by a family's real estate, tracking systems that might as well explicitly sort by race and class, and achievement measures that construe intellectual power in absurdly narrow ways. To dismantle these structures, we must first teach ourselves that our own children's advantage is not advantage at all if it is purchased at the cost of massive disadvantage for their peers and an irreparably fractured community.

Yet even if we teach ourselves to believe in all children rather than only in our own, we will still be only halfway there. We must also act on this belief, but common sense often gets in our way. My old teacher, a very wise man, pinpointed the problem immediately. "No blueprints, please," he told me, knowing that reformers typically draw blueprints first. That is, their common sense tells them to begin by investing energy in getting things right on some miniature scale—say, the scale of a book like this, some policy initiative, or a model school. Then they try to scale up the design, that is, to get it into place in many schools, to replicate it. "You think you have a good grasp of the problems," I imagine my old teacher saying, "but you cannot devise the right solutions. You can only assist others to devise them—more or less thoughtfully." That is because, as I have argued throughout this book, education is ultimately dependent upon teachers' and learners' beliefs; their habits associated with the exchange of power, energy, and information; and their relative openness and access to ideas not their own.

Many reformers today tend to approach the problem of redesigning school by formulating and polishing frameworks of new beliefs at the state or national level. To get educators in any widespread way to adopt these new beliefs, these reformers typically rely on in-service training programs for teachers, new textbooks, and new assessments intended to redirect practice. They oversimplify the challenge and implicitly demean practitioners. Other reformers rely on model schools of one kind or another. They presume that the models will "spread" in the way, say, that popular culture spreads. They ignore the fact that the core of schooling—that is, how teachers and students typically relate to knowledge and each other, and how the work of teaching and learning are typically organized—is nearly impervious to this kind of contagion (Elmore, 1996). Meanwhile, still other reformers urge the fashioning of a free and open educational marketplace within which the continuous revision of belief is the natural outgrowth of marketing—the effort to entice and satisfy customers. These reformers disregard the fact that education's customers have few incentives to shop around, and that the marketers have few incentives to innovate. Market-focused reformers may also conveniently ignore the fact that others besides parents have some stake in the education of all American children.

I believe there is a better approach than these. I think it is possible to provoke and support locally driven and nationally tuned reform. Indeed, I think nothing short of this combination will work. This is because we need on the one hand a radical redesign of the American school such that all children will be taught to use their minds well, a redesign informed by ideas and experiences that are not exclusively local. On the other hand, the redesign must be owned by the people closest to the children, whose ordinary beliefs and habits it puts at risk and whose openness to the possibilities in the redesign is indispensable to its realization. An approach that addresses both requirements is one I call *scaling down.* Simply put, it tries to arrange things so that the right people really care about doing the right thing.

Richard Elmore (1996) attributes the term *scaling down* to Heather Lewis, codirector of New York's Center for Collaborative Education. Lewis and Elmore both spoke at the Harvard Graduate School of Education in April 1995 on the subject of moving reform from policy designs and isolated models to widespread practice. Lewis described, and Elmore lauded, the effort in the New York Annenberg Challenge to create smaller schools, each possessing, in Elmore's words, a "tighter sense of mutual commitment" than bigger schools are capable of possessing (p. 20), each informed in its design by larger-than-local ideas and each bonded to the others in a scheme based on lateral accountability.

Scaling down involves working on the real problems of redesign at the actual sites, where new beliefs must be adopted, new structures and cultures worked out, and new ways imagined for productive interaction with a rich and increasingly information-laden external environment. This means no blueprints developed at a remote site, no models to be adopted, no leaving the whole problem to market magic. However, it does not mean leaving schools to do the designing all by themselves. It involves the invention of policy contexts that provide incentives for local design of a certain kind, and that support such efforts with intellectual, financial, and political resources.

There are good examples around today of scaling down. Elmore and Lewis referred to the small schools of the Annenberg Challenge in New York. I would also mention Lewis and her colleagues' work in New York to encourage the widespread use of the Primary Language Record (PLR). The PLR is an accountability tool originally developed by British educators, but in a spirit of policy inventiveness rather than implementation. It guides a teacher's observations of a young child's language development.[1] It also directs the teacher to call on parents' perspectives, to involve the child in recording his or her own progress, and in cases in which the child's first language is not English, to inquire about the child's development in that language. The overall purpose of the PLR is to help the teacher understand and teach to the child's unique developmental strengths and needs, and to communicate this understanding and the teaching strategies it suggests to the child's next teacher (Khattri, Reeve, Kane, and Adamson, 1996). In short, its purpose is felt accountability for each child, a purpose that transcends particular classrooms, one that might be realized within many different school designs. The champion of PLR in New York has been the New York Assessment Network (NYAN), itself a creature of three other networks—the Center for Educational Options, the Elementary Teachers Network, and Lewis's own Center for Collaborative Education. NYAN builds on the core beliefs of these networks and their capacity for providing technical as well as moral support to schools, in order to situate the experiments with the PLR in the actual sites where the PLR challenges ordinary beliefs and overloads ordinary wiring. At the same time, NYAN seeks to associate these experiments with the larger opportunities presented by the Annenberg Challenge in New York, with its support

---

1. The Primary Language Record, which focuses on early literacy, has an offshoot called the Primary Learning Record, which focuses on the other parts of the curriculum as well. The California Learning Record, yet another offshoot, has been used successfully in secondary as well as elementary classrooms. See Darling-Hammond, Einbender, Frelow, and Ley-King, 1993.

and encouragement of varied local experimentation and its insistence on lateral accountability.

The other Annenberg Challenge sites also offer good examples of scaling down, though they are still young and it will take time to judge their effectiveness. Young too is the effort by the Coalition of Essential Schools to create regional clusters of member schools bound by mutual support and lateral accountability. Other school reform networks like the League of Professional Schools, Accelerated Schools, and New American Schools are also engaged in similar efforts. Again, it will take time for these efforts to pay off, and we should be patient.

Meanwhile, to understand how scaling down might work as a strategy of school redesign, we might examine its success as a strategy of curriculum reform. The National Writing Project, arguably the most successful curriculum reform project of the last twenty years, has engaged in scaling down. That is, it is essentially a collective of local projects, each enrolling a band of local teachers committed to the exploration of new ways of teaching writing. Yet it skillfully combines local and national identities, local and national resources (including federal funding), personal and collective responsibility for change, and varied ideological viewpoints. One might say that it is evangelical in its method—using networks bound by faith and testimony to stimulate deeply personal evaluation.

By characterizing the work of the Writing Project as evangelical, I intend to suggest that it is every bit as sophisticated in its theory of action and in its structures and strategies as American evangelical Protestantism. Writing Project teachers—joining a local community of other teachers—learn again through practice how to be writers themselves, even as they take on a new identity as teachers of writing, an identity informed by ideas imported from other contexts.

Of course, the redesign of school to focus on teaching all students to use their minds well is a much bigger and more ambiguous undertaking than the redesign of writing instruction. Yet a massive conversion of belief is a necessary ingredient of both efforts, and requires a similar approach. This is one that takes teachers' actual contexts seriously, that nonetheless introduces the teachers to outside ideas, that offers them an appealing new identity rooted in new competencies, and that manages not only to forgive but to encourage and support learning on the job. I mean no disrespect for evangelical Christianity by suggesting that in this process teachers may be born again.

But scaling down takes too much time, say some school reformers. I understand their impatience, but I think that it belies the immensity of the task we face. Besides, I know that impatience cannot trickle down, yet "down" is where we need it most—down where the action is. Imagine more parents so impatient with the transition between elementary and secondary schools and what it does to their children that they demand secondary schools that are small enough and organized such that all personnel can know the students they teach. Imagine more teachers so impatient with the irresponsibility of some of their colleagues that they confront them and make them change their ways or get out of the profession. Imagine more citizens so impatient with the inattention of their local schools to the achievement of local children that they organize citizen action groups to force change.

Smart professional reformers will of course be necessary to cultivate such impatience and the knowledge of how to act on it to benefit children. That is, good new designs for school will no more appear spontaneously than desegregated lunch counters did in an earlier reform era. Parents, teachers, and other citizens will need ideas, networks, resources, and learning opportunities in order to have their impatience aroused and in order to act on it successfully. But the point of such assistance must be to enable *them* to become the redesigners of school. No blueprints please.

Can we have schools at last that educate all children to use their minds well? Certainly some critical mass of people must first want such schools, but this alone is not enough. It will also be necessary for those of us who want such schools to work very hard at getting them, and very patiently, because much unlearning and rewiring are involved. Finally, it will be necessary that we get clearer than we often are now about the nature of the overall work of redesigning school, about which parts of it can be done well at a distance from the actual children, and about which parts need to be scaled down—that is, brought into the closest possible contact with actual children. This too will take much work and much patience. As Myles Horton would have said, we are in for a long haul (Horton, 1990). Luckily, there is a whole new century just ahead.

Appendix: A Glossary of Terms

Accountability: A habit of caring about the intellectual achievement of every child. Necessarily a function of the entire educational system, accountability depends ultimately on the capacity of those closest to children to know them, on their power to act together on the basis of this knowledge, and on their willingness to feel responsible for the results.

Believing: An arena of school design concerned with the aims of schooling and with conceptions of knowledge, learning, and human capacity. Believing is more than a personal phenomenon; institutions have beliefs too, though these beliefs may lie submerged below surface structures, operational habits, and what is called common sense.

Cool perspectives: These are the perspectives that distance lends: what an outside observer might contribute to a school's policy deliberations, or what a colleague might say about the work of a student she herself had not taught. One premise of this book is that both cool and warm perspectives should be brought to bear on important questions of teaching and learning.

Curriculum: This is best thought of as a set of relations among students, teachers, and the knowledge and values the school promotes. As such it is not something already "possessed" by teachers, "covered" in lessons, or "mastered" by students. One consequence of this is that the curriculum cannot be fully laid out in advance. Another is that teachers must have opportunities for continuous learning on the job. A third is that students must have greater access to sources of knowledge than the dosage system of lessons and textbooks typically allows.

Exhibitions: These are performances of understanding, usually involving some public audience. The Coalition of Essential Schools advocates school designs in which students progress toward graduation on the basis of successful exhibitions rather than on the basis of course completion. Designing exhibitions entails creating systems that include not only the public performances themselves but goals for them, standards to use in judging them, contexts for coaching students to do their best in them, archives of previous performances that the coaches and the students may consult in the process, and mechanisms for the school to reflect on what particular performances reveal about the school's instructional strengths and weaknesses.

Lateral accountability: The effort to achieve accountability within the particular schools of a network by means of actions taken, supports provided, and commitments made across the network. So, for example, all the schools of a network might agree to a common set of indicators of achievement, and might regularly report to each other their progress with respect to these indicators. They might exchange and discuss student work samples, as in the use of the tuning protocol. And they might regularly visit each other using such protocols as those developed in New York and Illinois for the School Quality Review process.

Leverage-based reform: An approach to redesigning school that depends upon policy initiatives applied at key junctures of the overall educational system—for example, efforts to insist on higher standards in promotion and graduation decisions. One premise of this book is that this strategy often fails to account for the complexity of the redesigning problem—overlooking, for example, the need to transform underlying beliefs or to deal with the ordinary incapacity of schools to come to a collective understanding of new standards or to take collective action with respect to achieving them.

Moves: The strategies that leaders employ to shake up a school's prevailing beliefs, provoke the formation of new beliefs, and coax others in the school to adopt these new beliefs as their own.

Scaling down: A method of spreading school reform that aims to combine ideas and resources provided by outsiders with the ideas, resources, commitment, and mutual support of insiders. Usually dependent on networks, it may be said to be more lateral than either top-down or bottom-up in its dynamics. It may also be said to mimic non-hierarchical religions in its approach to changing beliefs and patterns of living.

Sighting: The opportunity, often sudden and striking as in an epiphany, to see and understand the beliefs that animate the behaviors or policies of a school. May result from mulling over what seems at first an incongruity.

Systemic design: An approach to redesigning school advocated here. It presumes that the school is both the node of a complex system and also a complex system in its own right. Redirecting school toward the serious intellectual education of all children therefore requires significant amounts of interior and exterior redesign. This work may best be conducted within arenas—the first focused on beliefs, the second on patterns of interaction (wiring), and the third on relations with local and remote stakeholders (tuning). Although the arenas may be worked on separately, each makes demands that must be accommodated.

Tuning: An arena of school design concerned with the access of schools to outside ideas and expertise, and with the accountability of schools to externally rooted standards of practice and performance.

Tuning protocol: A ritual that enlists outside perspectives in a school's inquiry into the qualities of teaching and learning evident in its students' work. The protocol supplies lubrication for the ordinarily difficult meshing of insiders' and outsiders' perspectives.

Warm perspectives: These are the perspectives that intimacy lends: what the child's own teacher or parent can say about the child, or what the school knows about itself. One premise of this book is that both warm and cool perspectives should be brought to bear on important questions of teaching and learning.

Wiring: An arena of school design concerned with the distribution of energy, power, and information within a school. One premise of this book is that the curriculum, accountability, and governance necessary for a school to teach all its students to use their minds well are not possible within the constraints of ordinary late twentieth-century school wiring.

References

Adler, M. *The Paideia Proposal: An Educational Manifesto.* New York: Macmillan, 1982.

Adler, M. *Paideia Problems and Possibilities: A Consideration of Questions Raised by the Paideia Proposal.* New York: Macmillan, 1983.

Adler, M., and the Paideia Group. *The Paideia Program: An Educational Syllabus.* New York: Macmillan, 1984.

Allen, D., and McDonald, J. P. *Keeping Student Performance Central.* Studies on Exhibitions, no. 14. Providence, R.I.: Coalition of Essential Schools, Brown University, 1994.

Apple, M. W., and Beane, J. A. *Democratic Schools.* Alexandria, Va.: Association for Supervision and Curriculum Development, 1995.

Archambault, R. *John Dewey on Education: Selected Writings.* Chicago: University of Chicago Press, 1974.

Barth, R. *Improving Schools from Within: Teachers, Parents, and Principals Can Make the Difference.* San Francisco: Jossey-Bass, 1990.

Belenky, M. F., and others. *Women's Ways of Knowing: The Development of Self, Voice, and Mind.* New York: Basic Books, 1986.

Bellah, R. N., Madsen, R., Sullivan, W. M., Swidler, A., and Tipton, S. M. *Habits of the Heart.* Berkeley: University of California Press, 1985.

Berger, R. *A Culture of Quality.* Providence, R.I.: Annenberg Institute, Brown University, 1996.

Boyer, E. L. *High School: A Report on Secondary Education in America.* New York: Harper & Row, 1983.

Briggs, J., and Peat, F. D. *Turbulent Mirror: An Illustrated Guide to Chaos Theory and the Science of Wholeness.* New York: Harper and Row, 1989.

Brown, A., and Campione, J. C. "Guided Discovery in a Community of Learners." In K. McGilly (ed.), *Classroom Lessons: Integrating Cognitive Theory and Classroom Practice.* Cambridge, Mass.: MIT Press, 1994.

Brown, R. *Schools of Thought.* San Francisco: Jossey-Bass, 1991.

Bruer, J. T. *Schools for Thought.* Cambridge, Mass.: MIT Press, 1993.

Bryk, A. S., Lee, V. E., and Holland, P. B. *Catholic Schools and the Common Good.* Cambridge, Mass.: Harvard University Press, 1993.

Burron, A. "Traditionalist Christians and OBE: What's the Problem?" *Educational Leadership,* 1994, *51*(6), 73–75.

California Center for School Restructuring. "Guidelines for the Protocol: Examining Student Work for What Matters Most." Unpublished paper, Redwood City, Calif., 1993.

Callahan, R. *Education and the Cult of Efficiency: A Study of the Social Forces That Have Shaped the Administration of the Public School.* Chicago: University of Chicago Press, 1962.

Clinchy, B. M. "Goals 2000: The Student as Object." *Phi Delta Kappan,* 1995, *76*(5), 383–392.

Cohen, D. K. "Origins." In A. G. Powell, E. Farrar, and D. K. Cohen (eds.), *The Shopping Mall High School: Winners and Losers in the Education Marketplace.* Boston: Houghton Mifflin, 1985.

Cohen, D. K. "What Standards for National Standards?" *Phi Delta Kappan,* 1995, *76*(10), 751–757.

Cohen, D. K., McLaughlin, M., and Talbert, J. *Teaching for Understanding: Challenges for Practice, Research, and Policy.* San Francisco: Jossey-Bass, 1993.

Collins, A., Brown, J. S., and Newman, S. E. "Cognitive Apprenticeship: Teaching the Craft of Reading, Writing, and Mathematics." In L. B. Resnick (ed.), *Knowing, Learning and Instruction: Essays in Honor of Robert Glaser.* Hillsdale, N.J.: Erlbaum, 1989.

Collins, A., Hawkins, J., and Carver, S. M. "A Cognitive Apprenticeship for Disadvantaged Students." In B. Means, C. Chelemer, and M. S. Knapp, *Teaching Advanced Skills to At-Risk Students.* San Francisco: Jossey-Bass, 1991.

Commission on the Skills of the American Workforce. *America's Choice: High Skills or Low Wages.* Rochester, N.Y.: National Center on Education and the Economy, 1990.

Conley, D. T. "Roadmap to Restructuring." *ERIC Review,* 1994, *3*(2).

Cuban, L. *Teachers and Machines: The Classroom Use of Technology Since 1920.* New York: Teachers College Press, 1986.

Damon, W. *Greater Expectations: Overcoming the Culture of Indulgence in America's Homes and Schools.* New York: Free Press, 1995.

Darling-Hammond, L. "Implications of Testing and Policy for Quality and Equality." *Phi Delta Kappan,* 1992, *73*(3), 220–225.

Darling-Hammond, L. "National Standards and Assessments: Will They Improve Education?" *American Journal of Education,* 1994, *102*(4), 478–510.

Darling-Hammond, L., Einbender, L., Frelow, F., and Ley-King, J. (eds.). *Authentic Assessment in Practice: A Collection of Portfolios, Performance*

Tasks, Exhibitions, and Documentation. New York: National Center for Restructuring Education, Schools, and Teaching, 1993.

Darling-Hammond, L., and Wise, A. "Beyond Standardization: State Standards and School Improvement." *Elementary School Journal,* 1985, *85*(3), 315–336.

Davis, A., and Felknor, C. "The Demise of Performance-Based Graduation in Littleton." *Educational Leadership,* 1994, *51*(6), 64–65.

Deming, W. E. *Out of the Crisis.* Cambridge, Mass.: MIT Center for Advanced Engineering Study, 1986.

Deming, W. E. *The New Economics for Industry, Education, Government.* Cambridge, Mass.: MIT Center for Advanced Engineering, 1994.

Denning, P. J. "Educating a New Engineer." *Communications of the Association for Computing Machinery,* 1992, *35,* 83–97.

Des Dixon, R. G. "Future Schools and How to Get There from Here." *Phi Delta Kappan,* 1994, *75*(5), 360–365.

Elbow, P. *Embracing Contraries.* New York: Oxford University Press, 1986.

Elmore, R. "Getting to Scale with Good Educational Practice." *Harvard Education Review,* 1996, *66*(1), 1–26.

Elmore, R., and McLaughlin, M. *Steady Work: Policy, Practice, and the Reform of American Education.* Santa Monica, Calif.: Rand, 1988.

Fine, M. *Framing Dropouts: Notes on the Politics of an Urban Public High School.* Albany, N.Y.: State University of New York Press, 1991.

Fine, M. *Talking Across Boundaries: Participatory Evaluation Research in an Urban Middle School.* New York: City University of New York Graduate School and University Center, 1996.

Fredericksen, J. R., and Collins, A. "A Systems Approach to Educational Testing." *Educational Researcher,* 1989, *18*(9), 27–32.

Freire, P. *Pedagogy of the Oppressed* (M. B. Ramos, trans.). New York: Continuum, 1981. (Original work published 1970.)

Fuhrman, S. H. (ed.). *Designing Coherent Education Policy.* San Francisco: Jossey-Bass, 1993.

Fullan, M. *Change Forces: Probing the Depths of Educational Reform.* London: Falmer Press, 1993.

The Futures Committee. *Looking to the Future: From Conversation to Demonstration.* Providence: R.I.: Coalition of Essential Schools, 1995.

Gardner, H. *Frames of Mind: The Theory of Multiple Intelligences.* New York: Basic, 1983.

Gardner, H. *To Open Minds: Chinese Clues to the Dilemma of American Education.* New York: Basic Books, 1989.

Gardner, H. *The Unschooled Mind: How Children Think and How Schools Should Teach.* New York: Basic Books, 1991.

Gardner, H., and Kornhaber, M. *Varieties of Excellence: Identifying and Assessing Children's Talents.* New York: National Center for Restructuring Education, Schools, and Teaching, 1993.

Goodlad, J. I. *A Place Called School.* New York: McGraw-Hill, 1984.

Goodlad, J. I., and others. *Behind the Classroom Door.* Worthington, Ohio: C. A. Jones, 1970.

Gould, S. J. *The Mismeasure of Man.* New York: Norton, 1981.

Gray, D. "Socratic Seminars: Basic Education and Reformation." *Basic Education,* 1988, *3*(4).

Gray, D. "Putting Minds to Work." *American Educator,* Fall 1989, pp. 16–23.

Greene, M. *The Dialectic of Freedom.* New York: Teachers College Press, 1988.

Gutmann, A. *Democratic Education.* Princeton, N.J.: Princeton University Press, 1987.

Gutmann, A. "Democratic Education in Difficult Times." *Teachers College Record,* 1990, *92*(1), 7–20.

Haroutunian-Gordon, S. *Turning the Soul: Teaching Through Conversation in the High School.* Chicago: University of Chicago Press, 1991.

Herrnstein, R. J., and Murray, C. *The Bell Curve: Intelligence and Class Structure in American Life.* New York: Free Press, 1994.

Hill, P. T. "The Future of Public School System Central Offices: Why Seek a New American School District?" In Education Commission of the States (ed.), *The New American Urban School District.* Denver, Colo.: The Education Commission of the States, 1995.

Hill, P. T., Foster, G. E., and Gendler, T. *High Schools with Character.* Santa Monica, Calif.: Rand, 1990.

Hock, D. Address to the Joyce Foundation, Chicago, October 11, 1993.

Horton, M. *The Long Haul: An Autobiography.* New York: Anchor Books, 1990.

Huberman, M. "The Model of the Independent Artisan in Teachers' Professional Relations." In J. Warren Little and M. W. McLaughlin (eds.), *Teachers' Work: Individuals, Colleagues and Contexts.* New York: Teachers College Press, 1993.

Johnson, B. *Giving the Kids the Keys: Using Advisories as a Vehicle for Change.* Providence, R.I.: Brown University, 1995.

Johnson, S. M. *Teachers at Work: Achieving Success in Our Schools.* New York: Basic Books, 1990.

Jones, B. F., and Idol, L. *Dimensions of Thinking and Cognitive Instruction.* Hillsdale, N.J.: Erlbaum, 1990.

Kaplan, G. R. "Shotgun Wedding: Notes on Public Education's Encounter with the New Christian Right." *Phi Delta Kappan,* 1994, *75*(9), Special Report: K1–K12.

Khattri, N., Reeve, A. L., Kane, M. B., and Adamson, R. J. *Studies of Education: Assessment of Student Performance.* Washington, D.C.: Office of Educational Research and Improvement, 1996.

Kliebard, H. M. *The Struggle for the American Curriculum, 1893–1958.* New York: Routledge & Kegan Paul, 1986.

Kozol, J. *Savage Inequalities: Children in America's Schools.* New York: Crown, 1991.

Lee, V. E., and Smith, J. B. *High School Restructuring and Student Achievement.* Issues in Restructuring Schools, no. 7. Madison: University of Wisconsin, Center on Organization and Restructuring of Schools, 1994.

Lewis, A. C. "An Overview of the Standards Movement." *Phi Delta Kappan,* 1995, *76*(10), 744–750.

Lortie, D. C. *School Teacher: A Sociological Study.* Chicago: University of Chicago Press, 1975.

Marshall, R., and Tucker, M. *Thinking for a Living.* New York: Basic Books, 1992.

Matthews, J. *Escalante: The Best Teacher in America.* New York: Holt, 1988.

McDonald, J. P. "Dilemmas of Teaching Backwards: Rescuing a Good Idea." *Teachers College Record,* 1992a, *94*(1), 152–169.

McDonald, J. P. *Steps in Planning Backwards: Early Lessons from the Schools.* Studies on Exhibitions, no. 5. Providence, R.I.: Coalition of Essential Schools, Brown University, 1992b.

McDonald, J. P. *Teaching: Making Sense of an Uncertain Craft.* New York: Teachers College Press, 1992c.

McDonald, J. P. "Three Pictures of an Exhibition: Warm, Cool, and Hard." *Phi Delta Kappan,* 1993, *74*(6), 480–485.

McDonald, J. P. "Below the Surface of School Reform: Vision and Its Foes." In R. Glaser and L. Schauble (eds.), *The Contributions of Instructional Innovation to Understanding Learning.* Hillsdale, N.J.: Erlbaum, 1996.

McDonald, J. P., and others. *Graduation by Exhibition: Assessing Genuine Achievement.* Alexandria, Va.: Association for Supervision and Curriculum Development, 1993.

McLuhan, M. *Understanding Media: The Extensions of Man.* New York: McGraw-Hill, 1964.

McNeil, L. M. *Contradiction of Control: School Structure and School Knowledge.* New York: Routledge & Kegan Paul, 1986.

McQuillan, P., and Muncey, D. *School-within-a-School Restructuring and Faculty Divisiveness: Examples from a Study of the Coalition of Essential Schools.* Working Paper, no. 6, School Ethnography Project. Providence, R.I.: Coalition of Essential Schools, Brown University, 1991.

Meadows, D. "Whole Earth Models and Systems." *Co-Evolution Quarterly,* Summer 1982, pp. 98–108.

Meier, D. "Why Kids Don't Want to Be Well Educated." Address to the Annual Meeting of the American Educational Research Association, Atlanta, 1993.

Meier, D. *The Power of Their Ideas.* Boston: Beacon Press, 1995.

Miller, G. W. "Getting Ready to Leave Adolescence Behind." *Providence Journal-Bulletin,* September 30, 1993, p. A8.

Mitchell, R. *Testing for Learning: How New Approaches to Evaluation Can Improve American Schools.* New York: Free Press, 1992.

Mitchell, R. *Sixth Grade Research Performance Assessment: Report on an Experience with South Brunswick, NJ, Public Schools.* South Brunswick, N.J.: Council for Basic Education, 1993.

New Standards Project. *Performance Standards: English Language Arts, Mathematics, Science, Applied Learning.* Pittsburgh, Pa.: National Center on Education and the Economy, 1995.

Newman, D. "Computer Networks: Opportunities or Obstacles?" In B. Means (ed.), *Technology and Education Reform.* San Francisco: Jossey-Bass, 1994.

Newmann, F. M., and Wehlage, G. G. *Successful School Restructuring.* Madison: Center on Organization and Restructuring of Schools, University of Wisconsin, 1995.

Niguidula, D. *The Digital Portfolio.* Studies on Exhibitions, no. 13. Providence, R.I.: Coalition of Essential Schools, Brown University, 1994.

Olsen, L. "Critical Friends." *Education Week,* May 4, 1994, pp. 20–23, 26–27.

Olsen, L. "Cards on the Table." *Education Week,* June 14, 1995, pp. 23–28.

Perelman, L. J. *School's Out.* New York: Morrow, 1992.

Perkins, D. *Smart Schools: From Training Memories to Educating Minds.* New York: Free Press, 1992.

Perkins, D. *Outsmarting IQ: The Emerging Science of Learnable Intelligence.* New York: Free Press, 1995.

Perrone, V. *A Letter to Teachers: Reflections on Schooling and the Art of Teaching.* San Francisco: Jossey-Bass, 1991.

Podl, J. B., and Metzger, M. T. "Learning by Teaching: An Exhibition Instead of an Exam." *English Journal,* 1994, *83*(4), 61–66.

Podl, J. B., and others. *The Process of Planning Backwards: Stories from Three Schools.* Studies on Exhibitions, no. 7. Providence, R.I.: Coalition of Essential Schools, Brown University, 1992.

Porter, A. "The Uses and Misuses of Opportunity-to-Learn Standards." Paper presented at a Brookings Institution conference, Beyond

Goals 2000: The Future of National Standards and Assessment in American Education, Washington, D.C., 1994.

Powell, A., Farrar, E., and Cohen, D. K. *The Shopping Mall High School: Winners and Losers in the Education Marketplace.* Boston: Houghton Mifflin, 1985.

Resnick, L. B. "Constructing Knowledge in School." In L. S. Liben (ed.), *Development and Learning: Conflict or Congruence?* Hillsdale, N.J.: Erlbaum, 1987.

Resnick, L. B. "Instruction and the Cultivation of Thinking." In E. de Corte, H. Lodewijks, R. Parmentier, and P. Span (eds.), *Learning and Instruction: European Research in an International Context.* Volume 1. New York: Pergamon Press, 1990.

Resnick, L. B., and Resnick, D. P. "Assessing the Thinking Curriculum: New Tools for Educational Reform." In B. R. Gifford and M. C. O'Connor (eds.), *Changing Assessments: Alternative Views of Aptitude, Achievement and Instruction.* Boston: Kluwer, 1991.

Sarason, S. *The Culture of the School and the Problem of Change.* (2nd ed.) Boston: Allyn & Bacon, 1982.

Saul, J. R. *Voltaire's Bastards: The Dictatorship of Reason in the West.* New York: Vintage, 1992.

Schlechty, P. P. *Schools for the Twenty-First Century: Leadership Imperatives for Educational Reform.* San Francisco: Jossey-Bass, 1991.

Schön, D. A. *The Reflective Practitioner: How Professionals Think in Action.* New York: Basic Books, 1983.

Schwartz, J. L. *The Prices of Secrecy: The Social, Intellectual, and Psychological Costs of Current Assessment Practice—A Report to the Ford Foundation.* Cambridge, Mass.: Educational Technology Center, Harvard Graduate School of Education, 1990.

Sedlak, M. W., Wheeler, C. W., Pullin, D. C., and Cusick, P. A. *Selling Students Short: Classroom Bargains and Academic Reform in the American High School.* New York: Teachers College Press, 1986.

Senge, P. M. *The Fifth Discipline: The Art and Practice of the Learning Organization.* New York: Doubleday, 1990.

Sizer, T. R. (ed.). *The Age of the Academies.* New York: Teachers College Press, 1964.

Sizer, T. R. *Horace's Compromise: The Dilemma of the American High School.* Boston: Houghton Mifflin, 1984.

Sizer, T. R. *Horace's School: Redesigning the American High School.* Boston: Houghton Mifflin, 1991.

Sizer, T. R., McDonald, J. P., and Rogers, B. "Standards and School Reform: Asking the Basic Questions." *Stanford Law and Policy Review,* 1992, *4,* 27–35.

Spady, W. G. "Organizing for Results: The Basis of Authentic Restructuring and Reform." *Educational Leadership,* 1988, *46*(2), 4–8.

Tyack, D. *The One Best System.* Cambridge, Mass.: Harvard University Press, 1974.

Tyack, D., and Tobin, W. "The Grammar of Schooling: Why Has It Been So Hard to Change?" *American Educational Research Journal,* 1994, *31*(3), 453–479.

Wasley, P. A., Hampel, R. L., and Clark, R. W. *Preliminary Findings: Report on the Research of the School Change Study.* Providence, R.I.: Annenberg Institute for School Reform, Brown University, 1995.

Weick, K. E. "Educational Organizations as Loosely Coupled Systems." *Administrative Science Quarterly,* 1976, *21,* 1–19.

Weick, K. E. "Administering Education in Loosely Coupled Schools." *Phi Delta Kappan,* 1982, *63*(10), 673–676.

Wheatley, M. J. *Leadership and the New Science.* San Francisco: Berrett-Koehler, 1992.

Wiggins, G. P. *Assessing Student Performance.* San Francisco: Jossey-Bass, 1993.

Wilson, T. A. *Reaching for a Better Standard: How English Inspection Provokes the Way Americans Know and Judge Schools.* New York: Teachers College Press, 1995.

Wolf, D., Bixby, J., Glenn, J., III, and Gardner, H. "To Use Their Minds Well: Investigating New Forms of Student Assessment." In G. Grant (ed.), *Review of Research in Education,* Vol. 17. Washington, D.C.: American Educational Research Association, 1991.

Wood, G. *Schools That Work: America's Most Innovative Public Education Programs.* New York: Plume, 1993.

Workforce Skills Program. *The Certificate of Initial Mastery: A Primer.* Rochester, N.Y.: National Center on Education and the Economy, 1994.

Woronov, T. "Six Myths (and Five Promising Truths) About the Uses of Educational Technology." *Harvard Education Letter,* 1994, *10*(5), 1–3.

Index

A

Academic, intellectual associated with, 10–12, 172
Accelerated Schools, 75, 247
Accountability: and assessment balance, 188–189, 191, 195–196, 198; and autonomy, 228–229; back door to, 125–126; in exhibition, 43, 44, 52, 102, 115–116; lateral, 218–219, 220, 223, 229, 231–232, 235, 245; and performance assessment, 116–118, 119; and standards, 113–116; and tuning protocol, 210–211; and wiring, 102–103, 113–118
ACORN, 227*n*
Action, in leadership, 55–58
Adamson, R. J., 246
Adler, M., 43, 62
Administration, and wiring, 107–109. *See also* Leadership
Allen, D., 45, 218, 230, 234, 235, 236
Allison, P., 229–230
Alverno College, 140
American Educational Research Association, 59–60
And, understanding, 41
Angelou, M., 162
Annenberg, W., 227–228
Annenberg Challenge, 227–228, 246–247
Annenberg Institute, 6, 59, 230, 234, 236
Apple, M. W., 200
Archambault, R., 103–104
Archimedes, 34
Arendt, H., 115
Art class, and beliefs, 30–31
Assessment: balance of state and local, 186–198; hypermedia for, 235–236; and ironic detachment, 191–196; middle ground for, 196–198; portfolios for, 126–127, 128, 136–137, 140–141; qualities of good, 189–191; state, 187–188. *See also* Performance assessment
ATLAS Seminar, 245
Audubon, J. J., 148
Authentic public space, and standards, 115
Authentic tasks, in exhibition, 44–45
Autonomy, and accountability, 228–229

B

Bard Writing Institute, 169
Barth, R., 56
Beane, J. A., 200
Belenky, M. F., 66
Beliefs and believing: aspects of, 21–85; background on, 23–24; conclusion on, 49–52; deep, 24–26; and defiance, 80–83; as design arena, 17, 19; for future, 50–52; and intellectual purpose, 23–52; leading with, 53–85; and leverage, 33–46; and planning backwards, 37–49; prevailing, 27–33; system of, 26–46; and tuning protocol, 217–218, 222–223; and wiring, 121, 130–131
Bellah, R. N., 4
Benchmarks: for graduation skills, 149; and performance assessment, 117; and standards movement, 36

Berger, R., 115, 165
Bixby, J., 9
Black Pride seminars, 63–65
Boston, tuning protocol in, 211–219
Briggs, J., 47–48
Brown, A., 10
Brown, J. S., 10, 45
Brown, R., 113
Brown University, 85, 116; network at, 75, 175; tuning protocol at, 215
Bruer, J. T., 9
Bryk, A. S., 15, 157
Budgets, and slack, 109–110
Burron, A., 124

C

California: networks in, 219–227, 247; Writing and Math Projects in, 220; year-round schooling in, 106
California Center for School Restructuring (CCSR), 219–227
California Learning Record, 246*n*
Callahan, R., 13
Calvin, J., 51
Campione, J. C., 10
Carver, S. M., 10, 44, 45
Cellular institutions, and central control, 13–14
Center for Children and Technology, 230
Center for Collaborative Education, 227*n*, 245, 246
Center for Educational Innovation, 227*n*
Center for Educational Options, 246
Central Park East Secondary School, 59, 140
Certificate of initial mastery (CIM), and beliefs, 36–37, 39
Chaos: and exhibition, 45–46, 47–48, 52; and leadership, 84–85
Charisma, and leadership, 66–73
Charter school, and community balance, 182
Chicago, networks in, 247
Children: belief in, 243–244; as sortable, 27–33; and trouble, 14–15
Civil discourse, 210
Classrooms: communication in, 99–100; new wiring in, 100–103; slack in, 202–203
Clinchy, B. M., 156
Coaching: cognitive, 10; for exhibition, 43–44, 192–193; and graduation skills, 140, 144
Coalition of Essential Schools: and accountability, 115, 196; and beliefs, 38–39, 43; and community balance, 174–186; Fall Forum of, 122, 219, 227; and leadership, 61, 73–77; principles of, 251–252; and scaling down, 247; and tuning protocol, 218, 219, 227
Cognitive apprenticeships, and authentic tasks, 45
Cohen, D. K., 5, 9, 15, 37–38
Collins, A., 10, 44, 45, 117
Comer, J., 51, 75
Commission on the Skills of the American Workforce, 12, 45
Communication: in classrooms, 99–100; informal, 99; wiring for, 97–100
Community: balance of parents and educators in, 170–186; defying expectations of, 77–83; policy reflections on, 181–182; purposeful, 15; reform agenda in, 173–175; strategy and vote in, 175–178; variation on, 183–186; wiring at stake in, 178–181
Competition, personal and economic, 12–13
Computer class, and beliefs, 32–33
Conley, D. T., 191
Content standards, 35
Continuous improvement, and quality review, 238
Control: and cellular institutions, 13–14; and information tools, 90–92; and productivity, 109–113

Cool: feedback, 204, 209–210, 213, 226, 232–233; perspectives, 162–164, 167–168
Cortes, C., 223
Critical friend role: and researcher role, 167–170; and tuning protocol, 212, 237
Cuban, L., 129
Culture, and restructuring, 223
Curriculum: constructed, 103–106; and wiring, 103–107
Cusick, P. A., 15

D

Damon, W., 85
Darling-Hammond, L., 8, 16, 156, 246*n*
Davis, A., 124
Defiance, and leadership, 77–83
Deficit, difference associated with, 9–10, 156–157
Deming, W. E., 14, 173
Democracy: and beliefs, 51–52; and tuning, 170–186
Democratic autocracy, and charisma, 70
Demonstration of Restructuring in Public Education, 219–220
Denning, P. J., 97–98
Des Dixon, R. G., 94
Development, belief in, 51
Dewey, J., 7, 28, 77, 103–104
Difference, deficit associated with, 9–10, 156–157
Digital Portfolio, 129, 137–138, 146–150, 151
Digital School Portfolio, 236–239
Disjunction, and leadership, 66–68, 73
Diversity, respect for, 10

E

Education Development Center, 236
Educational Video Center, 231
Einbender, L., 246*n*
Elbow, P., 213
Electronic portfolio, 111–112, 116
Elementary Teachers Network, 246
Elmore, R., 16, 71, 245–246
Energy, and wiring, 92–119
Escalante, J., 106
Evaluation, and exhibition, 42–43
Exhibition: accountability in, 43, 44, 52, 102, 115–116; and assessment, 191–193, 195; coaching for, 43–44, 192–193; concept of, 38; dimensions of, 39–46; and evaluation, 42–43; and graduation skills, 126–127, 128, 140–141; perspectives on, 159–164; and prompt, 41–42; reconsidered, 46–49; and reflection, 46; and student work, 44–46; in tuning protocol, 211–219, 232–233; and vision, 39–40
Exhibitions Project: and systemic design, 16; and technology, 129; and tuning protocol, 218, 234

F

Faith. *See* Intuition
Faithful witness concept, 240–241
Farrar, E., 15
Feedback, warm and cool, 204, 209–210, 213, 226, 232–233
Felicia, 95–97
Felknor, C., 124
Filing system, for graduation skills, 132–145
Fine, M., 25, 65
Fishbowl protocol, 210, 226
Foster, G. E., 25
France, wiring of Pompidou Center in, 92
Frederick Douglass Middle School, 235–236
Fredericksen, J. R., 117
Freire, P., 32
Frelow, F., 246*n*
Fuhrman, S. H., 8
Fullan, M., 19, 57, 62, 77, 223
Fund for Public Education, 227*n*
Futures Committee, The, 218

G

Gardner, H., 9, 10, 165
Gendler, T., 25
George, 132, 134, 135, 142–143, 144
Georgia, University of, 75
German Democratic Republic, telephoning in, 89–91
Glenn, J., III, 9
Goals 2000, 35, 36, 37–38
Goodlad, J. I., 13
Gould, S. J., 7, 9
Governance, and wiring, 102, 107–113
Governor's Task Force on Education, 128
Grading: and graduation skills, 133–135, 142, 144–145; and standards, 114–115
Graduation: by exhibition, 39; portfolio system for, 116–117, 118; skills for, 124–125, 127–128, 131, 132–145, 148–149
Gray, D., 62
Green, D., 36, 51, 236, 239
Greene, M., 115
Gutmann, A., 51, 115, 200

H

Haroutunian-Gordon, S., 62
Harvard Graduate School of Education, 245
Hawkins, J., 10, 44, 45
Hawkins, V., 236
Henry B. Smith School, 123–145, 146, 148, 151
Her Majesty's Inspectors (HMI), 236
Herrnstein, R. J., 8
Hill, P. T., 24–25, 182
Hock, D., 45
Hofstadter, R., 10
Holland, P. B., 15, 157
Horticulture class, and beliefs, 30, 31–32
Horton, M., 248
Huberman, M., 62
Hughes, L., 243

I

IBM Corporation, 129, 146, 211–213, 234
Idol, L., 9
Illinois: networks in, 247; School Quality Review in, 236–239
Information: tools for, 90–92; and wiring, 92–119
Institutions. *See* Schools
Intellectual: academic associated with, 10–12, 172; lockdown, 15, 100; purposes, 23–52
Intelligence: concepts of, 5, 9–10; hierarchical, 156–158
Intuition: and leadership, 58–62; rationality alternating with, 124–132
Irony: in detachment of wiring and tuning, 191–196; and moves, 32–33; of views on students, 94

J

James, W., 177
Janet, 169–170
Jennie, 122, 124, 127–128, 130–145, 147–148, 150–151
Jesus, 213
Johnson, B., 116
Johnson, J. W., 63
Johnson, S. M., 13, 94
Jones, B. F., 9
Joyce, J., 23
Jubb, S., 219, 220

K

Kane, M. B., 246
Kaplan, G. R., 124
Khattri, N., 246
Kliebard, H. M., 4, 7
Knowledge, construction of, 5, 9
Kornhaber, M., 10
Kozol, J., 14

L

Lakesha's school, 187–196, 201
Lasky, L., 183*n*

Leadership: action in, 55–58; aspects of, 53–85; background on, 53–55; and charisma, 66–73; conclusion on, 84–85; and defiance, 77–83; distributed, 108; dynamics of, 69–70; generalized, 123*n*; and intuition, 58–62; and networks, 73–77; and ritual, 62–66; spiritual, 85; by teachers, 70–72, 231–232; transition of, 68–69, 108–109; and wiring, 107–109
League of Professional Schools, 75, 247
Learning Research and Development Center, 36
Lee, V. E., 15, 157
Lehman College, Literacy Institute at, 230
Leverage: lure of, 33–34, 37; networks for, 76–77; strategies of, 35–46
Levin, H., 75
Lewis, A. C., 35
Lewis, H., 245–246
Ley-King, J., 246*n*
Listening, in communication, 97–98
Lortie, D. C., 94
Los Angeles, networks in, 247

M

Manhattan Institute, 227*n*
Marshall, R., 12
Math class, and beliefs, 32–33
Matthews, J., 106
McDonald, J. P., 13, 38, 39, 45, 103, 167, 231
McLaughlin, M., 9, 16, 71
McLuhan, M., 162
McNeil, L. M., 15
McQuillan, P., 48
Meadows, D., 41
Meier, D., 6, 11, 49, 59–60, 228–229
Melissa, 2–4
Miller, G. W., 10
Mitchell, R., 35
Moves: and irony, 32–33; in leadership, 54–84; thoughtful, 11
Muncey, D., 48
Murray, C., 8

N

National Center for Education and the Economy, 36
National Endowment for the Humanities, 104
National Science Foundation, 104
National Writing Project, 247
Networks: for assessment, 246–247; and community balance, 174–186; evangelical agency of, 247–248; and leadership, 73–77; of small schools, 227–234; and tuning protocols, 219–234; value of, 75–77
New American Schools, 247
New Standards Project, 36, 169
New Visions Project, 227*n*
New York Assessment Collection, 235–236
New York Assessment Network (NYAN), 246–247
New York City: Annenberg Challenge in, 227–234, 245–247; new wiring in, 100–101; School Quality review in, 237; tuning protocol in, 227–234
Newman, D., 91
Newman, S. E., 10, 45
Newmann, F. M., 15
Newton, I., 48
Niguidula, D., 129, 146, 147*n*
Noise: as catalyst, 40; and dissonance, 73

O

Olsen, L., 115, 236–238
Opportunity to learn standards, 35–36, 43–44, 135–136

P

Paideia network: and accountability, 43; and ritual, 62–64
Peat, D., 47–48

Performance assessment: and accountability, 116–118, 119; aim of, 8; technologies for, 35, 38–39
Performance standards, 35
Perkins, D., 9, 172, 177
Perrone, V., 100
Perspectives: balance of, 159–168; cool, 162–164, 167–168; and outside contacts, 164–167; warm, 161–162, 167–168
Philadelphia, reform efforts in, 247
Planning backwards: reconsidered, 46–49; strategy of, 37–46
Plato, 63
Podl, J. B., 39
Porter, A., 36
Portfolios: for assessment, 126–127, 128, 136–137, 140–141; digital, 111–112, 116, 129, 137–138, 146–150, 151, 236–239; for graduation, 116–117, 118; perspectives on, 164–165; school, 236–239; for tuning protocol, 232–233
Powell, A., 15
Power: private and collective, 62; of reflection, 26, 48–49; separate, 13; and wiring, 92–119
Preliminary Scholastic Aptitude Test, 185
Primary Language Record (PLR), 246–247
Productivity, and control, 109–113
Prompt, and exhibition, 41–42
Protocol: concepts of, 206–206; fishbowl, 210, 226; for reflective conversation, 117–118. *See also* Tuning protocol
Pullin, D. C., 15

Q

Quality review, 236–238

R

Reeve, A. L., 246
Reflection: and exhibition, 46; power of, 26, 48–49
Reflective conversation: and performance assessment, 116–118, 119, 143–144; on tuning, 200–201
Reform, anxiety about, 174. *See also* School redesign
Relationships. *See* Wiring
Resnick, D. P., 9
Resnick, L. B., 7, 9, 36
Rewiring: alternating pattern for, 124–132; aspects of, 120–152; case study of, 123–145; conclusion on, 150–152; details in, 132–145; and tuning, 123, 125, 128; unfinished, 145–147
Riconscente, M., 129, 146, 236
Rituals: and leadership, 62–66; and tuning protocol, 222–223. *See also* Protocols
Rogers, B., 13, 183*n*

S

San Francisco Bay Area, networks in, 247
Sarason, S., 55, 87
Saul, J. R., 240
Schön, D. A., 46, 52
School choice: and defiance, 78; and networks, 75
School Development, 75
School Quality Review, 236–238
School redesign: aspects of, 1–19; background on, 1–4; beliefs for, 21–85; conditions for, 243–248; environment for, 28–29; impetuousness in, 19, 57–58; leveraged, 35–46; process for, 18–19; scaling down for, 245–247; scaling up for, 244–245; tuning for, 153–242; wiring for, 87–152
Schools: cellular, and central control, 13–14; as custodial, 14–15; design arenas for, 17–18; designing against common sense for, 7–9; as hardwired, 3; information tools in, 91–92; outcomes-based, 124; portfolios of, 236–239; properties of, 17–18; as purposeful community, 15; purposes of, 4–6, 50–51; super-

visory model of, 199; systemic design for, 16–17; as tightly coupled, 123–124; unlearning agenda for, 9–16; year-round schedule for, 106
Schwartz, J. L., 188
Sedlak, M. W., 15
Seminars: as exhibition, 41–42, 43; and ritual, 63–66; on tuning protocol, 212–218
Senge, P. M., 14, 98
Shawn, J., 220
Sighting, and belief system, 23–24, 50, 191
Sizer, T. R., 13, 15, 17, 38, 180
Skepticism, and faith, 61–62
Skills, for graduation, 124–125, 127–128, 131, 132–145, 148–149
Slack: for classroom, 202–203; wiring for, 109–113, 119
Smith, J. B., 157
Smith School, 123–145, 146, 148, 151
Socrates, 62–63, 213
Southern High School, 183–186
Southern Maine, University of, 75
Southern Maine Partnership, 75
Spady, W. G., 124
Standards: and accountability, 113–116; constructed, 151; and leverage, 35–39; minimum, 141–142
Stanford University, 75
Student work: examining, 147–150; and exhibition, 44–46; meta-analysis of, 224, 226–227; tools for reflecting on, 234–239; in tuning protocol, 206–219, 224–227, 232–233
Students: and responsibility for skills, 139–140, 148, 150; and wiring, 94–97
Szabo, M., 219, 220

T

Talbert, J., 9
Taylor, F. W., 13
Teacher leadership: cultivation of, 231–232; patterns of, 70–72
Teachers: as cognitive coaches, 10; good, 106–107; as guides, 45; individualism of, 71–73; learning by, 104–105; voice of, 231–232, 233–234
Teaching: instrumental orientation for, 146; as telling, 27–33
Team teaching: and graduation skills, 126, 132–145; and wiring, 101–102, 107
Technology: for documenting achievement, 128–132, 137–138, 146–150, 151; for school portfolios, 236–239; and slack, 110–112
Tests, and standards, 113–114
Theater class: and beliefs, 30, 32; protocol in, 202–206
Thucydides, 41–42
Time, rewiring for, 105–106
Title I compensatory education, 35
Tobin, W., 128
Tocqueville, A. de, 10
Tolstoy, L., 42
Total Quality Management, 173
Tucker, M., 12, 36
Tuning: alternative designs in, 158–159; aspects of, 153–242; and assessment balance, 186–198; assessment collection for, 235–236; background on, 155–158; challenges of, 155–201; community balance in, 170–186; conclusion on, 198–201; as design arena, 17, 19; and hierarchical intelligence, 156–158; outsiders and insiders for, 168–170, 194–195; perspectives balanced in, 159–168; and rewiring, 123, 125, 128; school portfolio for, 236–239; strategies for, 175–176, 193–196; tools for, 234–239; and wiring, 178–181, 191–96
Tuning protocol: aspects of, 202–242; background on, 202–206; citywide, 227–234; concept of, 205; conclusion on, 239–242; debut of, 211–219; features of, 207–211;

generous moderation in, 214–216; open conversations in, 216; outsiders and insiders for, 208–209, 210, 233–234; schedules for, 213, 225, 230; standards in, 214; statewide, 219–227; as work in progress, 206–211
Tyack, D., 7, 8, 50, 128

U

United Kingdom: language development in, 246; school visitation in, 236
U.S. Department of Education, 191
Universal Declaration of Human Rights, 42
University Heights High School, 229–230

V

Values. *See* Beliefs and believing
Vargo, M., 220
Vision: and action taking, 55–58; and beliefs, 21; and exhibition, 39–40
Voice: of teachers, 231–232, 233–234; time to gain, 66

W

Warm: feedback, 204, 209–210, 213, 226, 232–233; perspectives, 161–162, 167–168
Wasley, P. A., 210
Weber, L., 100
Wehlage, G. G., 15
Weick, K. E., 123
Wheatley, M. J., 41, 48–49
Wheeler, C. W., 15
White, B., 186*n*
Wiggins, G. P., 35
Wilson, T. A., 36, 236
Wiring: and accountability and standards, 113–116; and administration, 107–109; antiquated, 93–97, 121–122; aspects of, 87–152; background on, 89–91, 120–122; case study of, 120–152; in classrooms, 100–103, 202–203; concept of, 92, 120–121; conclusion on, 118–119; and constructed curriculum, 103–106; and control and productivity, 109–113; as design arena, 17, 19; figurative, 92–93; fundamentals of, 89–119; and good teachers, 106–107; lessons on, 103–118; and performance assessment, 116–118; and tuning, 191–196
Wise, A., 16
Wolf, D., 9
Workforce Skills Program, 36–37
Workplace, high-performance, 45
Woronov, T., 129

Y

Yale University, 75